International Acclaim for
A Time to Die

"An emotion-packed and ultimately heart-breaking story that also sheds light on the Soviet military's decline. Moore provides a vivid account of the last desperate attempts to open the hatch. . . . Fast-paced."
—*Washington Post*

"What is striking is the human tragedy: the bravery of the crew, the effect of the tragedy on those ashore, the dramatic and doomed rescue attempts, and the chilling fate of the 23 survivors of the initial explosion. . . . Harrowingly detailed."
—*Times* (London)

"Remarkable for its subject matter and style . . . Written in the tight, lean style that exemplifies excellent journalism . . . Expertly narrated, and the story's excitement and drama persist through straightforward and unadorned language."
—Associated Press

"A bleak but thrilling history of the greatest naval bungle of our time."
—*Sunday Times* (South Africa)

"A harrowing account . . . a gripping read, written in the style of a thriller, which serves as a fitting memorial to the lost sailors and as an indictment of Russia's military and political leaders. The book crackles with the authority of two years' solid research."
—*New Zealand Herald*

"Combining forensic evidence with the laws of physics, Moore masterfully re-creates the doomed sailors' final hours. . . . Readers might find themselves ignoring what they already know about the outcome and hoping against hope that some of the trapped sailors will be found alive."
—*BookPage*

"[Moore] has made good use of his experience as a journalist and his contacts to write a gripping account that reads in parts like a well-researched thriller."
—*Times Literary Supplement* (London)

A TIME TO DIE

A TIME

The Untold Story
of the *Kursk* Tragedy

TO DIE

Robert Moore

 THREE RIVERS PRESS • NEW YORK

Published by Three Rivers Press, New York, New York.

Member of the Crown Publishing Group, a division of Random House, Inc.

www.crownpublishing.com

Originally published in Great Britain in slightly different form by Transworld, London, in 2002.

Originally published in hardcover in the United States by Crown Publishers,
a division of Random House, Inc., in 2003.

Three Rivers Press and the Tugboat design are registered trademarks of Random House, Inc.

Printed in the United States of America

Design by Leonard W. Henderson

Library of Congress Cataloging-in-Publication Data

Moore, Robert.

A time to die : the untold story of the *Kursk* tragedy / Robert Moore.

1. *Kursk* (Submarine) 2. Submarine disasters—Russia (Federation) 3. Submarine disasters—
Barents Sea. 4. Russia (Federation).

Voenno-Morskoaei Flot—Submarine forces. I. Title.

VK1282.R8 M66 2003

910' .9163'24—dc21   2002015802

ISBN 1-4000-5124-X

10 9 8 7 6 5 4 3 2 1

First U.S. Paperback Edition

To the crew of K-141
and the families they left behind.
Especially the seventy children.

And to Liz and Timothy,
For their inspiration.

THE KURSK

1. Propellers
2. Upper rudder
3. Lower rudder
4. Stabilizer
5. Escape hatch
6. Ninth compartment
7. Emergency buoy
8. Steam turbines
9. Nuclear reactors
10. SS-N-19 missile tubes
11. Masts and antennae
12. Escape chamber (VSK)
13. Command center (second compartment)
14. Fin (sail)
15. Escape hatch
16. Torpedo room
17. Torpedo tubes
18. Sonar

BOEING 747

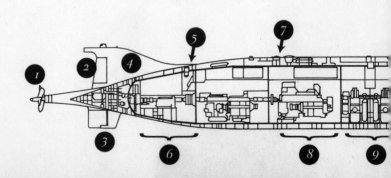

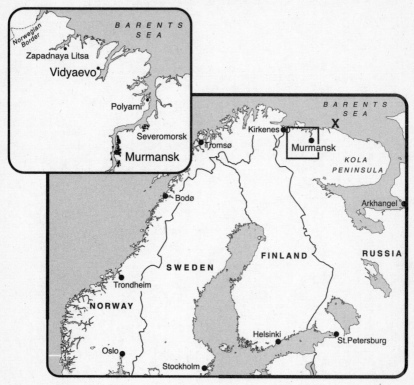

X = Kursk

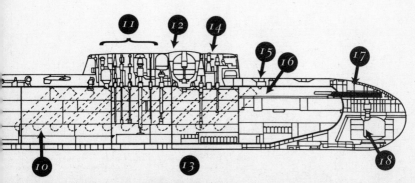

© A.D. Baker III March 2002

"Of all the branches of men in the forces there is none which shows more devotion and faces grimmer perils than the submariners."

—WINSTON CHURCHILL

Prologue

SATURDAY, AUGUST 12, 2000
Aboard the USS Memphis *in the Southern Barents Sea*

CAPTAIN MARK BREOR LISTENED closely to the flow of reports coming from the sonar and radio rooms. In the claustrophobic confines of the ship's attack center, the exchange of information was delivered in clipped and precise tones. Drawn, pale faces stared intently at the sensors and computer screens. After nearly two months of demanding duty in the Barents Sea, the tension was running high. The younger crew members were being taken to the very limits of their training, and beyond. Although the veterans' nerves were steadier, they also felt the pressure of knowing there was no scope for a single error or misjudgment.

Breor focused on the ever-shifting tactical picture on the surface. Keeping up with the movements of the Russian ships and submarines was like playing a high-stakes game of three-dimensional chess. The warships were never static, and the movement of each had to be meticulously plotted. He was determined to keep the USS *Memphis* at periscope depth for as long as he dared. There might be moments when he had to go deep to avoid detection, but very little information can be gleaned without a periscope or mast out of the water.

Gliding just sixty feet below the ocean surface, the submarine was intercepting Russian naval communications. The mission represented the perfect marriage of the sailor and the spy—navigating the submarine through hostile waters to collect high-grade naval intelligence. Despite all the technology contained within the hull of the *Memphis,* there is something very demanding, very human about driving a submarine into the shallow Barents Sea. Tactics and cunning, and a little artistry, are just as important as all the electronics.

Summer operations are complex missions, as oceanographic conditions constantly change. The Arctic Ocean, broiling and angry for the rest of the year, is calm. For a submarine on covert patrol, that brings hazards—benign seas combined with long hours of daylight mean a periscope can be more easily spotted by Russian lookouts. But Western submarine commanders like Breor have been taught how to use the summer months to their advantage. One of the tricks is to find where the Arctic ice is melting into the open sea. The fresh water flowing into the ocean creates different layers of salinity and temperature, confusing Russian sonar operators and providing Western submarines with an ideal hiding place.

Like the other officers on board, Breor viewed the Northern Run off the Kola Peninsula as the toughest and most exhilarating military patrol in the world. Nothing rivaled the challenge of a clandestine operation off Russia's Arctic coast. A single navigational blunder or tactical miscalculation could lead to collision or detection, either of which could provoke an international incident. But if all went well, the *Memphis* would leave no footprints on this invisible frontline, and the Russians would never even glimpse the sub's electronic shadow, despite her length of 362 feet and displacement of 7,000 tons.

For five decades, the frigid waters of the Barents Sea have played silent witness to the most classified espionage campaign in naval history. A generation of British and American submariners have monitored and tracked Russian ships as they left their lairs on the desolate Kola Peninsula and headed out on patrol. Over time, a bonanza of intelligence has been gathered on the capabilities and vulnerabilities of Russian submarines. The icy Barents Sea is still the red-hot center of operations in the lingering Cold War, the closest experience to combat for these American sailors.

On this long summer mission, Captain Breor was living up to his reputation as a commander who stayed calm under pressure. After eight adrenaline-driven weeks on patrol, he had never once shouted at a crew member, let alone lost his temper. The younger officers watched him closely and admired what they saw. He was going places in the U.S. Navy, no question about it. Twenty years earlier, he had won the Citadel Sword as the outstanding student in his naval course, and as captain of the *Memphis* he had just clinched the prestigious Battle Efficiency award for the performance of the submarine. But accolades don't count on a patrol like this, and a career can be lost in a moment's complacency. The lives of 130 American seamen, and the fate of a $2 billion boat, depended on Breor and his executive officer making the right judgments every hour of every day.

Two months earlier, in the second week of June, just before the *Memphis* slipped out of her home port of New London, Connecticut, the top-secret operational orders for the patrol had been hand-delivered by a courier from the Atlantic Fleet commander. Ever since, the document had been locked in Breor's personal safe. The key mission priority was detecting and monitoring the movement of the Russian nuclear ballistic-missile submarines—the giant boats known in U.S. Navy slang as "boomers." They can be tracked by their flow noise, the sound of eddies of waters sliding unevenly off the tiling of the hulls, disturbing the surrounding ocean. The sound waves from the cavitation of the propellers and the vibrations of machinery on the subs also betray them.

Tracking these ballistic-missile boats—or SSBNs, as they are properly classified—is of huge importance to the U.S. Navy. They comprise Russia's "strategic reserve"—Moscow's guarantee that in the event of a nuclear exchange it retains the retaliatory capability to destroy the United States. Should an all-out war erupt, targeting and destroying Russia's ballistic nuclear submarines would be the only way of saving the United States from annihilation.

Breor's mission orders did not stop there. Other objectives were carefully "stacked" by priority. In addition to keeping watch for a Russian boomer moving out on patrol, the *Memphis* was ordered to monitor the regular summer exercise in the Barents by the Northern Fleet. By the standard of recent years, the maneuvers this summer were on an impressive scale—with dozens of surface warships and, according to the sonar operators, at least four submarines.

The *Memphis* crew was feeling lucky. This was the submarine's second Arctic patrol in two years. The first had lasted three tension-filled months, from April to June 1999—the "best deployment ever," the officers agreed. And now they were up in the Barents again, in the high summer of 2000, watching the Northern Fleet with every piece of equipment that Navy intelligence could think of: acoustic sensors, an experimental fiber-optic periscope, and a state-of-the-art sonar that worked at greater range than ever before.

The *Memphis* is not only an attack submarine—she's an experimental platform for a range of these advanced technologies. In 1989, she was withdrawn from fleet service and modified before being reassigned to Submarine Development Squadron Twelve—DEVRON 12, as it's called—which specializes in improving submarine tactics. On this mission, a brand-new navigational system was also being tested that allowed the submarine to be maneuvered by measuring tiny differences in gravity along the ocean floor. The prototype technology was proving a major success, moving the U.S. submarine fleet a generation ahead of that being used by their Russian counterparts.

Throughout the patrol, Breor had kept his crew in a state of vigilance called "augmented watch section," often used while operating in the sensitive waters off Russia's northwest coast. Additional watch officers and enlisted specialists are placed on duty in the command center and in the sonar and radio rooms. The only state of alert higher is "battle stations," which mobilizes the entire crew.

Traveling at an ultra-stealthy three knots, the Los Angeles–class nuclear attack submarine was in her element. The diving officer stared intently at the consoles to gauge the submarine's angle and depth. At all costs, he wanted to avoid broaching, when the boat moves unexpectedly upward and breaks the surface—a disaster for the mission but one that can be easily caused by changing water temperatures or a lapse in concentration.

The forward part of the *Memphis* was crowded with intelligence "spooks." Some of these analysts and linguists were in the radio room recording intercepted communications; others were in the sonar room, seeking to track and decipher any acoustic anomalies.

This Northern Run, as the submariners call these spy missions in Arctic waters, had been scheduled to last six weeks but had been extended by another fourteen days. The USS *Toledo*, another Los Angeles—class boat, which was taking over sentry duty in the Barents Sea, had been delayed and was due to arrive on station by August 13. The *Memphis* was now on her final day's patrol. Tomorrow, Breor would give the order to withdraw to the northwest, and the *Memphis* would travel along a pre-designated corridor of sea around the North Cape, before heading due south down the Norwegian coast. The crewmembers were already excited, anticipating the long passage home. Tired minds were turning to thoughts of family reunions on the piers of the New London submarine base.

For the last several days, the *Memphis*'s radio and sonar rooms had been handling a huge amount of data. The communications traffic of the Russian naval exercise reached a peak as the warships and submarines performed their complex dance. For the last forty-eight hours, the *Memphis*'s sensors had been picking up and recording the sounds of numerous Russian missile launches and torpedo firings.

Four separate Russian submarines had been identified by their acoustic signatures and by their radio traffic: the giant Delta IV ballistic-missile sub the *Karelia*, the attack boats the *Boriso-Glebsk* and the *Daniil Moskovsky*, and finally the formidable Oscar II multipurpose missile attack submarine the *Kursk*. Above them, and to the northeast, was the flagship of the Fleet, the battle cruiser the *Peter the Great*.

Late that Saturday morning, the Russians seemed to be going through the final steps of the exercise, with their submarines launching their practice torpedoes. As the *Memphis*'s specialists covertly eavesdropped on these operations, nothing forewarned Breor of the startling sounds he was about to overhear. No intercepts or sonar plots suggested anything was amiss.

At precisely 11:28 A.M., a powerful shock wave rang through the hull of the *Memphis*. Even from a distance of sixty-five nautical miles, it was audible to those without earphones. Submarine sensors flared wildly, and sonar operators immediately reported the news to the command team in the attack center, unable to suppress the surprise in their voices. Then, just as Breor called for more information and a "classification," the *Memphis* was rocked by a second, even more powerful explosion.

What the hell had just happened?

Breor at first assumed the explosion was part of the naval exercise, probably a massive depth charge or the detonation of a SS-N-16 Stallion missile on an underwater target. Nothing in his technical training or command experience led him to question this belief. The spooks on board are partly there to make educated guesses about intelligence-gathering opportunities—to *anticipate* what is about to happen. But this time, they had heard nothing to prepare the *Memphis* for the giant blasts. There had been no intercepted communications suggesting test explosions on this scale were imminent.

For Breor, the event quickly coalesced into two related and equally pressing questions: Was the *Memphis* in immediate danger? Had her covert mission been compromised?

Signaling news of the mystery underwater blasts to his Fleet commanders was out of the question. Shooting high-frequency data into the Arctic sky and up to the military communications satellite overhead would only alert the Russians to the presence of an American spy sub. The absolute rule of Barents Sea patrols is to be invisible to the enemy and to do nothing that betrays your presence.

Breor would break strict radio silence only if he judged that matters of overwhelming national security were at stake. If he overheard the countdown to an act of war, such as the preparation for the launch of a nuclear missile, or if his submarine was under torpedo attack, he would send an emergency signal. Otherwise, jeopardizing your covert status or embarrassing your political masters back home is the ultimate submariner's sin. In any case, Breor knew that other U.S. detection systems would pick up the detonations.

The sonar operators aboard the *Memphis* replayed the sounds of the mystery blasts again and again, passing them through a low-frequency analyzer, trying to tease out any clues as to their source. Even after twelve long hours, the specialists were confused about what they had recorded.

Then late in the evening of August 12, just before Breor began the submarine's scheduled withdrawal to make way for the *Toledo*, the spooks in the radio room alerted him to a dramatic rise in Russian radio traffic to and from the exercise area.

All around the Barents Sea, on frequencies that were reserved for emergencies, naval communications circuits were bursting into life. Shore stations and surface warships transmitted a frenzied cacophony of signals. The Russian linguists in the *Memphis*'s radio room listened, almost overwhelmed by the volume, and quickly translated any messages that were not encrypted.

From the volume and content of the communications alone, Breor realized he was no longer watching over a routine naval exercise. Something extraordinary had happened out there, an event so sudden and troubling that it appeared to be generating a kind of panic among the seasoned Northern Fleet commanders.

I

I: 6 A.M., THURSDAY, AUGUST 10
Vidyaevo Garrison

IN A GENTLE CURVE of the hills, surrounded by pine and birch trees, and sandwiched between pristine lakes and the Arctic Sea, the brutal architecture of a Russian garrison town comes into view with first light. Dawn does no favors for Vidyaevo. Gray concrete apartment blocks squat in the valley, crumbling with neglect, and the roads leading to the central square are blistered and cracked. People live in this lonely corner of the Kola Peninsula only because someone has ordered them to do so. The only civilians allowed are the families of the sailors and naval officers, along with a few hundred local workers needed to support and supply the base. They are provided with documents and special passes to get through the security barricades and the perimeter fence. All other outsiders are strictly forbidden.

There are no bars or cafés, no cinemas or sports clubs in Vidyaevo. There is not even a church or a school. This secret, desolate outpost lies within the Arctic Circle, eighty miles northwest of Murmansk. Moscow sits a thousand miles to the south, and the nearest communities are all other submarine bases. The teenagers of Vidyaevo are sent off to the cities to live with relatives; the elderly have sought sanctuary where the geography and the climate are kinder. Only submariners, their wives, and those children too young to be sent elsewhere remain. Those who live in the town say it is a community without a soul. Vidyaevo has 18,000 residents, but no one calls it home.

During the long, brutal winter, the Arctic wind scythes through the town. There are naval ports along this coast where ropes are strung out along the roadsides to allow pedestrians to stay upright in the icy gales. In the humorous slang of the Northern Fleet, the sub base of Gremikha is also called "Flying Dogs," since the town's pets have been known to be blown through the air in the fierce wind. The locals wisely stay indoors or cling to the roadside ropes.

Founded in 1968, Vidyaevo is one of a string of such military towns that the Russian Navy built on the Kola Peninsula during the height of the Cold War. For decades, maps of the region showed no markings at all for the submarine bases. Careful scrutiny of Soviet-era charts reveals just a mass of inlets and fjords and an enigmatic coastline. Only some of the larger towns are marked with mysterious names that hint at military settlements: Base-35, Severomorsk-7, Shipyard-35, Murmansk-60. The official thinking was that if someone had to look at a map or ask directions, he had no business going there in the first place. For much of its short history, Vidyaevo did not officially exist.

The town was named after Fyodor Vidyaev, an impoverished trawlerman from the Volga region who became a legend during the Second World War as a fearless submarine captain. On April 8, 1942, his boat was severely damaged by a German destroyer, and Vidyaev attempted to limp home on the surface. With no power, he ordered the crew to stitch together a sail, tying it between the deck and the raised periscope. Unable to reach land, just as the crew was preparing to scuttle the submarine, they were rescued by another Soviet ship. After further combat patrols, each of them notching up successes against German shipping, in the summer of 1943 Vidyaev's *Shch-422* submarine was lost with all hands. In the skilled words of

Stalin's propagandists, Vidyaev made for a potent legend: the young fisherman from the south whose cunning and courage swung the battle in the Arctic against the Nazis.

A solitary road leads to the Vidyaevo base, winding through the low contours of the Kola Peninsula. The only signs of life along the route are the dwarf birch trees, frozen for much of the year, their growth stunted by the weight of snow and ice upon them. That they grow at all in this climate is an extraordinary achievement. The stark beauty of the land seems enhanced by knowledge of the destructive military power and nuclear weaponry that lie at the end of the road. For security reasons, no overhead lights and no markings delineate the route—there's just a strip of asphalt snaking through the woods. Reflective patches nailed to roadside trees at chest height assist drivers down the potholed route.

Most nights, an eerie silence falls over the base, although down at the docks the steady hum of pier-side generators is punctuated by the pacing of guards trying to stay warm. They protect the submarines around the clock against theft or espionage. In the town at night, the only noise is the occasional bark of a wild dog searching for scraps of food.

Shortly after dawn on August 10, that silence was broken as the base burst into life. In apartments and barracks, sailors quickly dressed and packed one spare set of clothes in their canvas bags. Minutes later, the young men emerged, striding out down the streets, shaking off the early-morning cold. Several buses and trucks arrived to take them down to the docks.

Twenty-four-year-old Sergei Tylik was among those early risers. Like many naval officers, his dislike of life on the base was outweighed by the sense of achievement he felt whenever he headed out to sea. As far as he was concerned, he traveled between two different worlds. There was the shame of living in a dilapidated and primitive base no one cared about, and then there was the pride of working on one of Russia's premier nuclear-powered submarines. The officers used to joke about why they liked the strenuous work aboard the

Kursk so much: *Why do we want to be on patrol? Because it means we're no longer ashore.*

The son of a submariner, Sergei had spent all his life on the Kola Peninsula. Serving in the Northern Fleet was like joining the family business. As a boy, he had loved to listen to officers gathered at his home talk of their adventures at sea. When his father was due to return from long voyages, Sergei's mother would take him down to the pier to wait for the first glimpse of the submarine. His earliest memories were of standing at the docks, wrapped up against the wind, eagerly scanning the horizon.

Sergei said a brief goodbye to his wife, Natasha, and to Lisa, their nine-month-old baby. A lingering farewell was reserved for longer voyages; this was a quick exercise, less than a week, and the submarine would not even leave home waters.

Moored to Pier Number Eight, lying low and menacing in the water, loomed the principal source of Sergei's pride. Russia couldn't offer much these days to inspire a young man with enthusiasm, but this submarine was different. With her huge double hulls and massive steel bulkheads dividing her into a series of sealed compartments, the *Kursk* was described by her designers as unsinkable.

She was the seventh of a class of boats that the Russian Navy designates as an Antey 949A-type and NATO calls an "Oscar II." Whatever you call these subs, they are easily the largest class of attack submarine ever built. Oscar IIs are designed to play a very specific role in combat: to hunt down and destroy American aircraft carriers and their battle groups. Their main weapon is the SS-N-19 Shipwreck, a supersonic anti-ship cruise missile designed to fly so fast and low that it can penetrate even the best Western naval air defenses.

Few other ships have been built amid as much turmoil as the *Kursk* was. During the three years of her construction, the nation she was designed to defend had self-destructed. She was planned under Communism, approved during Mikhail Gorbachev's era of reforms, and her keel was laid down under Boris Yeltsin. In the end, she was commissioned and launched into not the Soviet Navy but the Northern Fleet of the Russian Federation.

The construction of the *Kursk* began in the summer of 1992, on the slips of a White Sea shipyard in Severodvinsk, near Arkhangel. A canvas roof shielded the project from American satellite reconnaissance. Her design dated back to the late 1970s, when the Soviet Union hoped that a new class of giant attack submarine would guarantee victory in any future naval battle. She was a formidable machine the height of a four-story building and longer than two football fields. Submerged, she displaced 23,000 tons. Engineering on this scale was more than just impressive—it seemed outright audacious that anyone could design and build a submarine of this size.

The *Kursk*'s most distinctive feature was her double hull. The outer hydrodynamic hull was made from a high-quality material known as "austenitic steel," with a high-nickel, high-chrome content. Just a third of an inch thick, it was not only strongly resistant to corrosion but had a lower magnetic signature, making it more difficult to track through the water. The inner pressure hull was much thicker, about two inches of high-alloy steel, providing the boat with impressive strength and structural stability. Sitting amid some of the most resource-rich territories in the world, the engineers felt little need to economize on the quality of their steel. The double hulls, with a space of over six and a half feet between them, greatly improved the *Kursk*'s ability to survive a collision or torpedo attack.

Her internal design showed considerable flair and attention to detail as well. Compared with the earlier generation of claustrophobic and noisy Soviet submarines, the *Kursk* was fitted with extraordinary luxuries, including a relaxation area where the sailors could read or listen to music, a small aquarium, and a sauna.

One cool day in March 1995, a quiet ceremony was held in the docks of Vidyaevo. An Orthodox priest, Father Ioann, walked down the ranks of the sailors lining the pier. To each of them, he handed a small icon of St. Nicholas, the patron saint of sailors. In the new Russia, where Communist faith had collapsed and religion was filling the void, even a nuclear submarine needed to be baptized.

Father Ioann solemnly sprinkled holy water over the bow while an assistant murmured prayers and burned incense in a small cup.

Finally, after being given a tour of the submarine, the priest handed to the Fleet command a twelfth-century icon of Our Lady of Kursk. With reverence and pride, the medieval treasure was placed near the command center to act as the submarine's protector, guaranteeing safe voyages in defense of the Russian motherland.

II: 8 A.M., THURSDAY, AUGUST 10
Vidyaevo Naval Docks

ANYONE WATCHING FROM THE PIER would have noticed the men's high spirits as the officers and sailors clambered up the gangway and down the ladders and hatches of the submarine that bright August morning. A five-day voyage was the optimum length: sufficient to break up the monotony of life on the base, but not too long to be away from their families. They were dressed in their summer uniforms of black trousers, cream-colored shirt, and black tie and jacket.

Stooping through the bulkhead doors and quickly making their way along the maze of passageways, the sailors descended the narrow ladders that led into the bowels of the three-decked submarine. Once at their bunks, they quickly changed out of their uniforms into blue working overalls, which were worn for the duration of the voyage by all the men, sailors, officers, and the captain alike.

Once the crew members reported to their posts, and just before the hatches were sealed, they strapped around their waists the small, red emergency canisters that contained a mix of oxygen and helium, to be used if a fire or accident threatened their air supply.

One of the young officers making his way toward the aft of the submarine that morning was Dmitri Kolesnikov, a tall, broad man with a loping walk whose uniform always seemed a size too small. His rust-red hair and large six-foot-four-inch frame stood out in a crowd. Among the most popular officers on board, his good-natured character was forged by an adventurous boyhood in St. Petersburg and an insatiable appetite for stories about the sea. As he grew up, he took every opportunity to explore the city's canals and waterways. By the time he was a teenager, he dreamed of following in his father's footsteps and becoming an *atomshik*, as the elite nuclear submariners are known.

Kolesnikov had served on the *Kursk* for five years, joining the crew shortly after the submarine began operational patrols. He had been due to leave the Navy at the beginning of the year, but had decided to extend his naval career. His main reason to stay on with the Northern Fleet was to improve his pension rights; in March he had married Olga, a teacher from St. Petersburg, and the financial benefits of service mattered for the first time.

Another figure squeezing along the passageways, clutching his briefcase and heading toward his private cabin in the third compartment, was the *Kursk*'s commanding officer, Captain (1st Rank) Gennady Lyachin. At forty-five a little older than most submarine commanders, he was a highly regarded officer, although his relationship with his own naval headquarters was mixed. He had once been formally reprimanded for being rude to a visiting officer from Moscow, and he had been promoted slowly. His career had been saved by a spectacularly successful patrol in 1999, when Lyachin took the *Kursk* to the Mediterranean during the war in Yugoslavia to spy on the American Sixth Fleet. For the first time in nearly a decade, a Russian submarine had prowled around NATO's southern ports. After so many years of virtual confinement to their own bases due to severe budget cutbacks, the Northern Fleet was elated. The *Kursk* was at sea for three months, and, according to talk in the officers clubs, Lyachin had spent much of that time skillfully evading the best Western attempts to detect his submarine.

After the mission, Lyachin was summoned to Moscow and congratulated by Russia's military leaders. His name was put forward for the greatest honor that can be bestowed, the title Hero of Russia. The *Kursk*'s Mediterranean voyage was of no great intelligence value, but it had served as an important boost for the morale of the Northern Fleet. Moscow wanted to send out a message to the Russian armed forces that the years of decline and retreat were over, and the *Kursk* mission served that purpose perfectly.

Lyachin was comfortable in command, capable but not charismatic. Plenty of rumors circulated around Vidyaevo about him. Some people suggested that he drank too much, while others whispered of his wife's friendship with a local doctor. Kinder people knew better than to pry, for everyone has a secret in a place like Vidyaevo. There would always be malicious gossip—it was the price of living in a secretive and claustrophobic naval base. To those who worked under him, Lyachin was a demanding and exacting captain but also a man who cared for his sailors and their families. He made a point of writing to the parents of every young sailor who joined the *Kursk,* assuring them that he would keep an eye on the progress and safety of their son. In the world of the Russian military, where abuse is common, this gesture won him lasting gratitude among the crew and their families. "There is none of the usual bullying that new recruits face in the military," wrote one of the submarine's cooks, Oleg Yevdokimov, in a letter to his mother, telling her cheerfully of his recent transfer to the *Kursk.*

Facing constant staff shortages, Captain Lyachin tried his best to build a strong crew and keep them together as a team, cajoling his most talented young officers to stay with the submarine as well as poaching the best specialists from other ships. Fate played its own part in deciding who sailed on the *Kursk* that day. The *Voronezh* and the *Kursk* were sister submarines in Vidyaevo, even sharing the same pier, and when one was preparing to go to sea, a last-minute transfer of staff from one ship to the other was common. Andrei Polyansky normally served on the *Voronezh,* but that morning he boarded the *Kursk* as a replacement engineer. Other *Kursk* crewmembers avoided the voyage in the days just before departure: Nikolai Miziak was granted compassionate leave to look after his dying mother; Oleg Sukharev had fallen ill.

* * *

The *Kursk* crew came from many different parts of Russia. Some hailed from the traditional maritime cities along the Baltic and the Crimea, others from inland towns and villages scattered across the steppes. They had first met at submarine training colleges in St. Petersburg or Sebastopol, and they had forged close friendships, personal bonds that transcended all other loyalties.

Among those serving in the aft compartments, alongside Kolesnikov, were Sergei Lybushkin and Rashid Ariapov. All aged twenty-eight and sharing the rank of captain-lieutenant, the three men were inseparable. They had known one another since cadet school, and after graduating they had requested that they serve together. At first, the friends were sent to different bases on the Kola Peninsula, but they had badgered their commanders until the Fleet assigned them to the same base. By sheer good fortune, they ended up in the same submarine.

The *Kursk* crew was linked not just by friendship but also by a complex mix of emotions. They were patriotic and believed in the need to defend the Russian nation, but they also shared a brewing anger and frustration. Many saw their principal day-to-day enemy as not the West but their own corrupt military bureaucracy, and several members of the *Kursk* crew loyally served in the submarine even while they took legal action against the Northern Fleet. Andrei Rudakov, the *Kursk*'s senior communications officer, was pursuing a case in Vidyaevo's military tribunal, demanding that the submarine crew be paid their salaries on time. For several years, he had also been attempting to sue the Navy for lost pay during the mid-1990s. Unable to afford a lawyer, he had studied military law in the evenings so that he could handle the case himself and provide assistance to his crewmates. Far from being discouraged by senior officers, Rudakov was surprised to receive the open support of commanders on the base, including Gennady Lyachin.

The issue of pay was one that worried commanders as much as their crews. After returning from one recent patrol, the *Kursk* sailors had gone to the Salaries Office in Vidyaevo to pick up their checks and been told that the wages owed them could not be paid—there was no money left in the bank. Lyachin was determined that would not happen again. So, as the sailors gathered on the pier on August 10, he ordered a midshipman to stay ashore, charged with the task of collecting the crew's salaries on payday, before the Navy had time to divert the money to other uses. The least his men deserved when they returned was a salary.

The pitiful wages did not reflect the sacrifices the men made. The commander of a nuclear submarine in the Northern Fleet was earning the same money as a tram driver in Moscow. Captain-Lieutenant Dmitri Kolesnikov earned a salary of 2,700 rubles a month, the equivalent of just over $1,000 a year. He received a token increase when at sea, and had been granted a bonus of just $100 for his three-month mission to the Mediterranean in 1999.

His father's generation of submariners was sustained by Communist faith and a set of privileges that gave their profession meaning and respect. Now both the ideology and the rewards had vanished, and the young naval officers were motivated primarily by loyalty to one another.

Many had signed up—like sailors all over the world—to improve their education, and to escape the crushing boredom of life in the provinces. These young men wanted to strike out on their own, to see something of Russia beyond the grim monotony of hometown life.

The Navy was a path to opportunity. It might offer a harsh life—living in a bleak military base in the Arctic Circle and serving in the claustrophobia of a submarine—but compared with where these young men had grown up, in communities blighted by alcoholism and economic decay, the Northern Fleet represented freedom.

III: 10.00 A.M., THURSDAY, AUGUST 10
Ara-Guba Bay

THE *KURSK* WAS GENTLY maneuvered away from Vidyaevo's Pier Number Eight by two weatherbeaten tugs. The bay was tranquil, bathed in a watery sun, and with a gentle breeze blowing from the north. A small swell slapped across the tiles on the steel hull, barely noticeable.

She was one of a dozen submarines in the Seventh Division that came under the command of the First Flotilla. The division commander was away on holiday that week, and his deputy, Captain Oleg Yakubin, commander of another submarine, was on duty. Yakubin had glimpsed the final preparations for departure as he worked from his office overlooking the dock. In one glimpse, he had noticed the mooring lines being thrown back onto the pier. The next time he looked out of his window, the pier was empty, and out in the bay, edging toward the open sea, the *Kursk* stood, ink-black against the sea, her upper rudder rising from the water like the tail of a whale.

Once out of the Ara-Guba Bay and past the little settlement of Port Vladimir, founded by traders at the end of the nineteenth century, Captain Lyachin ordered the *Kursk* to dive to periscope depth and head due east to join the final phase of the Fleet exercise. He must have been greatly relieved to be under way, for the preceding days had been plagued with maddening bureaucratic tangles. When Lyachin had docked the submarine at the loading pier in the nearby port of Zapadnaya Litsa to take on the practice torpedoes, they were not ready. When the torpedoes finally arrived, the crane needed to load them was broken. After hours of delays, another crane was finally used, and the *Kursk* took on both the torpedoes and a full complement of twenty-four Shipwreck cruise missiles, each gingerly lowered into the tubes on either side of her double hulls. Although the *Kursk* was only participating in an exercise, she still took on her warload of weapons. She was one of an elite group of submarines kept ready at all times for combat operations.

The "weapons fit" of a submarine—the exact configuration of missiles and torpedoes carried on a particular deployment—is regarded as an important military secret. The *Kursk*'s official "table of arms" for that day showed that when she set sail, in addition to the Shipwrecks she was carrying eighteen torpedoes, including a mix of

SS-N-15 Starfish missiles, fired through the smaller 533mm torpedo tubes, and heavier SS-N-16 Stallion missiles, launched through the 650mm tubes. Two of the regular torpedoes had been converted for training purposes, fitted with flotation devices and dummy warheads.

Lyachin knew that the *Kursk* would not be alone under the waves. Three other Russian submarines were part of the exercise, and he also suspected that there would be another unidentified boat, a British or American submarine on patrol, keeping an eye on the exercise. With a further thirty warships and auxiliary vessels taking part, watched over by a couple of Western surface spy ships, the shallow Barents Sea would be unusually crowded.

2

Northern Fleet Headquarters, Severomorsk

SUMMER WAR GAMES IN THE Barents Sea date back as far as any officer can remember. Even in the darkest years, during the mid-1990s, when fuel was in critically short supply, the Fleet command managed to choreograph small exercises.

The year 2000 was going to be different. Plans were in place for maneuvers on a scale not seen since the collapse of the Soviet Union a decade earlier. The Northern Fleet admirals were eager to impress the newly elected Russian president, Vladimir Putin, who had come to power promising to boost the prestige and morale of the military. Even better, Putin had grown up in St. Petersburg, the birthplace of the Russian Fleet, and it was widely hoped he would seek to restore naval pride. Several sycophantic gestures were made by the admirals in an attempt to curry favor with the young president, including firing a ballistic nuclear missile from a submarine to "celebrate" his election.

There was also an operational reason for a more extensive exercise. Training was essential in advance of a deployment of Russian warships to the Mediterranean later in the year, projected as the boldest Russian naval activity since the end of the Cold War. The imminent exercise to prepare for this deployment would involve low-level air strikes against surface ships, missile firings from warships, and a third phase that would test the tactical skills of submarine commanders. The training would culminate with the submarines executing ambushes and launching torpedo attacks. The *Peter the Great,* the Northern Fleet's cruiser and flagship, would steam through the exercise area and act as the main target.

The leadership of the Northern Fleet in the summer of 2000 was in the hands of just two men, both larger-than-life submariners widely respected by their own sailors and officers. They were not naval bureaucrats from Moscow. They had earned their position and rank the hard way, excelling on long voyages and on dangerous missions.

Admiral Viacheslav Popov is a craggy-faced, chain-smoking commander who likes to remind people that if the durations of all his submarine patrols are added together, he has spent a total of eight years under the sea. Almost all his time has been with the Northern Fleet. His only other naval experience was a few months in 1996 as the third-ranking officer of the Baltic command. He laughs at the memory of being called back to the Kola Peninsula after that brief assignment. "I arrived back in Murmansk. It was minus eighteen degrees Celsius; there was an Arctic blizzard; the wind was ferocious. I knew I had arrived home." Those who know him best say that there are two parts to his love affair with the navy: the Northern Fleet and the submarine flotillas.

Popov occupies a unique status within the Russian military, not only because of the length of his service as a submarine commander but also because he is part of a legendary naval family. Both his younger brothers are also senior submarine officers. Captain Alexei Popov serves under his older brother at the staff headquarters of the Northern Fleet, and Vladimir Popov, the youngest of the three, commands a naval training college on the Black Sea.

Admiral Popov's staff officers say that he cannot be bribed—a remarkable tribute in the new Russia. Popov is proud, emotional, and patriotic. He wears the Order of the Red Star and the Order of the Motherland prominently. He also insists on bringing along to naval parades his six-year-old grandson, Slava, wearing his own little uniform. But the sentimental side of Popov does not disguise his deep dismay at the state of his beloved Fleet or the suppressed fury that the American and British navies have turned his home waters into their intelligence playground. For Popov, the extent of Western submarine espionage around the Kola Peninsula is a constant reminder of Russia's naval decline.

His deputy is Vice Admiral Mikhail Motsak, a former commander of attack submarines, who won the title Hero of Russia for a famed patrol under the North Pole. As the Northern Fleet's chief of staff, Motsak had direct responsibility for planning the summer exercise. Privately, some senior naval staff officers grumbled that the maneuvers were a charade. Moscow liked to pretend that the Fleet was a major naval presence, when in reality it barely had the resources to act as a coastal defense force. Only the nuclear submarines possessed global importance, and that was because the ballistic missiles could reach their targets without the boats leaving the Barents Sea. The idea of projecting power into foreign oceans struck those who knew the Fleet best as hopelessly overambitious, a fantasy drawn from the world of Potemkin, where everything was dressed up to impress a new tsar.

Charade or not, that August's naval exercise featured a clever twist, a tribute to Russian cunning and to the abilities of Admiral Popov. The plan, known to only a handful of the most senior Russian naval planners and strategists, was to use the exercise as a smoke-screen. Under the disguise of the war games, one of the Northern Fleet missile submarines—a boomer, fully armed with her nuclear missiles—would attempt to sneak out of her home port and slip under the summer ice, undetected by the Americans. Russian admirals use the pristine Arctic world as a place to hide their submarines from American surveillance.

The plan had Popov's fingerprints all over it. He made his name as a commander of ballistic-missile submarines who prided himself on an ability to outfox the Americans. He believed that the American spy submarines would be drawn to the exercise like bees to honey. If the Americans fell for the trick and decided to monitor the missile and torpedo firings, that would leave a crucial gap in their surveillance of the route up to the icepack. The routine August naval maneuvers were important in their own right, but of much greater strategic significance was this question of whether Russia could deploy its missile submarine without being trailed. Many ruses had been used in the past, such as Russian submarines following in the wake of a large merchant ship, hoping the acoustic disturbance would disguise the submarine's presence, and the stakes behind such diversionary games have always been high. In a war, detection can mean destruction, and destruction of the entire SSBN fleet would represent the loss of Russia's strategic nuclear reserve.

For many years now, the Russians have excelled in under-ice submarine operations. Throughout the Cold War, they studied the unique oceanography and acoustics of the Arctic, learning how best to exploit the conditions to compensate for the superior sonar technology of the American boats. Under the thick pack ice, the odds favor the submarine trying to hide, not those pursuing her. She is invulnerable to detection from aircraft and satellite reconnaissance. No sonar buoys can be dropped into the water to try to track her. In addition, the sophisticated American seabed sensors that are deployed in other ocean areas are very difficult to install and maintain under the ice. Furthermore, the water is extremely tranquil; there are no waves, no shipping, and very little marine life. The result is that any approaching U.S. attack submarine can be detected. But there is a very obvious problem: An SSBN is unable to fire her missiles through thick ice. The icepack may be a good place under which to hide, but it is no place to be when war breaks out.

Instead, the Russian submarine fleet has learned to operate patrols in another part of the Arctic waters, an area known as the Marginal Ice Zone (MIZ). Here, open patches of water vie with slabs of ice, and some of the most complex games of hide-and-seek between Western and Russian boats are played out. The MIZ is a totally different acoustic environment in comparison to the world under the pack ice. The ocean here is filled with noise: It is rich with marine life and crackles with the sounds of colliding ice floes. The seals and whales, the walruses and other marine mammals, combine to produce a cacophony that confuses the spy submarines. The Russian boats have the opportunity to use these background acoustics to hide from the American hunters while still having sufficient open water through which to fire their ballistic missiles.

The American and Russian admirals want this gamesmanship to be a private affair, part intelligence gathering, part probing and testing, part psychological warfare. The quiet dance, the elaborate choreography of rival submarine operations in Russia's Arctic seas, goes on to this day, invisibly, as it has for half a century.

II: 8 A.M., SATURDAY, AUGUST 12
Southern Barents Sea

FOR FORTY-EIGHT HOURS, from early on Thursday, August 10, until Saturday, the Northern Fleet exercise went broadly according to plan, although there were a number of highly visible technical problems and weapons failures. Several surface warships fired missiles at target barges over the horizon to test the launch systems and the crew training. The *Peter the Great*'s first firing went spectacularly wrong, an SS-N-19 missile crashing into the sea a short distance from the ship. Engine failure was suspected, since commanders deliberately chose to use their oldest missiles first. The second launch went much better, the dummy warhead landing extremely close to the target, near enough for observers in patrol boats to describe it as a "complete success."

The pressure to send positive news to the Defense Ministry was intense, and Admiral Popov obliged by giving a prerecorded television interview expressing deep satisfaction with the performance of the ships and submarines and describing the maneuvers as a resounding success. The crews, he added, were heading home.

As premature congratulatory statements go, this would take some beating, for the exercise was not quite over. All four submarines—the attack subs the *Kursk,* the *Boriso-Glebsk,* and the *Daniil Moskovsky* and the SSBN the *Karelia*—still had to go through their paces.

The attack submarines were tasked to fire torpedoes, and the *Karelia* was to launch a ballistic missile. On board the Northern Fleet submarines, the commanding officers were preparing for the tactical phase of the war games, when they would maneuver within their pre-assigned "patrol boxes" and try to avoid detection by the Russian surface ships. The Fleet gave prizes to the submarine crew that performed best, and there was a good-natured rivalry between the commanding officers for the awards.

As the sun rose higher in the clear Arctic sky that Saturday morning, the *Peter the Great* and her support ships surged through the sea on a westerly heading. The group's exact movements were kept secret, to introduce an element of surprise. Before long, the ships turned around, sweeping back on a southeasterly heading. All the submarines were now deployed in their firing areas, and each captain signaled to the Fleet command that he was waiting for the final phase of the exercise to begin.

The *Kursk* signal—"We are ready for torpedo firing"—was received at 8:51 A.M.

This would be the final communication from the *Kursk* until she reported the completion of the test. Each submarine was under strict instructions to stay within her specified exercise area. This eliminated the possibility of a collision and would also help the surface ships detect the presence of a Western spy sub. Any acoustic contact moving quietly below the waves but outside the designated patrol boxes could be regarded as a hostile Western submarine.

The whole focus of the *Kursk*'s operations now shifted to the forward two compartments, which housed the command center and the torpedo room. The rest of the submarine simply existed to transport the weapons to the firing point, and now the flair, tactical skill, and cool nerves of the commander took center stage.

Captain Lyachin liked to stand in the heart of the central command post in the run-up to a torpedo launch, watching over his team and absorbing information from those around him. The officers were excellent professionals, and their mood was upbeat. In each compartment, there were men he completely trusted, a bond forged during the long Mediterranean patrol nine months before. He had the comfort of knowing that extra technicians were working in the torpedo room, and he was not bothered by the presence in the control center of several senior, shore-based staff officers, who had joined the sub for the exercises.

In a properly worked-up submarine, the atmosphere is calm and professional at this time. Submarine commanding officers say that the perfect attack is conducted in a taut, efficient, and ruthlessly clinical manner. But for Russian submarine COs, with much less training than their Western counterparts, a weapons launch is an anxious affair. Despite his confidence in the crew, Lyachin was well aware of the heightened risks that resulted from the atrocious condition of the Fleet's infrastructure. Even as he concentrated on the flow of orders and preparations leading up to his imminent order to fire, he had to wrestle with a number of disturbing questions. These were doubts that preoccupied all Russian sub commanders. Were the test torpedoes being reused too often? Had a warhead been destabilized during poor handling? Were the safety rules about weapons storage being strictly enforced?

Once the *Peter the Great* penetrated the *Kursk*'s designated area, and Lyachin was satisfied with his line of attack, he would order the launch of two special practice torpedoes in quick succession. The warheads had been removed from the weapons, and in their place devices had been installed to record the speed, direction, and depth of the torpedoes. In addition, a safety feature was fitted to each, which ensured that they would run too deep to risk hitting a surface ship. Flotation devices would bring the torpedoes to the surface at the end of their runs.

An alarm rang throughout the submarine, one short burst, then a long one lasting twenty seconds, the signal for the crew to man their battle stations. A voiced command from a senior officer then explained the reason for the alarm:

"*Uchebnaya trevoga. Torpednaya ataka.*"

"Practice alarm. Torpedo attack."

The *Kursk* moved into position for the launch. A torpedo slid into the larger 650mm tube, on the starboard side, with a sharp hiss of air and the sound of the tube's breech door closing behind it. In the torpedo room, all appeared well. In keeping with common practice during firings, the reinforced, watertight doors between the command center and the torpedo room were opened, which helps to minimize the change in pressure and to dissipate the noise of a weapon's launch.

Just before 11:30 A.M., Lyachin was making the final calculations of the firing geometry and choosing the precise timing of the attack.

The chain of events that would soon unfold was triggered not by Lyachin but by an unforeseen development in the first compartment's torpedo room, a crowded workspace filled with weapon racks. With their distinctive green-and-gray steel casings, the torpedoes lie on shelving, their propellers wrapped in protective covering. A narrow walkway down the center allows the technicians to inspect the weapons, but it's a tight squeeze.

Modern torpedoes are built with the same basic design as the primitive versions of eighty years ago: At the front lies a warhead, and behind that is a propulsion system to drive the torpedo through the water as well as a guidance system to steer the weapon to its target. In the earliest days, when the torpedo was proving itself as a weapon during the First World War, the warhead featured a fuse that was triggered to explode when it collided with a ship's hull. The torpedo's propulsion was driven by either compressed air or an electric motor. The new generation of underwater weapons are much more devastating, designed to travel much faster, to carry greater destructive power over increased range, and to pursue a target actively. They are ultra-high-performance machines that, once released, engage in a dramatic sprint toward an ever-shifting target in the ocean. Some naval engineers compare the race to a cheetah's pursuit of an antelope—the hunter following every desperate twist and turn of the prey, all the time closing in for the kill.

The search for extreme performance in an underwater weapon has heightened dangers. High-speed and long-range torpedoes require huge quantities of energy; the energy stored in the propulsion section of a modern high-performance torpedo exceeds even that of the warhead. The engineering challenge is how to tame this energy until the moment of launch.

In the 1920s, propulsion engineers came up with the idea of powering a torpedo by using a conventional fuel, such as kerosene, and giving it an immense energy boost by mixing it with an oxidant. That combination would result in a furious but contained chemical reaction. The best theoretical choice was liquid oxygen, but it was judged far too dangerous and volatile to store inside a submarine. Second best was hydrogen peroxide, known in its highly concentrated form as high-test peroxide (HTP).

The first Russian HTP torpedo was known by the strictly functional name of "53-57," the 53 referring to the diameter in centimeters of the torpedo tube, the 57 to the year it was introduced. Moscow's military leaders, adhering to a deep-seated belief that bigger was better, committed themselves to building ever more powerful weapons. Driven by Cold War competition, they ordered the development of a larger, more potent HTP torpedo. The result was the 65-76 torpedo. As the name suggests, the weapon would be launched from 65cm tubes, and it was introduced in 1976. The torpedo found a place throughout the Russian fleet of nuclear-powered multipurpose submarines. The *Kursk* was carrying two of them on the morning of the test. One had just been loaded into the star-board's tube number four, and would be the first practice torpedo fired. The second weapon due to be launched that day was a USET-80, a smaller but powerful torpedo that uses an electric propulsion system.

Once the firing countdown is under way, the launch technicians run through a strict checklist of preparations:

- confirm the outer torpedo tube door is securely shut; double-check it by opening a valve and making sure the water is not under high pressure;
- secure the inner door in the open position; check if the empty torpedo tube is clear of debris;
- check the torpedo's latch claws are attached; remove the safety covers and pins in the torpedo's nose;
- observe closely as the hydraulic lifts align the torpedo with the 65cm tube on the starboard side.

At this point, the weapon glides forward into the torpedo tube, immense power contained within a deceptively simple casing. The intercom to the command center is kept open to allow for a constant dialogue with officers in the second compartment as the final series of checks continues in the torpedo room:

- remove the protective covers from the propellers and from the steering at the rear of the torpedo;
- allow the torpedo to slot home; connect the control cables;
- shut the inner door; flood the tube.

Seawater rushes into the torpedo tube until the pressure is equal to that of the outside ocean. The torpedo room then waits for the captain's instructions to open the outer door in the external hydro-dynamic hull, breaking the clean shape of the submarine's bow.

Then they wait for the order to fire.

In the command post at this time, all eyes are on the captain. Perhaps only a fighter pilot has the same single-handed ability to shape the outcome of a mission as that of a submarine commander. Although there is an intense camaraderie on board—more than one hundred highly trained professionals working as a team, each with a very specific responsibility—as soon as a torpedo launch or missile firing is being prepared, or when a submarine is involved in combat or an emergency, the commanding officer makes all the big decisions. One man alone in the attack center determines the fate of the submarine and the success of the mission.

In no other walk of life can a man in his thirties or early forties be thrown into such a demanding and lonely job as commanding a nuclear submarine, where panicking under pressure can have catastrophic results. Once at sea on covert patrol, submarines are expected to communicate only in absolute emergencies. The commanding officer of a ballistic-missile submarine is on his own, with sufficient power to annihilate large parts of the planet.

Lyachin opted to launch his exercise attack on the *Peter the Great* cruiser from periscope depth. Firing a torpedo from deeper is an option, and in war, when preserving the submarine's covert status is a matter of survival, that may be the most desirable tactic. But it is much easier to engage a target when your periscope and masts are breaking the surface—like going into a fight with your eyes open. Lyachin tracked the *Peter the Great* with all the *Kursk*'s sensors: the periscope, the sonars, and the electronic intercepts of the surface ship's radar. He confirmed the identity of the target, matching the *Peter the Great*'s passive sonar signature to his library data. Everything was ready for the attack.

The latest target information flashed down the control cable attached to the torpedo's guidance system. On the appropriate command, the motor of the 65-76 would start up, and as it gathered momentum, compressed air would eject the torpedo from the tube and hurl it into open water. Then, once safely clear of the submarine, the propulsion system would kick in, the HTP and the kerosene igniting in their virulent chemical reaction, driving the torpedo toward its target at thirty knots.

Captain Lyachin had no reason to know the service history of the practice weapon that lay in tube number four, which at any moment he would send hurtling on its way toward its target. The torpedo was manufactured in 1990 in the Mashzavod factory in Alma-Ata, the biggest city in Kazakhstan and lying deep in Soviet Central Asia. In the possession of the Northern Fleet since January 1994, when it had last been serviced, the torpedo had never been used before, unlike so many of the other practice weapons. Technical documents refer to this particular 65-76 torpedo by the factory manufacturing number 298A 1336A PV. But no paperwork revealed its greatest and most terrifying secret: Deep within the casing, over a period of six years, corrosion had invisibly begun to weaken internal metal and plastic components, including gaskets perilously close to the tank that contained the HTP.

The torpedo had been loaded onto the submarine on August 3 by two of the *Kursk*'s technicians, Senior Midshipman Abdulkhadur Ildarov and Senior Lieutenant Alexei Ivanov-Pavlov. The base supervisor was absent, so they signed the required document themselves, confirming that the weapon was now the responsibility of the *Kursk* crew.

From the moment they signed for the torpedo and winched it through the loading hatch and into the first compartment, Ildarov and Ivanov-Pavlov unwittingly transformed the *Kursk* into a potential disaster zone. The horrifying destructive power of a compromised HTP torpedo had become devastatingly clear forty-five years earlier.

On a sparkling midsummer's morning in 1955, the British Royal Navy's submarine *Sidon* was in Portland harbor, moored alongside a depot ship. With her crew at "harbor stations," HMS *Sidon* was about to proceed to sea, and all her hatches were shut except at the conning tower.

Suddenly, inside her number three tube, a twenty-one-inch torpedo known by its nickname, "Fancy," exploded without warning.

Debris was hurled backward into the torpedo room, and toxic fumes swept through the submarine, killing twelve men. HMS *Sidon* began flooding. Nearby ships made desperate attempts to keep her afloat, but less than thirty minutes after the explosion, she sank.

The accident triggered an exhaustive investigation by the Royal Navy, and for many years the results of the inquiry were kept secret. The Admiralty Board believed that high-test peroxide had leaked out of a pipe and reached the catalyst chamber of the torpedo. Its top-secret report concluded that HTP droplets may have ignited on "an oily or greasy surface . . . [and] violent combustion and consequent rise of pressure burst open the torpedo tube." Six men died from blast and burn injuries; the other six were killed by the thick, poisonous fumes of carbon monoxide that quickly filled the submarine.

At first glance, hydrogen peroxide, H_2O_2, seems an extraordinarily benign liquid, colorless and odorless. As the chemical formula indicates, it is just water (H_2O) with an extra oxygen atom. But when it comes into contact with certain metals, such as copper, the reaction is fast and furious as it tries to eject the additional oxygen atom, producing immense amounts of heat. Copper is found in brass and bronze, both of which were used in the construction of the torpedo tube, and investigators realized that if the hydrogen peroxide leaked while a torpedo was in position for launch, the chemical reaction would begin.

What shocked the investigators was the fact that twelve men had died and a submarine had been lost—without the torpedo warhead even detonating. All the destructive power had been in the propulsion system. The Royal Navy decided then and there that hydrogen peroxide was too volatile to be stored within the unforgiving confines of a torpedo room, and never again did a British submarine go to sea with weapons that used HTP.

Russia's Northern Fleet had issued no such edict. Aboard the *Kursk*, the 65-76 torpedo lay silently in its tube. Poised for launch, the potent HTP chemical cocktail was ready for ignition.

* * *

Seven men were crammed into the small passageways of the torpedo room that day, including Mamed Gadjiev, the only civilian on board. He was from Dagestan in the Russian Caucasus, and he worked in a rundown factory that produced many of the Navy's torpedoes. A talented and serious man in his mid-thirties, Gadjiev's engineering background was in aeronautics. He had studied in the Ukraine before switching to the plant on the shores of the Caspian Sea, to be close to his wife and two teenage daughters. Gadjiev was aboard the *Kursk* to supervise a test of a new battery for the USET-80 torpedo, the second weapon that was to be launched that Saturday morning.

As he stood in the torpedo room, listening to the crew run through the launch checklist, his technical knowledge and engineer's instinct would have given him no advance warning that something was going terribly wrong. The reservoir of colorless HTP was seeping through gaskets deep inside the casing of the 65-76 torpedo. Although an inexorable chemical reaction had begun, it must have been invisible to those in the torpedo room.

The explosive power needed to drive a thirty-five-foot-long, five-ton torpedo at a speed of thirty knots for up to fifty miles was about to annihilate the forward compartment of the *Kursk*. As the reaction accelerated, Gadjiev may have experienced a few seconds of paralyzing horror, fleetingly aware of the enormous destructive forces that were building.

The torpedo exploded in a massive fireball at exactly 11:28.27, with a force equivalent to 220 pounds of TNT. The blast registered 1.5 on the Richter scale—the size of a small earth tremor.

With the torpedo doors still shut, the energy burst backward into the compartment, traveling at more than a thousand feet a second, engulfing all seven men in a rush of flames.

Mamed Gadjiev, Abdulkhadur Ildarov, Alexei Zubov, Ivan Nefedkov, Maxim Borzhov, Alexei Shulgin, Arnold Borisov.

They were incinerated with merciful speed, by forces of overwhelming power.

* * *

Immediately behind the torpedo room, in the second compartment, lies the operational heart of the submarine, where thirty-six men were at their posts. Normally, the command center is manned by thirty-one officers and sailors, but on this voyage an additional five senior, shore-based officers were monitoring the performance of the submarine and her command team. In the control room, at the periscope or close by, stood Captain Lyachin. Next to him sat Sergei Tylik, the twenty-four-year-old with submarining in his blood, watching over his sonar and acoustic equipment.

The explosion ripped through the second compartment with fury, throwing men from their posts and hurling them against the machinery and pipework that surrounded the control room. Submariners who have experienced depth charges talk of their harrowing psychological impact: the fear, the uncertainty of what happens next, the sense of having nowhere to hide. This explosion was on a much greater scale, and *inside* the submarine.

Security forces use stun grenades to incapacitate people because the intense noise and flash of light overwhelms and numbs the human mind. Lyachin, Tylik, and all those around them had been subjected to the shock of a stun grenade multiplied a hundred times. Their shock and disorientation must have been complete. They were in no position to halt the sequence of explosions, ruptures, and avalanching electrical failures that doomed the submarine.

No one who has experienced explosions in a submarine on this scale has survived to relate the horror. The firsthand accounts that come closest are therefore those of the explosions of close-range depth charges. Few have recalled the unique psychology of being in peril in a submarine more vividly than Lothar-Günther Buchheim, who sailed in the German U-boat fleet during the Second World War. He has described the horror of successive concussions, the crew waiting for the hull to rupture, and the fatal rush of the icy ocean:

> The impact has knocked two men down. I see a mouth shrieking, flailing feet, two faces masked in terror. . . . My skull seems under the same extreme pressure as our steel skin. . . . I see and feel every-

thing going on around me with astounding clarity. . . . I hear screams that seem to be coming from a long way off. . . . I want to lie down and hide my head in my arms. No light. The crazy fear of drowning in the dark, unable to see the green-white torrent of water as it comes bursting into the boat. . . .

Lyachin had no time to assess events. Even if he had shouted out orders, he would not have been heard. The explosion ruptured the eardrums of all those in the forward areas of the submarine. The noise of the detonation was itself intensified as hydraulic and compressed air running in pipes throughout the submarine burst into the compartments.

Behind the command center, in the third compartment, lay the *Kursk*'s radio room, the most secretive part of the submarine, accessed only with special keys and codes. Experienced Oscar II officers say that the communications equipment is set up so that when the submarine is at periscope depth, with her antennae extended, an emergency signal can be sent by punching just four or five keys. Commanding the radio room was Andrei Rudakov, the officer who was taking legal action against his own admirals to ensure the sailors were paid on time. Trained in the Pacific Fleet, regarded as tenacious and capable, Rudakov is described by his friends as a man who would have excelled in a crisis.

The *Kursk*'s masts were all extended, just penetrating the ocean surface. At this depth and position, Rudakov appeared to be in an excellent position to dispatch an immediate SOS. But no emergency communication was sent—neither on Northern Fleet encrypted channels nor on international distress frequencies. The radio room must have been badly damaged and Rudakov incapacitated, probably thrown to the deck and severely disoriented.

In the few seconds after the explosion, in horror and confusion, Lyachin and some of the men in the command center must have struggled to regain their bearings. Despite injuries, they would have scrambled to assess the damage and open the air valves in order to bring the *Kursk* to the surface. Blowing air into the ballast tanks is a simple task that requires merely pressing a button on the control console. This would certainly have been the first action of any senior officer on board. But apparently it was already too late for that. If someone did reach and press the button, the submarine was too damaged to respond.

Even the emergency buoy, which is recessed into the casing of the outer hull, failed to function. The device is linked to sensors that detect a range of emergency conditions, such as increasing pressure inside the submarine, flooding, or fire, all of which should automatically trigger the buoy's release, sending it shooting upward on a cable. On reaching the surface, an antenna begins to transmit distress signals. Once the buoy is located, rescuers need only follow the cable down to the seabed to locate the missing submarine. Some Northern Fleet specialists claim that the *Kursk*'s buoy had malfunctioned so many times that it had been welded down; others suggest that the sensors were destroyed by the explosion before they could trigger the buoy's release. The startling truth is that during the *Kursk*'s 1999 Mediterranean voyage, there had been so much concern that the buoy would accidentally deploy and reveal the sub's position to Western naval forces that the release mechanism in the third compartment had been overridden. Even during this summer exercise in home waters, the mechanism lay deliberately disabled. The operating key in the machine that controlled the buoy had been removed.

If Lyachin and his senior officers had time to think that their predicament could not get any worse, they had only to glance at the depth gauges, which were still operating, to discover that the *Kursk* was now being driven downward by her own power and by the weight of the water that was pouring into the forward compartments through broken internal pipework.

The shallow water of the southern Barents Sea now presented its

own grave danger. A lack of depth is a hazard in submarine operations, depriving a commanding officer of any margin for error. Even
if Lyachin managed to make command decisions, he was desperately
short of time. The average depth of the Barents Sea is 720 feet, and
there are areas south of Bear Island where it reaches just under
2,000 feet. But the *Kursk* was in water only 375 feet deep. Instead of
several minutes in which to save his submarine, Lyachin had only
seconds.

In the wrecked torpedo room, the laws of physics were remorse-
lessly at work. The inexorable reaction of fuel and HTP cannot be
halted; it is self-sustaining, like an avalanche. Torpedoes give you no
second chance. Extinguishers and other firefighting equipment,
even if you have time to deploy them, are worthless. The reaction will
only stop only when the chemicals—in this case, 2,200 pounds of
HTP and 1,100 pounds of kerosene—are used up. The forward compartment became a giant combustion chamber: the fuel-fire of the
torpedo, the mix of kerosene and high-test peroxide, raging to an
incredible heat. The torpedo racks, the patchwork of wiring, the
steel bulkheads, and the casings of the remaining twenty-three
weapons began to melt. The torpedoes—not the practice weapons,
but the actual warload—were either still lying jammed on their racks
or were strewn among the debris from the explosion.

The warheads were, essentially, cooking.

Explosives suffer spontaneous combustion at around four hundred degrees Celsius (725°F.). The temperature in the torpedo room
was soaring well into the danger zone.

The uncontrolled dive of the submarine lasted exactly 135 seconds,
before the second explosion tore through the compartments. It is
estimated that the *Kursk* traveled around a quarter of a mile between
the detonations, descending 350 feet. The 23,000-ton ship crashed
into the seabed at only a slight angle but with shuddering force.

The second detonation was a truly seismic event, nearly 250 times greater than the initial blast. All the warheads and the fuel in the remaining torpedoes ignited almost simultaneously, an explosion that registered 3.5 on the Richter scale. Scientists who have studied the seismic patterns generated by this second explosion say that it occurred at the same depth as the seabed—at 375 feet. That suggests, but does not prove, that the second detonation was triggered by the crash into the seabed rather than the warheads reaching spontaneous combustion. In fact, either could have been true. The fire inside the torpedo room was generating an inferno, temperatures now reaching several *thousand* degrees.

The pressure hull is far stronger than the internal bulkheads that separate the compartments. The high-strength, high-yield steel of the hull can withstand pressure up to a depth of 3,200 feet, whereas the bulkheads would yield at a tenth of that. But the scale of this second explosion made such distinctions barely relevant. The second blast ruptured the hull only a fraction of a second after the forward compartment's bulkhead was demolished. Directly above the torpedo storage area, on the starboard side, the shock wave tore out ten square feet of the pressure hull. The thick steel was punched out, as if by a giant fist. The outer hydrodynamic hull, just a third of an inch thick, stood no chance.

The shock waves then raced through the ocean, hammering into the seabed. Into a compartment that had been devastated by fire and explosion now roared icy Arctic waters, just a few degrees above freezing and under sufficient pressure to cut a man in two. Had the boat been close to the surface, the torpedo compartment, with its twenty-one-square-foot hole in the hull, would have filled up at a rate of 24,000 gallons a second; at a depth of nearly 375 feet, under the additional water pressure, the compartment filled up much faster. In just sixteen seconds, it was entirely flooded. The sailors and officers in the command center who had survived the first explosion stood no chance now. With the bulkhead destroyed between the torpedo room and the second compartment, they faced a crushing wall of water.

The second blast left all four forward compartments shattered.

Rudakov and his team of twenty-four officers and sailors in the third compartment were protected only by the steel bulkhead that separated them from the control room, and that was ripped open as if it were made of paper. The fourth compartment, home to the kitchen, the canteen, and many of the living and sleeping quarters of the submariners, was wrecked. Those trapped here included Oleg Yevdokimov, the young chef who had regarded his transfer to the *Kursk* as a blessing because Captain Lyachin's watchful eye meant he would escape the bullying that was so prevalent elsewhere in the Russian armed forces.

As the shock wave punched its way through the large fourth compartment, the successive internal bulkheads began to slow the velocity of the blast. The explosion now became a titanic contest between the tremendous force of the blast and the engineering rigor of the submarine. The question was how far the destruction would extend back into the aft of the *Kursk*. The fifth compartment housed the twin nuclear reactors. They were encased by walls of extraordinary strength, surrounded by five inches of hardened high-grade steel, capable of resisting pressure to 3,200 feet, the same resilience as that of the inner hull.

The shock waves wreaked havoc in the first four compartments, smashing through the bulkheads up to the nuclear reactors. There, the bulkhead held. It was buckled and twisted, but, astonishingly, the steel held. An earlier generation of Russian *atomshiks* had scornfully described their submarines as "nuclear tractors," because of the rudimentary engineering that surrounded the reactors. But there was no mocking the construction of the *Kursk*. Against all the odds, a team of designers and engineers had built in a huge safety margin, and their work had passed the supreme test. The blast was halted at the most critical point, before the shock waves dislodged the control rods. If those rods had not been driven safely home in time, the reactors would have continued running, and without proper water circulation they would have become hotter and hotter. In a short time, the fuel could have melted its way through the reactor, a highly radio-active lump burning into the seabed and poisoning the ocean.

The world had come one bulkhead away from a nuclear disaster. Five inches of precious steel made sure this was a submarine acci-dent, not a regional disaster.

In the event, the control rods were driven safely home, either by an automatic safety mechanism or by a sailor reacting with lightning speed to the impending disaster. Either way, the nuclear reactors "scrammed," automatically shutting down. The pressure in the steam plant plummeted as the turbogenerators stopped. The batteries in the forward compartments were destroyed. The *Kursk* now lay inert on the seabed, without electrical power.

Broken bodies floated in flooded passageways. Driven into the upper part of the bow compartment's ceiling were the remnants of the 65-76 torpedo that had been in the starboard tube. One of the sailors in the command center was blown backward and upward with such power that his corpse was later found embedded in the ceiling of the second compartment.

The submarine herself was over 500 feet long, so she was resting at a depth far less than her own length. Had she done the impossible and ended up resting vertically, some 130 feet of the submarine would have reared above the surface. The escape hatch over the ninth compartment would have been several yards above the waves.

With compartments one to five flooded, both hulls punctured, and her twin 190-megawatt reactors shut down, the *Kursk* was fatally wounded. The crowning achievement of the legendary Rubin design bureau in St. Petersburg and the Sevmash shipyard on the White Sea lay devastated on the bottom of the Barents Sea.

She had taken a decade to design, three years to build, and just 135 seconds to destroy.

For the survivors in the stern compartments of the crippled subma-rine, the ordeal was just beginning. One hundred meters separated the point of the explosion and the sixth compartment just aft of the nuclear reactors. The engineers at the shipyard on the White Sea had spoken of the boat's "survivability," and in one sense they had been proved right. It seems inconceivable that any other submarine in the world would have afforded the chance of life to so many of her crew after twin explosions of this size. What occurred to the *Kursk* was the worst nightmare imaginable for the Sevmash shipyard and the Rubin design bureau, but it was also their most remarkable achievement.

The sixth compartment was manned by five sailors led by Captain-Lieutenant Rashid Ariapov, the young married officer from Uzbekistan whose wife had told him just a few weeks earlier that she was pregnant with their first child. He was in charge of the submarine's propulsion systems. The seventh and eighth compartments housed the team in charge of the main engines and turbogenerators, a further sixteen men, led by Ariapov's friend Dmitri Kolesnikov and Sergei Sadilenko, both men with the rank of captain-lieutenant. In the final compartment, the ninth, three more sailors served as mechanics.

Just before the torpedo launch, we know, two of the sailors in the stern had moved forward, and one crew member had come aft, leaving twenty-three men behind the protective wall of the reactors. They had heard the standard warning bell and listened to the command post notifying them of the imminent firing.

The sailors in the aft must have been thrown to the deck by the shock waves, and waited in horror as the submarine buckled and convulsed, alarms ringing out. The sound of tearing steel screeched through the ship. In all four aft compartments, depth meters would have told them that the *Kursk* was rapidly plunging downward. Communication links with the control room were severed, leaving the sailors in the aft isolated and terrified. They can only have guessed at the horrors that were being inflicted on their colleagues and friends farther forward. There was no way for them to know what had happened, but they must have deduced that either there had been a massive collision with a ship or submarine, or else one of their own torpedoes or missiles had detonated.

For the first few moments after the second explosion, they were thrust into a world where survival was completely out of their own hands. Had the pressure hull ruptured over the stern, they would have faced instant death. The physics of the explosions and the work of designers in St. Petersburg and engineers in an Arctic shipyard several years earlier were determining whether they would be alive in a few seconds' time. They must have stared desperately at the bulkheads and hatches, waiting to see if these protective barriers would withstand the shock waves and the crushing pressure of the outside ocean.

By the time the submarine had slammed into the seabed, carving a shallow channel in the silt, the *Kursk* had lost communications, heating, ventilation, and all but emergency lighting. The hydraulic and electrical systems had collapsed. The twenty-three sailors were entombed.

As they lay on the deck, or clutched at machinery to maintain their balance, the deafening echoes of the detonations faded away. Amid the baffling horror of what they were facing, they still had no comprehension of the ordeal that now lay ahead.

3

I: 11:28 A.M., SATURDAY, AUGUST 12
On board Delta IV submarine the **Karelia,**
northeast of Kildin Island

THIRTY-TWO NAUTICAL MILES FROM the *Kursk,* the Russian ballistic-missile submarine the *Karelia* glided through the water at periscope depth. At the age of thirty-six, her commanding officer, Captain Andrei Korablev, is one of the young stars of the Northern Fleet's submarine flotilla. The *Karelia* is a giant Delta IV–class SSBN, one of the "boomers" that the U.S. Navy seeks to track at every available opportunity. On board, at least a dozen missiles were sitting silently in their launch tubes, each with multiple warheads capable of destroying large swathes of the United States. In addition, several others had been converted for test firings.

Calm and methodical, Korablev's self-belief and confidence would be regarded as arrogance in any other profession. His father was the captain of a Soviet diesel submarine, and he grew up on the Baltic base of Kronstadt with the sounds and smells of a naval port all around him. Joining the submarine fleet seemed the most natural step. He lives and breathes the Navy, relishes the responsibility of being on patrol with Russia's nuclear-deterrent force, and enjoys the challenge of evading the American submarines with their superior technology. To outwit the Americans requires the oldest of Russian military skills: cunning, improvisation, stamina.

The *Karelia*'s crew was working with consummate professionalism. Of all the boats in the Fleet, the *Karelia* has the reputation for being the most popular submarine, with the lowest turnover of sailors in the Russian flotilla. Other crews began calling her "the president's submarine" after Vladimir Putin visited the *Karelia* for a brief training exercise a few months earlier. Enjoying their celebrity status, the sailors came up with their own motto: "If not us, then who?"

In less than an hour, Korablev would order a ballistic-missile test firing, set for 12:08 P.M.

The shock waves of the *Kursk* explosions rocked the *Karelia,* sending a shiver straight down her hull. Shouts of alarm resounded through the submarine, and even as he struggled to understand what had happened, Korablev ordered immediate damage reports from all of his compartment commanders. He assumed that the *Karelia* had struck an underwater object, or a depth charge had detonated close to the submarine. From the control room, demands for immediate information were shouted to the sonar operators. The two distinct shock waves had been felt a couple of minutes apart, the second far more powerful than the first. The compartment reports all came back negative, detecting no leaks or other damage.

Korablev wanted a second opinion, and he consulted Rear Admiral Shchegolev, a division commander who was aboard the *Karelia* to monitor the performance of the senior officers, a role known as "command riding." Both men arrived at the same conclusion: The source of the shock waves must have been an underwater explosion linked to the exercise. With a total of thirty surface ships and four submarines reaching the final stage of the exercise, a weapons detonation or depth charge seemed the most likely explanation. During Korablev's briefing at Northern Fleet Headquarters five days earlier, he had been told only about his specific tasks, and he was not privy to the orders for the other warships.

Korablev relaxed a little and decided that the *Karelia*'s missile launch would go ahead as planned. The Fleet admirals would not thank him for radioing in an alarmist report, and Korablev certainly did not want to be blamed for unnecessary communication or for panicking over a weapons test that had nothing to do with him. After all, the *Karelia* was a nuclear-weapons platform, not a coast-guard vessel. There would be no prizes for sending signals that could betray her location to American or British submarines almost certainly lurking nearby.

Forty minutes later, at 12:08 P.M., exactly on schedule and without incident, the *Karelia* fired her ballistic missile with its dummy warhead. It burst out of the ocean depths and, for a moment, appeared to hover in the air. Then the rocket's first-stage motor kicked in, and the missile roared into the Arctic sky, programmed for a target on the Kamchatka test range a thousand miles to the east.

A short time later, Korablev brought his submarine up to periscope depth and sent a brief signal to announce that the *Karelia* had completed her task and was ready to return to her home base on the Kola Peninsula, the port of Gadjievo. He made no mention of the mysterious shock waves that had rocked the *Karelia* less than an hour earlier.

II: 11:30 A.M.
The Norwegian Arctic

THE MOMENT THE SHOCK WAVES fractured the *Kursk*'s outer hull, the secret of the blasts was out. Nothing in the world could stop the seismic information racing through the water and the bedrock of the ocean floor. The pressure waves traveled at extremely high velocity, four miles every second. Sixty seconds after their journey began, after nearly 250 miles, the waves passed under the remote Norwegian village of Karasjok, high in the Arctic Circle.

A short distance outside Karasjok, deep in the forest and away from local roads, lie twenty-five fiberglass, cone-shaped containers.

Securely fixed to slabs of concrete, they are spread out over an area of two square miles and linked by underground fiber-optic cables. A compact satellite dish lies in the middle of the network, constantly transmitting data. The Karasjok facility is known as ARCESS, for Arctic Experimental Seismic Station. Seismographs, capable of registering the slightest tremors deep in the earth, are positioned inside the fiberglass containers. The equipment is so sensitive that it can pick up the vibrations of roadworks across the Russian border a hundred miles away. Built in 1987 and upgraded in 1999, the station is deliberately positioned close to the frontier, designed to alert the West to any Russian underground nuclear tests.

At 11:30, the seismographs of ARCESS suddenly twitched, registering first a smaller pulse, then a much more violent one. This information was automatically relayed in real time by satellite to the headquarters of the Norwegian Seismic Array (NORSAR) just outside Oslo. All such data are recorded on computer disks and kept for analysis.

In Oslo, Frode Ringdal scanned the computer readings from the six seismic arrays spread out across Norway. A patient, soft-spoken man, he has worked at NORSAR for more than thirty years. As the institute's scientific director, his specialty is distinguishing between the seismic patterns of earthquakes and those generated by explosions.

The spike of seismic activity picked up by the Karasjok array puzzled him. What made the data interesting was that they appeared at first to make no sense. The epicenter seemed to be situated in the southern part of the Barents Sea, which he knew was virtually impossible. There is almost no earthquake or volcanic activity in these waters. The Mid-Atlantic Ridge is the only seismic fault line in the region, and that lies far to the west, running close to the archipelago of Spitsbergen and through Iceland. Scrutinizing the data, Ringdal thought he could discern two separate sets of shock waves a couple of minutes apart. He shook his head in surprise and pondered what besides an earthquake might have caused them. Sometimes the Russian military blew up old ammunition stocks. Perhaps they had detonated some powerful experimental depth charge as part of a naval exercise.

Seismology has made huge strides since its modern origins a century ago. Encouraged by the view, now largely discredited, that earthquakes can be accurately predicted, substantial resources have been directed toward understanding the movements of the earth. The 1906 San Francisco quake was a decisive moment for the field, prompting the infusion of the considerable scientific resources of America into the discipline. But the major funding boost for the science came in the 1960s, when the U.S. Defense Department recognized that seismology was the key to detecting underground Soviet nuclear testing. Even after nearly a century of study, and the recent dramatic growth in computing power, many types of seismology data remain extremely difficult to analyze, especially those from small-scale seismic events like the one that caught Ringdal's attention on the morning of Saturday, August 12, 2000.

His curiosity piqued, Ringdal decided to continue to analyze the mysterious Barents Sea data.

III: SATURDAY AFTERNOON
Southern Barents Sea

THE *PETER THE GREAT,* accompanied by the warships *Admiral Chabanenko* and *Admiral Kharlamov,* steamed through the operational areas of the three submarines tasked to fire practice torpedoes. Deep within the flagship's command center, the chief acoustics specialist, Senior Lieutenant Lavrinuk, reported a powerful underwater explosion, which he carefully logged at 11:29 A.M., in the direction of 096 degrees. Others aboard the *Peter the Great* later said they felt the giant warship tremble in the water at this time. Senior officers took note of Lavrinuk's report, but they were preoccupied with other logistical concerns, and they quickly put it to one side. No importance was attached to the event, and no one took responsibility for probing it further. The *Peter the Great* moved to the southern perimeter of the exercise zone.

Both the *Daniil Moskovsky* and the *Boriso-Glebsk* had launched torpedoes successfully. Small utility boats, known appropriately as "torpedo catchers," had tracked and ensnared the weapons as they floated up to the surface, retrieving them for future use. But from the *Kursk* there was no sign of an "attack," and no signal was received explaining her failure to launch her 65-76 and USET-80 torpedoes.

Communication problems are relatively common on Russian submarines. Many commanding officers have encountered technical faults at some point in their career, caused by equipment failure or unusual atmospheric conditions. Admiral Viacheslav Popov recalls that as a submarine captain he had once been unable to make radio contact with the Fleet's command ship, triggering an alert. With these precedents in mind, the admirals were not alarmed by the silence from the *Kursk*.

A final designated time for communications with the *Kursk* was scheduled for 11 P.M., when she was due to report her departure for Zapadnaya Litsa, the naval base and weapons depot to the west of Vidyaevo. So the Fleet commanders took no immediate action, just continuing the exercise. By the end of the day, the ships and submarines would be heading back to base, mission accomplished.

The question is: How could the *Kursk* have suffered twin explosions, the second of a huge magnitude, right in the midst of a naval exercise without anyone grasping what had happened? The answer, already glimpsed in the reaction of Andrei Korablev on board the *Karelia,* provides an insight into the Northern Fleet and the mentality that is one of the greatest weaknesses in the Russian military: a reluctance to probe and question and an unwillingness to pass bad news up the chain of command.

Even in tsarist times, military officers were deterred from raising troublesome issues. Battle reports from the naval war with Japan in

1905 were heavily edited before being sent back to St. Petersburg for scrutiny by court officials. The problem became far more serious during the Red Army's massive purges in the 1930s, when identifying problems and criticizing the system involved taking great personal risks. In the Second World War, many officers were punished for accurate dispatches that hinted at operational failures at higher levels. Serving officers today in Russia are familiar with the story of the Russian pilots who spotted German tanks and armored columns approaching Moscow in 1941. One after another, the pilots reported the Nazi advance to their commanders in the capital; one after another, they were berated for generating panic through inaccurate aerial reconnaissance. Reporting an unpalatable truth in the Russian military is a dangerous activity.

The Northern Fleet's lack of response to the mystery explosions deeply confused the host of watching Western intelligence experts monitoring the Barents. Russian commanders could not have done better at hiding the disaster if they had actually been trying to.

Naval analysts in the United States and Britain rely heavily on signals intelligence—SIGINT—especially communication and electronic intercepts. The West would understand that a major event had happened in the Barents Sea not so much by the occurrence itself but by the Russian reaction to it. U.S. Navy intelligence is constantly watching out for a surge in communications between ships of the Northern Fleet and the shore headquarters in Severomorsk. Such signals might be encrypted and impossible to decode, but the activation of circuits alone would tell Western governments that an emergency was unfolding. If the Russians had launched an immediate search-and-rescue operation that Saturday lunchtime, the West would have noticed. Norwegian shore stations would have detected the increased flow of Russian communications; U.S. reconnaissance satellites would have seen warships converging on a specific point; the spooks aboard the USS *Memphis* might have intercepted signals. Yet for many hours none of this occurred. The Fleet exercise proceeded as if everything were normal.

Few people outside the world of naval intelligence are aware of the extraordinary resources poured into monitoring these few thousand square miles of remote and icy waters. Whatever happens in the Barents Sea, it certainly shouldn't go unnoticed.

Around the North Cape, and in many other waters where hostile submarines are known to transit, the U.S. Navy has deployed a secret underwater detection system known as SOSUS, or Sound Surveillance System. The network comprises hydrophones secured on the ocean floor, acoustic devices designed to gather precise information on the movement and activity of Russian submarines. Lightweight fiber-optic cables interconnect the arrays at sea and provide U.S. naval intelligence with real-time data. They are concentrated at "choke points" outside the submarine ports and around the North Cape and the channel leading from the Barents Sea to the open Atlantic, submarine passages known as the Greenland–Iceland–United Kingdom (GIUK) Gap. If the sensors detect major submarine movements—a "surge deployment"—the data can be used to alert other Western anti-submarine warfare assets such as aircraft, surface ships, and attack submarines. Since the 1960s, SOSUS has been used to help track Soviet ballistic-missile submarines as they head out on patrol. Cued by the sensors, U.S. submarines pick up the scent and follow the trail.

SOSUS is today complemented by a concentration of extremely high-quality electronic and satellite intelligence over the Kola Peninsula. Reconnaissance satellites look down on the piers of the Russian submarine bases, constantly relaying the status of the boats. For this reason, in the docks of Gremikha, the home port of the giant Typhoon-class strategic submarines, the pens were carved deep into the base of mountains to allow the Russians to hide their patrol preparations. Shore stations run by the Norwegian Intelligence Service also intercept Northern Fleet communications, with help from America's National Security Agency and Britain's communications-intelligence service GCHQ. There are also secret experimental programs to test if submarines can be tracked through the ocean by satellites with infrared capabilities. As nuclear submarines travel underwater, heat from the machinery escapes upward and raises the temperature of the surrounding water by a tiny amount, a phenomenon called a "thermal scarring." The debate continues about whether this is a feasible method of tracking submarines.

Despite all this unmanned technology, the U.S. Navy seeks to keep at least one attack submarine on constant patrol in the Barents Sea, or at least within easy reach if other systems detect that a Russian deployment is imminent. The best means of tracking a submarine is still with another submarine.

There was certainly no shortage of Western intelligence assets off the Kola Peninsula in August 2000. Sailing to the northwest of the exercise was, of course, the USS *Memphis,* commanded by Mark Breor, watching carefully for the movement of Russian missile submarines. On the surface, the Norwegian spy ship *Marjata* also monitored the exercise. Although officially classified as a research ship, the *Marjata* reports directly to the Norwegian Intelligence Service. The data she collects are sent for analysis by NIS experts in Oslo.

Farther away, sailing in the northern part of the Norwegian Sea, was the unarmed American surveillance ship USNS *Loyal.* She is run by the U.S. Navy but managed by a mix of civilian and Navy technicians who analyze the information flowing into the ship from a hydrophone-packed array that's towed through the water. A vast quantity of acoustic intelligence is recorded on board, then passed by data link to U.S. shore stations for analysis. The *Loyal*'s task is to detect, track, and report on submarine contacts at long range.

Almost all the American expertise and technology invested in monitoring the Barents Sea is directed at detecting the mechanical, electrical, and flow-related sounds associated with the normal movement of submarines, but the explosions registered around 11:30 A.M. on August 12 were so unusual that they baffled Russian and U.S. analysts alike. Despite the concentration of intelligence-collection systems, there was a complete and startling failure to understand the nature of the emergency that was unfolding in the middle of the Barents Sea.

4

I: The Kola Peninsula

THE NORTHERN FLEET WAS CREATED not as a showcase of military strength but in response to a naval weakness. For much of the eighteenth and nineteenth centuries, Russia was tormented by a strategic vulnerability. The tsar's two major fleets—based in the Baltic and the Black Sea—could easily be prevented from reaching the open sea, because they had to pass through narrow straits that could either be blocked by ships or attacked with shore-based artillery. Enemies controlled both sea routes: The Ottoman Empire could keep the Black Sea Fleet contained, and Germany dominated the Baltic. Russia's other great coast was on the Pacific, but it was too distant from the heart of the empire to be of much value. In the days before the Trans-Siberian Railway was completed in 1904, many weeks' travel were required to reach the port of Vladivostok.

In an attempt to escape this handicap, in 1894, the final year of his reign, Tsar Alexander III looked with yearning northward, toward Russia's Arctic seas. The region's climate appeared too brutal for human settlement, with its sub-zero temperatures and polar winters that stripped the land of natural light. But eighteenth-century explorers had found that the waters off the Kola Peninsula exhibited a remarkable and inexplicable characteristic: However cold the temperature on land and in the air, the water never froze. Investigation by some of Russia's earliest oceanographers yielded a solution to the riddle: A tongue of the warm Gulf Stream lapped around northern Norway and kept the sea temperature a few degrees above freezing.

This scientific discovery carried stunning military implications. Russia could develop unrestricted, ice-free access to the open ocean from the Arctic, via the North Cape. The vast waters of the Atlantic beckoned; Turkey and Germany could no longer strangle Russian maritime power. All that was needed was a good harbor and a band of sailors tough enough to cope with the inevitable hardships.

In the summer of 1894, Alexander III dispatched the ablest administrator in the empire, Finance Minister Sergei Witte, to visit the lonely Kola Peninsula and see whether he could build a port and the infrastructure to support it. At that time the local population comprised fishermen and hunters, as well as a few brave traders living in the settlement of Kola, surviving on a local vodka brew through the bitter winters. After a journey by river barge, coach, and ship into the northern Russian wilderness, Witte gazed out in wonder over an inlet known as St. Catherine's Bay. Instead of the anticipated problems, he saw only vast potential. In his diary, Witte wrote, "Such a grand harbor I never saw before in my life. It never freezes, it could be easily defended, and from this place our Fleet would have direct access to the ocean."

Gradually the area was developed. The port of Alexandrovsk, later to be the submarine base of Polyarni, was founded in 1899, providing the Kola Peninsula with its first piers and docking facilities. Without a railway connection, however, the port remained an isolated outpost. Only the logistical necessities of the First World War—the need to move troops and bring in war supplies—pushed tsarist officials to develop an infrastructure for Russia's Arctic coast. In 1917, the city of Romanov-on-the-Murman was founded at the mouth of the Kola Bay, its imperial name changed by the Bolsheviks to Murmansk just four months later.

By 1922, the Fleet of the Northern Seas was established with a small group of ships that were brought up from the Baltic. It was renamed the Northern Fleet over a decade later by Josef Stalin. The focus of Soviet naval power now shifted to the Kola Peninsula.

Throughout the Second World War, Allied convoys repeatedly ran the gauntlet of German U-boats to bring crucial military supplies through the Barents Sea and into the Soviet Union. Often battling atrocious Arctic storms, these convoys were highly successful. Of the 811 ships that headed for Stalin's Arctic ports, only fifty-eight were sunk. The strategic importance of the Kola Peninsula was reinforced.

The Cold War energized the Northern Fleet, providing it with a whole new purpose. The Soviet Navy used the ports of the Kola Peninsula to deploy submarines into the Atlantic and, in a time of war, would threaten Western convoys, hunt down American carrier battle groups, and deploy to within striking distance of the U.S. eastern seaboard. Moscow ordered the expansion of the Fleet beyond all recognition, and the Kola Peninsula was transformed to house the greatest concentration of naval power anywhere in the world. At the height of its power, in the mid-1980s, the Northern Fleet deployed as many as 180 submarines, operating from a dozen bases that stretched from the Finnish border to inlets on the White Sea three hundred miles to the east.

The dramatic rise of the Northern Fleet made the speed and scale of its collapse all the more shocking. As the Soviet Union imploded and descended into economic chaos, the Fleet was starved of funds, suffering almost complete neglect from Moscow, a thousand miles to the south. By the mid-1990s, fewer than forty submarines remained in active service, and the ports and docks were littered with the carcasses of decommissioned submarines and surface ships, many rusting and in danger of sinking.

By 1995, the more isolated Northern Fleet bases were even running short of basic food and provisions. In some ports, at one point, there was no bread for two weeks. Some senior naval officers improvised, providing manpower and military trucks to local companies in return for their products. The Kola Peninsula had been largely reduced to a barter economy. In the remote outpost of Gremikha, the base commander cabled the town up to a submarine's nuclear reactor so that the Navy families, at least, would have heating and electricity.

The whole network of economic links in the Arctic North unraveled. Fuel and spare parts were in critically short supply. The Northern Fleet admirals did their best to keep the Navy alive as a viable military force, using ruthless measures to prioritize the needs of its fighting arm. The auxiliary and standby forces were cut back. If the ships were to be kept seaworthy and missiles at the ready, no money could be spent on infrastructure or backup services. The submarine piers, the torpedo-loading cranes, the repair shops, the training centers, the housing stock—all rapidly deteriorated.

Funds earmarked for transfer from Moscow to the Northern Fleet simply never materialized. There was almost no money for training purposes. In 1995, the Fleet's annual budget was spent in the first half of the year, which meant that the payment of salaries was suspended for several months. The nadir of the Fleet's period of humiliation was during the summer of 1995, when several Victor III–class submarines, highly regarded by Western naval experts, were converted to carry fruit and potatoes from Murmansk to the Yamal Peninsula in northern Siberia. The torpedoes were unloaded to make room for the food supplies. As late as 1999, the commander-in-chief of the Russian Navy wrote to Parliament pleading for extra funds, complaining that of seventy-seven cranes in the Northern Fleet, just twenty were operational. Admiral Vladimir Kuroyedov concluded that "as a result, loading torpedoes and missiles could not be conducted in the Fleet." Even for a Navy lurching from crisis to crisis, this was a startling admission. An urgent request went to the Defense Ministry to spend millions of rubles repairing the cranes during the year 2000, but by the time the defense budget was agreed upon, the money was no longer available.

If the bases and main naval forces were suffering, the fate of the search-and-rescue forces of the Northern Fleet was even more disastrous. For the admirals, the rescue assets were the easiest forces to cut without damaging their careers. If the major warships and strategic submarines were stranded at port, that would be a national and very public embarrassment. But no one in Moscow would ever know, much less actually care, if the rescue submersibles and their mother-ships were kept in port, slowly decaying.

On shore, inside the disintegrating and underfunded bases, the decay and neglect led to widespread misery and frequent tragedies in the main prompted by that perennial, demoralizing issue, lack of pay. In Vidyaevo, one naval officer took his own life, leaving for his superiors a one-sentence suicide note of such simple power it became the whispered and shocked talk of the Northern Fleet: "Please pay my salary, what's owed to me, and pass the money on to my wife and two hungry children." The Russian Navy seeks to hide the statistics, but in 1999, on Northern Fleet bases alone, at least twelve sailors committed suicide. In the year 2000, eighteen men took their own lives, most shooting themselves in the head with their service pistols.

Crime emerged as a problem too. During the *Kursk*'s patrols, while Captain-Lieutenant Dmitri Kolesnikov was away from base, his small apartment was repeatedly ransacked. His furniture, his uniform, and his prized *kortik* naval dagger were stolen. He told his father in St. Petersburg that, on returning from one voyage, even the toilet seat was missing. In Vidyaevo in late January 1999, a conscript sneaked into the reactor compartment of a submarine and removed some wiring, hoping to sell it on the black market. The young sailor knew that semiprecious metals were sometimes used as key components. He was arrested shortly after the technicians noticed that some coiled palladium wire was missing, a vital component in the nuclear reactors.

The collapse of morale did not, however, mean an end to the nuclear threat posed by the Northern Fleet. The submarines them-selves were still highly capable. They were among the best-engineered ships in the world, and they still carried extremely powerful weapons. The U.S. Navy stayed vigilant, gravely uncertain about Russia's future political direction and recognizing her potential for regalvanizing the Fleet.

II: NOON, SATURDAY, AUGUST 12
The Kursk's *Ninth Compartment*

NOW, THE PRIDE OF the Northern Fleet was fatally wounded. But in the machinery sections, to the aft of the reactor compartments, twenty-three officers and sailors had not only survived—they were physically unscathed.

After the horror of the detonations and the crash into the seabed, the men must have been astonished that they were still alive. Several factors allowed the sailors in the aft of the submarine to avoid life-threatening impact injuries. One of the aims of the designers of the Oscar IIs was to reduce the risk of detection by minimizing the machinery noise emanating from the submarine. Instead of rigidly fastening the three decks to the hull, they were simply suspended, attached at key points. The vibrations of the machinery no longer passed through the pressure hull. In this catastrophe, the design also served to protect the sailors in the machinery compartments from the force of the shock waves as they tore through the submarine.

Relief at their own survival must have been mixed with a desperate uncertainty about the fate of their colleagues farther forward. They had no means of communicating with the command post and no way of finding out what had happened. Dmitri Kolesnikov's best friend was Sergei Lybushkin. Now Kolesnikov was on one side of the reactor bulkheads and Lybushkin was on the other. They were separated by only a few inches of steel, but they might as well have been in different universes.

At some stage in the first hour or so, Kolesnikov took control. He had no means of knowing that 80 percent of the crew were already dead, but what was plain was that, along with two other officers, he held the most senior rank of those serving in the stern.

Kolesnikov's first instruction was dictated by the basic training taught to submariners serving behind the reactors: In the event of an emergency, collect your special breathing equipment and move to the ninth escape compartment. There the men would gather to consider their options and to formulate a plan.

The primary escape route from a stricken Oscar II submarine is from the second compartment, which contains within the conning tower a pressurized chamber that acts as an escape "lifeboat." Known to Russian submariners as the VSK *(Vsplyvaushchaya Spasatelnaya Kapsula,* or ascending safety capsule), the pod has positive buoyancy even when packed with a submarine crew. Once the sailors are safely inside, the capsule can be detached from the submarine using either a hydraulic or a manually operated handle. The capsule, which can take up to a hundred sailors—virtually the entire crew—surges to the surface when released and serves as a life raft until rescuers reach the scene. Trapped in the aft of the *Kursk,* however, and unable to move forward of the reactor compartments, let alone reach the command post in the second compartment, the *Kursk* survivors could not make use of the safety capsule.

Other ways of escaping from a Russian submarine include an emergency route through the large 65cm torpedo tubes. Some Russian submariners have practiced sliding into the tubes wearing their emergency breathing kit, three men at a time, closing the inner and outer torpedo-tube doors, flooding the tube to equalize the pressure to that of the outside ocean and then swimming to the surface. The procedure requires strong nerves and a great deal of training, but it has worked in the past. Thirty-four sailors from the Pacific Fleet diesel submarine *S-178* were saved this way from a depth of 131 feet. Despite that success, many Northern Fleet submarine crew members are deeply skeptical of this procedure, viewing it as an unrealistic option because the required techniques are rarely taught. Certainly Kolesnikov and the other survivors must have given it only momentary consideration. If they couldn't reach the command compartment, they certainly couldn't struggle through to the torpedo room.

They must have guessed that the detonations had originated in the bow area and that the first compartment was in all likelihood destroyed.

They had only one feasible route out of the submarine: the gray-green escape hatch just above them in the ninth compartment. A steel ladder lay invitingly against the wall, providing access to the escape tower.

The tower above the hatch is ten feet high and just wide enough for a man to enter while wearing a full escape suit. The technique for evacuating is designed to be simple. One sailor at a time opens the bottom hatch and enters the tower. He closes the hatch behind him, sealing himself in the escape chamber, and switches on his individual breathing system. He then flicks open an equalization valve inside the tower, allowing ocean water to pour in and fill the chamber until the pressure inside the tower is equal to that of the water outside. He begins breathing, using his respirator, before pushing up against the upper hatch, swinging it open. He then kicks upward into the open ocean, his lifejacket helping to bring him rapidly to the surface.

That is the theory. In practice, the engineering of the hatches presents a daunting challenge. By definition, the escape system is only used by people under extreme stress, in deteriorating mental and physical condition. During an evacuation from depths of over 325 feet, even the best-trained submariner faces disorientation. (The *Kursk* hatch lay at 350 feet.) As he stands in the tower and opens the valve to let in the ocean and equalize the pressure, a sailor may enter "cold shock" as his body is submerged in the near-freezing water. Even if he is able to continue with the procedure and push open the upper hatch, the ascent is likely to rupture his eardrums and cause "face squeeze" as the brutal water pressure presses his mask against his face, breaking fragile blood vessels around his eyes and nose. As he goes through rapid pressure changes, a sailor's lungs may also rupture. Furthermore, a condition known as compression arthralgia attacks the joints and is potentially fatal unless treated immediately. Even if he reaches the surface, at a water temperature of about three degrees Celsius (37.4°F.), and without a life raft, he could expect to stave off hypothermia for a few hours at most.

During the Second World War, very few air crews that ditched into Russia's northern seas were rescued. Even in summer waters, and with clothing to help preserve core body temperature, pilots succumbed to hypothermia with frightening speed.

Had the situation inside the *Kursk* at this time been even more desperate—had the survivors faced a fire, or noxious fumes pouring into the escape compartment—the decision would have been made for them. They would surely have grasped the chance of survival by an escape attempt, however risky, over the certainty of death. But at noon that Saturday in the ninth compartment, the twenty-three sailors and officers found themselves in relative comfort, despite the enormity of the disaster farther forward. They were dry and benefiting from the residual heat still coming from the reactor compartment. Above all, they were drawing strength from one another. If they evacuated the submarine, each man would be on his own, abandoned to an unknown fate on the surface.

Had they traded their relative comfort for the shock of an ascent through 350 feet of Arctic water, they would have been taking a remarkable gamble. Huddled in the extremely cramped space on the upper deck of the ninth compartment, the survivors must have intensely debated the decision, tormented by their lack of information about the state of the submarine.

As they had moved to the aft of the submarine, the survivors had brought with them their special "hydro-suits" with escape hoods and flotation devices. In theory, the suit and breathing system allow for an ascent from a maximum depth of just under 500 feet. Known as ISP-60s (*Individualnoe Sredstvo Podvodnika*), they are kept close to the battle stations at all times, and now they were lying in a pile in the crowded ninth compartment.

The largest open area in the compartment is the passageway, just a narrow corridor, that runs past the machinery from the eighth bulkhead and underneath the escape tower, fifteen feet in length and three feet wide. Here the survivors stood shoulder to shoulder, debating their choices. Should they evacuate the submarine and take their chances, or should they wait for rescue? They had no means of knowing if rescue was on its way, no way of telling if the emergency buoy had been released. Did the exercise commander even know what had happened? Was there a submersible heading toward them even now? Was the Fleet gathered above them, putting together a rescue plan? Might the explosions have damaged the upper hatch, effectively barring any escape option at all? If the shock waves had caused the release mechanism to distort, as it well might have, they were entombed.

A serious submarine accident, even in relatively shallow water, presents multiple problems simultaneously, each one with the potential to kill. So many survival issues flow from an underwater accident that it's been compared to being caught in an avalanche, trapped in a blaze, adrift in outer space, and lost at sea—all at the same time.

The Royal Navy has put special emphasis on studying the problem of how submariners can make lightning-fast decisions in a crisis. Their experts in submarine escape have come up with a radical solution, simple enough to be applied almost without thought: If conditions are deteriorating fast, don't even discuss the merits of evacuating the submarine—just do it. The objective of this technique, called a "rush escape," is to try to cheat death by taking immediate and drastic action, before you are physically or psychologically overwhelmed by the disaster.

Such a precipitous emergency escape involves deliberately flooding the entire submarine compartment to equalize pressure with the outside sea. Amid the chaos of water cascading in and air escaping during the procedure, the sailors breathe using a device known as BIBS, or built-in breathing system. Masks hang down from the pipework leading to the escape tower. Once the compartment is flooded and the upper hatch is opened, the man nearest the tower takes a last deep breath, zips up his escape hood, and evacuates, his buoyancy aids taking him rapidly to the surface. Back in the submarine, in a process known as "fleeting," the sailors shift down the line, moving forward one place at a time. As they edge closer to escape, they take over the mask discarded by the man in front of them. Every ten or fifteen seconds, a man evacuates the stranded sub.

Russian submarine training does not embrace the theory of rush escape. It favors a slower, more cautious approach. The process of evacuating through the ninth hatch of an Oscar II, requiring each sailor to individually enter the escape tower for pressure equalization, is a laborious one. Instead of a man escaping every ten or fifteen seconds, as Royal Navy practice allows, the Russian technique might take as long as ten or fifteen *minutes* per sailor. Some submarine-rescue specialists describe the Russian method as more "pure" and better grounded in good science. In a calm and controlled environment, it may well be a superior system, but it runs the risk of the escape attempt being overtaken by the speed and chaos of the accident.

Kolesnikov must have concluded that his men would drown or die of hypothermia if they attempted an escape through the hatch. In theory, they wouldn't even need to get wet if they waited for a submersible rescue and transferred through the hatch to one of the Northern Fleet's rescue subs. Surely the exercise commander would realize that a disaster had befallen the *Kursk* and order the search-and-rescue forces to begin an emergency evacuation of the submarine?

No submarine-rescue specialist now suggests that the *Kursk* survivors made the wrong decision in opting to stay where they were. Many point out that without knowledge of the precise circumstances of the ninth compartment, without personal experience of the multiplying, multidimensional horrors unfolding inside the sub, no one is qualified to second-guess Kolesnikov's choice.

Even as they grappled with the disaster, the twenty-three sailors would have recognized that their situation, though grave, was not hopeless. The men decided to put their faith in the Fleet. Rescue would have to come through external intervention.

* * *

The *Kursk* survivors faced four immediate problems: falling oxygen levels as they breathed the air in the compartment; rising carbon-dioxide levels as they exhaled; plummeting temperatures; and the risk of rising pressure. All four were life-threatening. The decision to stay in the ninth section and wait for rescue did not mean, however, that the men were consigned to be passive victims.

They could boost their survival prospects by improving the atmospheric conditions in the compartment with emergency equipment. Each of them had a bottle of emergency air, a system called IDA-59M *(Individualny Dykhatelny Apparat),* which would last them about fifteen minutes.

Dmitri Kolesnikov would certainly have known he had to act quickly to improve the atmosphere, and it was probably he who gave the order to activate the air-regeneration cartridges stored on board all Russian submarines. The chemicals used in these cartridges are known as "superoxides," which react with the moisture in the air, absorb the CO_2, and replace it with fresh oxygen. The cartridges—which look like rectangular cassettes—are loaded one at a time into a blower that circulates air through the compartment. The system is easy to use and is designed to buy trapped men precious extra days of life.

If the blower cannot operate because of a power failure, the cartridges can simply be opened and hung up to allow the air to circulate through them. The result is the same: The foul air arrives and moves over the chemicals, and the departing air, though it may not be pleasant, is once again supportive of life.

As the survivors started opening up the cartridges in the ninth compartment, they took their first action to help themselves. In the aftermath of the explosion and in such a perilous situation, taking some positive steps must have been a morale boost. Now they had only to hang on and wait for the rescuers who would surely arrive before long at the hatch just above them.

Using the emergency life-support equipment was certainly extending their survival time. The failure of the electrical power led to the shutdown of all the air-purification systems inside the submarine. Normally, they ran continuously, removing the carbon dioxide and replenishing the oxygen. In fact, they were designed to run forever, using electricity and the seawater outside. But without power, the normal machinery that preserved the atmosphere was dead and useless. The survivors knew that with every breath they took, the oxygen levels in the aft compartments were falling and the carbon-dioxide levels increasing. The cruel reality of being trapped in a sealed environment is that the most natural action in the world, breathing, can be the cause of your own death.

Even with the superoxide cassettes, the predicament was bitterly ironic: The survival of so many people considerably lessened the chances for all of them. There was plenty of air for one or two men to live in this atmosphere for many weeks, but the twenty-three sailors, each consuming oxygen and exhaling carbon dioxide with every breath, knew they would be confronting a deadly atmosphere much sooner than that.

Many different factors determine how long a trapped man can survive. If he is taking relaxed and shallow breaths, his consumption of oxygen and production of carbon dioxide will be less. For example, if a sailor is sitting calmly, leaning against a bulkhead, or lying down on a bunk, he will consume about 0.4 quart of oxygen per minute and breathe out around a third of a quart of CO_2. If he falls asleep, those figures are reduced by up to 50 percent. But if the survivor is panicking and hyperventilating, or if he's engaged in heavy physical activity such as moving debris, hammering an SOS against the hull, or dragging others to safety, he may well consume as much as two quarts of oxygen a minute. The first sign for sailors of a critical shortage of oxygen would be a sense that their minds were slowing down as they struggled with ordinary tasks. Next, they would slip into a twilight world where colors faded, everything appeared grayer, and they experienced tunnel vision. Gradually, the survivors would become detached from their predicament and lapse into unconsciousness.

As serious as the danger from oxygen depletion was, the survivors knew from their basic training that the amount of oxygen in the *Kursk*'s atmosphere was not the most pressing concern. The more immediate priority was to try to lessen the buildup of carbon dioxide. The human body can tolerate a far greater depletion of oxygen than it can an increase in carbon dioxide. A buildup of CO_2 will kill long before a shortage of oxygen. The men would have known that carbon-dioxide poisoning is a terrible fate, one that would provide a harrowing and agonizing end to their ordeal. With oxygen deprivation, there is at least a merciful feature: The brain fades before the body collapses. But a buildup of carbon dioxide triggers a much more traumatic cycle of physiological reactions.

As the CO_2 reaches a level above 3 percent of the atmosphere, the human body begins to experience what doctors call "respiratory distress." "Distress" is a medical euphemism, however, and considerably understates what the body undergoes. The body craves fresh air, and breathing becomes deeper and faster. As the level of CO_2 continues to build, the body loses the ability to get rid of the carbon dioxide it is producing. The mind cannot understand why inhaling more air is not providing relief, and breathing becomes more and more desperate. With every breath comes a more intense craving for oxygen. Finally, the realization hits that it is impossible to achieve the intake of air. The torture is psychological as well as physical: There is a constant cycle of the expectation of relief followed by the hope being dashed. The mind, lungs, and body are effectively embroiled in a life-and-death struggle with the atmosphere. Unless the atmosphere can be very rapidly improved, there is only ever one winner.

The simple arithmetic facing the *Kursk* survivors was potentially devastating. Ninety percent of the oxygen breathed in was being exhaled as carbon dioxide. Even if the twenty-three survivors were breathing lightly, they were still exhaling almost two gallons of carbon dioxide into the atmosphere every sixty seconds.

5

EXACTLY TWO HOURS AND six minutes after the first explosion, Kolesnikov carefully tore out a blank page from one of the submarine's notebooks, a vertically and horizontally lined pad normally used by a supervising officer to write out a checklist of safety recommendations. Kolesnikov would put it to a very different use. With a blue pen, he wrote the date—"12.08.2000"—in the top left-hand corner, and the time—"13.34"—in the top right-hand corner. What followed was a list of great coherence, a sheet of information written with such precision and clarity that it is immediately apparent that Kolesnikov was at the time in complete control of his mental and physical faculties. It might well have been written in an office. That it was written amid the ruins of the *Kursk* two hours after the explosions is a remarkable tribute to the professionalism of the twenty-eight-year-old officer.

Below the date and time, Kolesnikov wrote: "List of 6th, 7th, 8th, 9th sections, of people who are in the 9th compartment after evacuation." The choice of the word *evacuation* is striking. In Russian, the word is *evakuatsia,* similar to English in sound and usage, implying an orderly, planned process. Kolesnikov then wrote down twenty-three names, a different survivor on each line, starting with the service "tag" number that revealed their compartment, position, and shift. Then he wrote each survivor's family name and at the end of the line made a little cross, which indicated that each was present with him and properly accounted for. The survivors were listed in order, compartment by compartment, starting with the sixth compartment.

The first name he wrote down was that of Chief Petty Officer Viacheslav Maynagashev. On the next line of the page was Seaman Alexei Korkin, a young sailor from Arkhangel. The third name must have been especially difficult for Kolesnikov to write: It was that of his good friend Rashid Ariapov. They had been together many years, through so much together, and now he was writing Ariapov's name on a list of those stranded.

After those three names, Kolesnikov calmly listed those from the seventh compartment, starting with Midshipman Fanis Ishmudatov, who worked as a general technician. At no stage did his handwriting deteriorate. It appears that he was speaking to them as he wrote, asking the sailors to shout out, section by section, their number and name and then simply writing out their replies one by one. This was an accomplishment of impressive discipline. Then Kolesnikov wrote down his own name, using his rank rather than his tag number, and the cross next to it on the right-hand side of the page.

After this, he moved on to the eighth and ninth compartments. The first name from this section was its commander, Captain-Lieutenant Sergei Sadilenko, an officer from the Ukraine; the last name he wrote was that of Alexander Neustroev, an electrician from the far-flung Siberian city of Tomsk. At the end of the page he wrote the time: "13.58."

The list had taken him twenty-four minutes to compile, and it tells us many things about conditions in the ninth compartment several hours after the disaster. At this stage, there was clearly light, either from overhead emergency lighting that was still functioning despite the collapse of the ship's power or from flashlights that were pre-positioned at various points around each compartment. Everyone who was in the aft of the submarine at the time of the disaster had survived. Only two people who should have been serving in the *Kursk*'s aft compartments were not on Kolesnikov's list of survivors, Alexei Balanov and Alexei Mitiaev. Both worked as specialists on the propulsion system, and they must have moved forward to another part of the submarine during the torpedo launch. Conversely, Kolesnikov listed Dmitri Leonov as a survivor even though he normally served in the forward end of the submarine, in the second compartment. Perhaps he was running an errand for the captain or had come to speak to one of his friends.

The contrast between the catastrophic predicament of the men and the inner calm of Kolesnikov's list has led some Russian experts to ask whether the young officer was in deep shock, a dreamworld in which he acted almost like an external witness to the disaster. One submarine captain has said that Kolesnikov's state of mind reminded him of a car-crash victim, someone who is badly injured, covered in blood, wandering around the vehicle wreckage insisting that everything is fine and worrying about being late for work.

After the first few hours, the temperature inside the aft compartments of the *Kursk* began to fall sharply. The heating systems had collapsed with the loss of power, and the ocean outside was now counteracting the residual warmth from the reactors, chilling the giant double hulls. The machinery areas inside a nuclear submarine are normally hot—the heat from the steam plant and turbines keeps the temperature high. As a result, the submariners in the *Kursk* were all lightly dressed in blue work overalls. Fortunately, though, the Northern Fleet had learned one lesson from its catalog of accidents.

On April 7, 1989, the submarine the *Komsomolets* was due south of Bear Island in the Norwegian Sea and heading back to her home port on the Kola Peninsula. She was an experimental boat with a titanium hull that allowed her to dive to the remarkable depth of over 3,280 feet. She carried not just her atomic reactor but two torpedoes tipped with nuclear warheads.

Just after 11 A.M., electrical equipment in the seventh section short-circuited, igniting a fire. The crew waged a desperate battle to contain the blaze for several hours, but as the submarine lost power and wallowed in the heavy seas, the captain gave the order to abandon ship. In disarray, the sailors tried to evacuate into two life rafts, but there were not enough places for all sixty-four of them. Then one of the rafts overturned. Fifty men ended up in the near-freezing water. Some jumped into the sea. By the time Russian surface ships arrived on the scene, only twenty-seven men were able to be saved.

In the aftermath of the *Komsomolets* disaster, with the Soviet Union having to acknowledge the sinking of its prototype submarine and the loss of nuclear weapons, a number of safety measures were implemented. All submariners would henceforth be issued with adequate emergency clothing to combat hypothermia, which would be stored in each compartment. The *Kursk* sailors had therefore been provided with thick, green thermal clothing that greatly increased their chances of survival. Even so, hypothermia remained a major risk. Many of the tricks to stay warm, such as moving around or stamping feet, were denied them because exercise increased both oxygen intake and carbon-dioxide production. The men faced a classic survival dilemma: By warding off one problem, they only increased the hazards from another. The air temperature was now just above freezing, and the core temperature of their bodies was beginning to fall. In addition, the cold must have been sapping their spirits, slowly diminishing their desire to survive.

II: 5 P.M.
Severomorsk Naval Headquarters

ADMIRAL POPOV WAS INFORMED of the loss of communications with the *Kursk* while in his office in Severomorsk, surrounded by his favorite possessions, including a massive map of the world's oceans and a traditional icon of the Russian saint Nicholas. Popov was not overly worried, remembering his own past problem with submarine communications. As a precaution, though, he ordered a staff officer to put a helicopter on standby in case he needed to join his flagship the *Peter the Great*.

On board the warship, which had been the *Kursk*'s "target" in the torpedo tests, a discussion was under way among staff officers about why the submarine had apparently failed to fire her practice torpedoes. The talk centered on the assumption that Captain Lyachin was experiencing temporary problems with his communications. If it were merely a torpedo fault, Lyachin would have signaled that he was unable to launch the weapons.

Communication systems between surface headquarters and nuclear submarines are perhaps the most secretive part of all naval operations. Signals from a submarine expose the boat to the risk of detection. The *Kursk*'s next routine communication was set for 11 P.M., when all the submarines were due to confirm that they were transiting out of the exercise area and returning to port. This would be a crucial moment: Failure to communicate once suggested a technical problem or human error; a second missed signal pointed to the possibility of a disaster.

As the afternoon passed, and as commanders argued about the possibilities, the level of anxiety slowly rose. Five hours had passed since the submarine should have launched her torpedoes. Rather than wait for the 11 P.M. signals deadline, the officers running the exercise aboard the *Peter the Great* made contact with Fleet headquarters and requested that a systematic effort to communicate with the *Kursk* be made. From shore stations as well as surface ships, the submarine was repeatedly asked to report her position and status.

In the operations center at Northern Fleet Headquarters in Severomorsk, Alexei Palkin was the acting duty officer. Just after 5 P.M., his deputy took a call from the flagship and turned around in alarm. "A submarine is missing," he told Palkin.

In a flurry of signals between headquarters and the *Peter the Great,* officers re-examined the exercise timings and the movements of the four submarines. At 6 P.M., Palkin gave the order for an Ilyushin-38 anti-submarine aircraft to get airborne and conduct a rapid surface search during the last few hours of daylight. At this stage, naval commanders still believed that the *Kursk* was wallowing on the surface without communications. The Il-38 plane scanned the exercise area, passing over the dozens of warships that were cruising across the placid summer waters. The crew on board the Ilyushin also searched for any debris or oil spill that might indicate the location of an accident. With her emergency systems, sophisticated communications, and rescue marker buoys, the *Kursk couldn't* simply go missing. This was not a combat patrol in the remote Pacific; this was an exhaustively planned exercise in home waters with thirty-two Northern Fleet surface ships and three other friendly submarines.

The head of the Fleet's search-and-rescue forces, Captain Alexander Teslenko, had also been notified at 5 P.M. A veteran Navy officer, he had been in charge of the Fleet's rescue service for five years. The coincidence of the alert struck Teslenko immediately: He had been due to practice submarine escape drills with his men on August 15, the day after the Fleet exercises ended.

Teslenko was in command of grossly deficient search-and-rescue forces. His main ship, the *Mikhail Rudnitsky,* was twenty years old and had been designed to carry timber. A little under 8,000 tons and 426 feet in length, she had been acquired by the Northern Fleet from the Black Sea Fleet in 1998. When she had first edged around the North Cape into the Barents Sea, pulling into her new home port of Severomorsk, Northern Fleet officers realized immediately why their Black Sea colleagues had not fought to keep the *Rudnitsky.* One naval official watching her dock described her condition as "pitiful." For a year, Teslenko's team worked to make the *Rudnitsky* seaworthy. The decision was made then to convert her into the mother-ship for the Fleet's two rescue submersibles. She was not an ideal choice—the derricks on her deck that had loaded and unloaded timber on so many voyages were suitable for lowering the ship's rescue submersibles into the water only in calm conditions. The *Rudnitsky* was also not equipped with stabilizers capable of keeping her in position in stormy weather.

While Teslenko was realistic about the ship's capabilities, he also believed that she was a great deal better than nothing.

The *Rudnitsky* is normally on four hours' notice to respond to an emergency. At 5:40 P.M., Teslenko ordered the ship's captain to be ready to leave Severomorsk within just sixty minutes. A junior officer in the headquarters telephoned the *Rudnitsky* sailors at their homes with the brief statement, "Your ship has been placed on one-hour standby for sailing. Report to the docks immediately." Many of the younger sailors, living in barracks or sharing apartments on the outskirts of the base, do not have telephones, so naval messengers were also sent out to find them and bring them to one of Severomorsk's three muster points. From there, trucks took those men down to the docks.

Almost without exception, the sailors assumed this was a drill. Knowing that the *Rudnitsky* was due to sail on August 15 on a search-and-rescue exercise, they believed the exercise had merely been brought forward by forty-eight hours. A few thought Teslenko was testing them to see how quickly his rescue forces could be assembled, and that once they reached the pier, he would just send them home again.

Jumping from the trucks, still bemoaning interrupted plans for that Saturday night, they were greeted by an unexpected frenzy of activity. Several generators were operating alongside the ship, and two mini-submersibles were being carefully winched on board. Gathered there along the pier, the young sailors, many just eighteen- or nineteen-year-old conscripts, first heard the rumor that a submarine was in trouble. No mention was made of any name. One cadet said they were going to act as a tug and take a submarine in tow back to the shore. Another overheard an officer say that a ship's lookout had spotted oil and debris out at sea and that the *Rudnitsky* was being mobilized just in case there had been an accident. Another smaller ship, the *Altai*, which acts as a multipurpose rescue tug and firefighting vessel, was also put on standby.

At 7 P.M., Fleet command issued its first orders to redeploy and divert ships. The tug *SB-523*, which was nearing Kildin Island, a point where the Bay of Severomorsk dissolves into the open sea, was ordered out to the exercise area. With a top speed of fourteen knots, she wouldn't arrive until around 10:30 P.M.

The Ilyushin-38 search plane had returned to the Severomorsk airfield by 8 P.M. having spotted nothing out of the ordinary. Just after 8, Admiral Popov instructed his staff communications officers to make contact with the *Karelia*, the Delta IV submarine that had been operating closest to the *Kursk*. Captain Andrei Korablev was asked to report any contact or communication he might have had with other submarines. Facing such an unusual request, Korablev consulted other officers on board, including Admiral Shchegolev, the "command rider" and deputy flotilla commander.

Only now did it dawn on Korablev that the shock waves they had felt just before midday might be linked to the radio request for news about the *Kursk*. He immediately sent a signal to Fleet headquarters stating that there had been no communication with any other submarine but that the *Karelia* had been struck by two powerful underwater shock waves, probably the result of a series of detonations, forty minutes before his own missile launch. Almost instantly, the request came back to provide all possible information about that event: "Provide data on your course, speed, and depth at the time and any possible estimate for direction and range of the source of the detonation."

Korablev ordered the sonar team to assemble all the data and told his radio room to prepare for a second, longer transmission. For the first, time the young submarine commander worried that the exercise might have gone badly wrong.

Some hours later, the *Karelia* edged toward a pier at the Gadjievo naval base. Normally, returning home after a successful missile test firing would be a cause for celebration; instead, the command room was somber, the silence broken only by Korablev's orders as he brought his boat in. The officers now suspected that the shock waves were linked to the disappearance of the *Kursk*, which would mean a probable disaster. They had heard the radio traffic between the *Peter the Great* and the Fleet's shore stations and the urgent calls for Captain Lyachin to report his position.

The officers of the submarine flotillas are a small, tightly knit cadre of men. Korablev had last seen Lyachin five days earlier, on August 7, when all the submarine commanding officers had attended Vice Admiral Motsak's pre-exercise briefing at the naval headquarters in Severomorsk. The two men didn't know each other well. They were different ages; they served on different bases and commanded very different types of submarines. But Korablev and Lyachin had exchanged a warm smile and friendly greetings that day. They had laughed as they saw that each of them was carrying instructions from Motsak in a sealed envelope that they would open only once the exercise was under way.

As the *Karelia* was secured to the pier with ropes, Korablev was still several hours away from being able to leave his post, but he asked a fellow officer to pass a message to his wife. He knew it would not be long before word spread among the naval bases about a missing submarine. Soon the families would hear the first cruel news. "Please call my wife right away," he said. "Tell her I'm back safely."

As Saturday evening dragged on, the anxiety and helplessness in the communications center at Northern Fleet headquarters grew; officers stared first at the clock and then at their signals operators. For the chief of staff, Motsak, the situation was much more than a strictly professional nightmare. Motsak had once commanded a division of the Oscar II boats, and his own son Anatoly now served in the *Voronezh,* the *Kursk*'s sister ship. He felt extremely close to the Fleet's attack submarines and their crews.

Nor was Popov unfamiliar with naval tragedies—when the submarine *K-8* sank in the Bay of Biscay in April 1970, he was aboard the submarine that saved the crew; when *K-219* went down, Popov was on patrol nearby and could hear the frenzy of emergency radio traffic. In 1972, he had returned from a voyage and had been embraced with tearful astonishment by his mother. She had heard rumors that he had died. In fact, it was another submarine, *K-19,* that had suffered a severe fire that had killed twenty-eight sailors. Despite this constant proximity to Russia's underwater disasters, he was regarded as a lucky and crafty commander, a brilliant exponent of submarine tactics.

For Popov, the consequences of the disaster they feared had occurred were potentially devastating. As commander of the Northern Fleet, he had ultimate responsibility for the safety of the ships and their crews. He had done what any naval commander would do with limited resources by giving priority to his combat elements, but as he watched the Fleet's rescue ships' steady decline, he had known that every deployment decision was a calculated risk. His calculation now threatened to explode in his face; he would be held responsible for any accident. The disgrace would be his. Popov must have felt a surge of bitterness toward Russian political leaders at that moment. They had deprived his beloved fleet of resources, even while demanding that the Navy become "visible" as a sign of resurgent Russian power.

As all now feared it would, the critical time for the next planned communication from the *Kursk*, 11 P.M., passed with no signal from the submarine. Further attempts to contact her were made from the flagship's radio room, from military headquarters in Severomorsk, and from several shore stations along the coast, but after thirty more fruitless minutes, Popov could delay the order no more. At 11:30 P.M., exactly twelve hours after shock waves from the twin explosions were first registered, he issued the *boevaya trevoga*, the battle or emergency alarm. The signal was received by all naval facilities across the Kola Peninsula, including the base at Vidyaevo.

The submarine *Kursk*, tactical number *K-141*, commanded by Captain 1st Rank Gennady Lyachin, is missing. A search-and-rescue operation is being launched.

III: 12:30 A.M., SUNDAY, AUGUST 13
Southern Barents Sea

SHORTLY AFTER THE EMERGENCY ALARM was officially sounded, and nearly seven hours after she had been put on standby, the *Mikhail Rudnitsky* pulled away from her pier. She left Severomorsk just after midnight on August 13, twelve and a half hours after the explosions had shattered the *Kursk*.

As the ship left port, the crew could see to starboard the outline of a giant ghostly image of a Northern Fleet marine clutching his rifle. The white stone monument pays tribute to the troops who fought in the Russian Arctic during the Second World War against invading German forces. Further up the Severomorsk channel, the *Rudnitsky* steamed past Polyarni, where a century ago, in 1899, the first port on the Kola Peninsula was founded, now a home to diesel submarines and the graveyard for dozens of rusting ships. Within an hour, the *Rudnitsky* was into clear water, passing the missile batteries on Kildin Island at the mouth of the Kola Bay. Frontier guards watched the ship steam by, unaware of the crisis toward which she was heading.

The precious cargo inside the *Rudnitsky*'s hold comprised two rescue submersibles. The first was known by the clumsy name *Avtonomny Rabochy Snaryad,* or "autonomous working apparatus," but was referred to simply as AS-32 after its construction code. This minisub was adequate for searching and basic underwater work using a pair of manipulator arms, but it had no rescue functions and could not evacuate sailors from a crippled submarine. The *Kursk* sailors' main hope was the second vehicle the *Rudnitsky* was carrying.

Priz is a fifty-ton submersible, just over thirty feet in length with a maximum speed of two knots, and the equipment to attach itself to the escape hatch of a submarine. It has two compartments, one for the operators and another for between sixteen and eighteen rescued submariners. But Priz has major flaws, long recognized by the Russian Navy's search-and-rescue specialists. In particular, its batteries are poor performers, severely restricting the submersible's underwater endurance. The mechanism that is supposed to make a watertight seal with the submarine hatch is also flawed. To compound those problems on this mission, there had recently been a rotation of Priz's "pilots." Some of the most experienced operators had left the Northern Fleet and were serving elsewhere in the Navy. New specialists were waiting to be trained.

A third mini-sub in the Fleet, known as Bester, was slightly larger and five tons heavier than Priz, but its mother-ship had been decommissioned in the mid-1990s, and the rescue vehicle now sat in a warehouse. If it was to be deployed, Bester would have to be brought to the scene independently. As the *Rudnitsky* sailed into the Barents Sea, all hopes rested with Priz.

By now, many other ships were mobilizing. As the first glint of the Arctic dawn broke through on the horizon, sailors on the *Peter the Great* were ordered on deck. Their officers instructed them to look for an emergency buoy on the surface. As the young men stared out, searching for signs of oil and wreckage rising with the swell, all they saw was an empty blue-gray stretch of water. Two other warships joined the search, the *Admiral Chabanenko* and the *Admiral Kharlamov,* both of which had been taking part in the war games.

Along the guardrails of the *Peter the Great,* rumors spread like wildfire. What had happened to the *Kursk?* Had there been a fire on board? Were the men alive, banging out emergency signals on her hull? Had she collided with an American submarine? Had surface ships mistakenly struck her with missiles during the previous day's exercise? Warnings were issued throughout the ship not to speak openly about the incident, and officers from the Russian security service, the FSB, who served in the ship kept a careful eye on the radio room and the command center.

Very early that morning, a triumphant shout rang out from a sailor in a lookout post who had seen a buoy half-submerged in the water, lost in the whitecaps. A small boat was launched to bring it on board for examination, but by the time the sailors had reached the spot, the buoy had vanished. Just below the surface they saw some medusa, the giant, formless, milky white jellyfish that hover in the waters of the Barents Sea.

Locating the largest attack submarine ever built in one of the shallowest seas in the world might seem like a relatively easy task, but, like all submarines, the *Kursk* was designed—very purposefully—to be difficult to detect. Now, all the features designed to make her stealthy were working against the rescuers. The rubber tiles that surrounded her outer hull, designed to prevent the sonar echoes of hunters from giving her position away, kept her acoustic profile low. The Northern Fleet warships tried to track any sounds emanating from the *Kursk,* but a stricken submarine with her machinery out of operation makes little noise. She lay virtually silent and invisible on the seabed. The failure of her emergency buoy to deploy to the surface and the absence of an SOS message ensured that the twenty-three survivors spent their first night missing without a trace.

As the search began in earnest, the ghost of a bizarre earlier Barents Sea submarine disaster haunted the rescuers, one that had been one of the most closely guarded secrets of the Northern Fleet for more than three decades.

Deep in the polar winter of 1961, a Romeo-class Soviet submarine carrying a crew of sixty-seven was powering through the roiling surface of the southern Barents Sea. Known by her tactical number *S-80,* she had just successfully completed maneuvers, and the captain had signaled for permission to return to base at Severomorsk. But when the Fleet command radioed back agreeing to the request, *S-80* failed to acknowledge. Repeated efforts to restore communications failed. Staff officers on shore at first assumed that the submarine's radio mast had been damaged in the mountainous seas. They waited for the submarine to return, but she never did.

An all-Fleet alarm was raised on February 28, one week after she went missing, and an armada of search-and-rescue vessels plied the seas looking for the sub. No trace was found. The search for the wreckage of *S-80* stretched through March and April and all summer, and then all year. In fact, shrouded from public gaze, the Northern

Fleet's hunt for their missing submarine went on for an astonishing seven years, suspended only during winter storms. Russia's leaders demanded that the submarine be found. *S-80* was the first of her type, two hundred further diesel submarines of a similar construction had been built, and finding *S-80* was of the highest national importance, so that she could be raised to determine what had caused her to sink. The admiral who led the search, Yuri Senatsky, remembers being told by Moscow: "You can lose men and vessels in the search, but you must find the submarine. There can be no excuses."

As ships scoured the seabed looking for *S-80* using fishing nets and primitive hydroacoustic systems, the Barents Sea gave up plenty of its dead—dozens of ships sunk during the Second World War, an oil tanker from the First World War, endless amounts of military junk—but there was no sign of *S-80*. The secret was kept from the outside world. Relatives of the dead were told that the submarine sank on a secret operation and were ordered not to reveal the news to anyone outside the Fleet.

Finally, in August 1968, a diving bell was lowered into the water to inspect some unexplained wreckage, and *S-80* was found. The search had lasted for 384 weeks. When *S-80* was lifted from the seabed and towed into port in July 1969, investigators discovered the reason for the tragedy. In the storm, water had started to enter through an open hatch while the submarine was rolling on the surface. A young sailor was quickly ordered to close it, and he applied himself to the hatch wheel with all his strength, unable to understand why the mechanism wasn't working. Seawater continued to rush into the sub with successive waves. All the time, the sailor was simply turning the hatch wheel the wrong way. Salvage experts looking at the wreck saw that the hatch wheel was twisted with desperate force, the thread worn thin. Navy investigators discovered that the sailor had been assigned from another submarine, on which the hatch wheel rotated the opposite way from the one on *S-80*. In the Northern Fleet ships, some of the wheels and valves opened clockwise, others counterclockwise. The lack of design consistency had confused one young sailor and exacted a terrible price.

News of the loss of the submarine and the length of the search emerged only in 1996, when some of those involved in the hunt told their story after a silence that had lasted thirty-five years. As the hunt for the *Kursk* began, this long-hidden secret seemed like a bad omen to the superstitious Fleet commanders. Especially as the *Kursk* had been lost in almost exactly the same place as *S-80*.

6

AS HEAD OF THE Russian Navy's search-and-rescue forces, Rear Admiral Gennady Verich knew that predawn telephone calls never brought good news. Just after 5 on Sunday morning, the duty officer in the Navy's Moscow Command Center called. The conversation was short and to the point. Verich was told that the Northern Fleet's exercise had encountered a major problem: The commanders had mysteriously lost contact with the *Kursk,* and repeated efforts to re-establish communications were proving unsuccessful. Verich instructed the duty officer to call him if there were any fresh developments but chose to stay at home. He was convinced that the problem would turn out to be either a technical fault with the boat's communications mast or the product of confusion over when the *Kursk* was due to report her position. Verich was reminded that peculiar oceanographic and atmospheric conditions in the Barents Sea during the summer months sometimes hindered submarine communications.

Verich is a pugnacious, aggressive commander, balding and heavy in build. Even his friends concede that he lacks diplomatic skills, but he has built a career out of driving tough decisions through the military bureaucracy, which in Russia is a very considerable achievement.

Several hours after that call, still with no news from the *Kursk,* Verich reported to his command post inside naval headquarters. His first action was to gather a team of staff officers and start planning a response if the loss of the *Kursk* was confirmed. He also decided to fly up to Severomorsk and assume direct command of the operation, taking over from Alexander Teslenko, who was in charge of the Northern Fleet's search-and-rescue team.

Each of Russia's four fleets—the Northern, the Pacific, the Baltic, and the Black Sea—has its own separate search-and-rescue unit. Verich's task was to coordinate the resources, manage the budgets, and respond to any national emergencies at sea. He got the job in 1991, the year the Soviet Union collapsed, and he had struggled in vain to keep intact four viable search-and-rescue forces. Year after year, throughout his tenure, the budget of the department was slashed. In 1999, the Northern Fleet rescue service requested 27 million rubles (about $1 million) in an attempt to revive its capabilities. It received just 400,000 rubles ($14,000). As naval officers commented bitterly, the money was barely enough to buy a car.

In the strictly hierarchical world of the Kremlin, only two men had the right to call the Russian president to discuss military affairs: Marshal Igor Sergeyev, the Defense Minister, and General Anatoly Kvashnin, head of the General Staff. Not even the head of the Navy, Admiral Vladimir Kuroyedov, is permitted to contact President Putin directly.

At 7 A.M. that Sunday, Sergeyev assumed the deeply uncomfortable task of interrupting the president's holiday to inform him that the country's newest nuclear-powered, multipurpose submarine was missing in home waters and that the Northern Fleet could not explain her disappearance.

Although the transcript of this crucial conversation between the minister of defense and the president remains locked in the Kremlin's files, it seems clear that the gravity of the situation was underplayed. At the end of the conversation, Putin knew there was a "problem," but he had no understanding that the crew of the *Kursk* was probably in grave danger. Later in the day, Putin was filmed in shirtsleeves, smiling broadly, hosting a barbecue on the grounds of his official dacha in Sochi on the Black Sea. This was not a leader who recognized that he was facing the first crisis of his hundred-day presidency.

The politics of the Russian Defense Ministry are always turbulent, with many departments fighting over a rapidly shrinking budget, but they were especially poisonous in the summer of 2000. A concerted campaign was under way to replace the elderly Sergeyev as defense minister. Groups of highly ambitious young officers were circling, their spirits buoyed by the new president in the Kremlin. The question was how to topple the savvy minister, who had made his reputation by running Russia's Strategic Rocket Forces, the nation's land-based nuclear-missile arsenal. Sergeyev had good reason to view top naval officers with suspicion: Kuroyedov, the head of the Navy, was the man widely expected to replace him.

Sergeyev now believes that key information about the *Kursk* accident was deliberately kept from him in the critical first few hours. If Navy officials could make Sergeyev appear inadequately briefed, make him seem incompetent and foolish in front of the president, that might be sufficient to undermine his hold on the Defense Ministry.

The overall picture that Sunday morning was certainly a sorry one. The president was on holiday, the defense minister suspected he was being misled by the Navy as part of an internal political battle, and the head of the search-and-rescue forces was first notified a full seventeen and a half hours after the *Kursk* was lost.

II: SUNDAY MORNING
Vidyaevo Naval Base

A MIDDLE-AGED WOMAN SITTING through a dull night shift in the early hours of Sunday morning was the first civilian to realize that a full-scale submarine emergency was under way. Valentina Kozelkova was the telephone operator in Vidyaevo. A widow in her mid-forties, with three young daughters at home, this night job was her only way of earning a meager salary. She worked in the switching center, handling much of the telephone traffic for the town. Around midnight, she was puzzled to be handling a mounting number of calls between Vidyaevo and Severomorsk. Calls were also coming in from Zapadnaya Litsa, the headquarters of the Seventh Submarine Division. There was always one duty Fleet officer at the Vidyaevo base, but now several others were also there, fielding a mounting number of calls.

Valentina could not suppress her curiosity, and she listened in on snatches of conversation as she made the connections. The voices she overheard were devoid of courtesies. Orders were barked. Information was demanded. She detected fear. Soon she had gleaned just enough to realize that a submarine was in trouble. Commanders were insisting that officers report to their bases immediately. Then someone mentioned the *Kursk,* and she gasped. She knew many of the sailors. Her closest friend was Olga Chernyshov, whose husband, Sergei, served on the submarine as a communications officer.

Valentina kept the secret to herself those first few hours. In the morning, she visited Olga, intending to tell her what she had overheard, but Valentina's courage deserted her, and instead she distracted Olga by taking her for a long walk to pick some mushrooms in the open fields behind Vidyaevo. Perhaps by the time they returned, she thought, the *Kursk* would have signaled that all was well.

When tragedy breaks in a small community, the news travels with remarkable speed via a whispered exchange at the entrance to an apartment, a chance encounter in the street, a hastily made phone call between friends. And if that is true of news, it is doubly so when it comes to rumor. Many of those in Vidyaevo who describe how they first heard the *Kursk* was in trouble say the rumors spread furiously. "Wildfire in the jungle" was how Natasha Tylik put it.

> *Have you heard?*
> *What's happening?*
> *Is it true? Is it possible?*
> *Who can we call? How can we check the information?*
> *Who would know the truth?*

A small knot of women gathered in Vidyaevo's little square, and the odd snatch of anxious conversation was audible as wives waited to buy fish and vegetables in the shabby kiosks that line the square.

> *What's the news?*
> *Has it sunk?*
> *No, but it's lost power.*
> *I heard it's on fire.*
> *No, everything is fine.*
> *Are they trapped?*
> *Who knows? God help them.*

At midday, Natasha Tylik, with her baby daughter on her lap, was having tea with Irina Korobkov, whose husband was one of the *Kursk*'s sonar officers. They were the closest of friends. Natasha was stronger, Irina fragile and more vulnerable, but together they were a team, learning to cope with their husbands' long absences and the harsh conditions of the garrison. In the small apartment, the friends were chatting about their plans for when the men returned ashore. They agreed that they would all go for a picnic in the hills.

The phone interrupted their planning.

Irina said hello and then lapsed into silence, clutching the handset, listening to the wavering voice of a friend whose husband also served on the *Kursk*. She turned around to stare at Natasha, unable to speak. Moments passed. Finally, she sat down.

"What's happened?" Natasha pleaded.

Irina could not find the words.

"What's wrong?"

"The *Kursk* has sunk," Irina blurted out.

Natasha was the first to break free from the shocked silence, declaring that she would call her father-in-law, who lived just a mile away. Nikolai would know what was going on. He was a veteran submariner himself and maintained strong links with the present generation of officers. If there had been an accident, Nikolai Tylik would know.

Nikolai's wife, Nadezhda, answered Natasha's call.

"People are saying the *Kursk* has sunk," Natasha said. "Have you heard anything?"

"Who told you this? Don't listen to such nonsense!" Nadezhda shouted. "No such thing can happen. It is the wild talk of lonely wives, and you must not believe it. The *Kursk* cannot sink. You know that."

"Are you sure?"

"Of course I am. Calm down! Nikolai will ring some friends to confirm everything is well."

But Natasha then phoned other wives of the *Kursk*'s crew, and they had also heard something was wrong. No two pieces of information were the same: Some had been told by friends at the base that the submarine had sunk to the seabed, others that the *Kursk* was disabled on the surface, still others that everything was now under control and their husbands were heading back home. Natasha wasn't sure what to think. Part of her believed that something had gone terribly wrong. Who would start such a rumor without reliable information? But the *Kursk* was so big and so strong that she had to wonder what could possibly have gone wrong. She wanted to believe that all was well, that the submarine was just taking part in a last-minute twist to the maneuvers, perhaps a search-and-rescue drill.

Despite the confusion, the clue that something was indeed seriously wrong was there in plain sight for the wives to see. The community was too small to hide it: The naval base on the outskirts of the town had been placed on full alert.

Nadezhda Tylik did not believe that her son was in trouble, or that the *Kursk* was on the seabed, but she desperately wanted to establish why the rumor was circulating and who had started it. Leaving her home, she spotted Irina Lyachin, the wife of the *Kursk*'s captain. They stopped in the street and spoke for a while. Both women had heard the reports; neither was sure what to think. As they were talking, Mikhail Kochegub, the deputy to the base commander and a leading military figure in Vidyaevo, walked by. Kochegub promised to check at headquarters and report back on what he found. He returned a short while later with good news. "Half the headquarters is closed, and the other half is filled with officers just passing the time of day. Relax. Everything is fine. We would know if there was an emergency."

III: Ninth Compartment

ONE HUNDRED AND TWENTY-FIVE miles northeast of Vidyaevo, in the aft compartment of the *Kursk,* the twenty-three men continued their valiant battle for survival. The submarine was essentially a steel drum on the floor of the sea. When they chose not to make a free-ascent escape from the ninth hatch, they must have been calculating that a rescue submersible would quickly reach the scene of the disaster.

As long as the ninth compartment was hermetically sealed off from the ocean, the pressure inside would remain constant, at what submariners and divers call "atmospheric," or surface, pressure, and the *Kursk* survivors could still attempt an escape to the surface on their own, through the emergency hatch. Their bodies would be at the same pressure as on the surface, so there would be no risk of decompression as they kicked out of the hatch and shot up. Physiologically, they could cope with the ascent, since they would be moving, in effect, from surface pressure to surface pressure. At some stage, if all hope of an outside rescue evaporated, it was still a last-ditch, life-or-death gamble they might have to take. Although escaping through the hatch was a terrifying option given the dangers—ranging from cold shock to face squeeze to hypothermia—it was still a possibility, so long as their bodies stayed at atmospheric pressure.

Unfortunately for the *Kursk* survivors, however, the structural integrity of the ninth compartment was not good. From very shortly after the explosions, the survivors had heard water seeping in through the stern glands, where the propeller shafts enter the aft compartment. Drowning was only a distant threat—the narrow stream of water forcing its way through the stern pipework would take many days to fill the cavernous aft compartments. But a much more immediate danger was developing within their own bodies. As water entered the compartment, it was pushing the air into a smaller and smaller space, steadily increasing the pressure. And as the pressure in the ninth section rose, so did the pressure on the air in their lungs. Gradually, invisibly, bubbles of gas in soluble form were entering their bloodstream, a process that is known as "saturating" the human body as it adjusts naturally to the rise in pressure. Even that did not in itself represent a problem, but there was one potentially catastrophic consequence: They would no longer survive a free ascent from the escape hatch to the surface.

If they attempted an escape now, the pressure would rapidly change in their bodies, and the gas in their bloodstream, previously in a soluble form, would be transformed into a gaseous state. The bubbles would catch in the joints, spine, and brain, giving rise to a condition known as decompression sickness or, much more commonly, "the bends." With pressure rising in the ninth compartment, an attempt to surface from 350 feet would only guarantee a rapid and agonizing death, unless they were placed immediately in decompression chambers—facilities that neither the Northern Fleet surface ships nor the rescue service possess. Even if they reached the surface, gulping down fresh air and savoring life, the triumph of survival would be illusory. Within seconds, they would be in the grip of crippling, explosive decompression sickness; within minutes, they would die in unimaginable pain as the gas bubbles expanded and destroyed nerves and tissues.

The rising pressure was changing not only the state of their bodies but the very physics and chemistry of their environment. As the pressure rose, one result was a rapidly increasing risk of fire. If a blaze was ignited, perhaps by a spark as water came into contact with electrical equipment, it would burn with much greater ferocity than at surface pressure. Meanwhile, the potency of the carbon dioxide was increasing.

As they sat there in the ninth compartment, or possibly spreading out into the much larger eighth section, they understood all too well the implications of the steady stream of water forcing itself into the ninth compartment. The noise would have echoed eerily through the pipework, hissing through the shafts on its way through the submarine. They must have prayed for the sound of an approaching submersible. Perhaps inside the double-hulled *Kursk*, they would not hear its quiet approach, and the first they would know of a rescue would be a mini-sub scraping along the upper hatch as it came in to dock. They must have imagined many times the echoing of steel as first the outer and then the inner hatches swung open and the gleaming faces of rescuers peered down the escape tower.

The men had been adhering to their survival training in combating the insidiously rising carbon dioxide and falling oxygen levels. The large cartridges containing superoxide chemicals were filtering the atmosphere, just as they were designed to do. But these life-support measures incurred other risks. The chemicals are designed to react with the moisture in the air to produce oxygen, but with too much water the reaction can become violent and uncontrollable. In common with all systems that produce oxygen, there is a danger of fire.

As the aft compartments slowly flooded, the rising water began to cover machinery and seep into oil filters. Oil now rose to float on the top of the water. It wasn't just water that was now rising up in the gloom. There was also a volatile and potentially lethal cocktail of oil and lubricants. As the men worked to keep the atmosphere breathable, the *Kursk* was now highly vulnerable to another disaster. Even with their bodies numbed by cold and fatigue, even as their exhausted, frightened minds slowed down, they knew that they had to exercise extreme caution as they replaced the chemical cassettes. If they fumbled and dropped one in the water, it could trigger an uncontrollable inferno.

Their situation was grim, and it was about to become a whole lot worse. At some point, probably in the early hours of Sunday morning, Dmitri Kolesnikov and his twenty-two colleagues were plunged into darkness. Their flashlight batteries faded, and the last glimmer of the emergency lights above them failed. This must have been a severe psychological blow. The men were now reduced to feeling their way around the compartment by touch and memory. Some of them might have chosen to lie down on several bunks that were positioned to one side of the bulkhead in the eighth compartment, hoping to preserve their strength and minimize the uptake of oxygen. In the cold dark of the compartment, Kolesnikov pulled out the piece of paper on which he had recorded the names of the survivors. He turned it over and with the same blue pen wrote a new note:

> *It's dark here to write, but I'll try by feel. It seems like there are no chances,*
> *10–20 %. Let's hope that at least someone will read this. Here's the list of*
> *personnel from the other sections, who are now in the 9th and will attempt to*
> *get out. Regards to everybody, no need to be desperate. Kolesnikov.*

Kolesnikov's first note had been neatly written, perfectly following the paper's evenly spaced lines. These four sentences were an irregular scrawl, veering wildly across the margins. His earlier list had a date and time written above it; this one had no such reference. In the darkness, perhaps Kolesnikov could no longer read his watch. He still had the energy to try and communicate, and he was still in sufficient control to calculate the chances of survival. Folding the note several times, he tightly wound a waterproof wrapping around the paper and placed it deep in the breast pocket of his overalls, below the layer of his thermal suit.

The most intriguing part of the note was the penultimate sentence: "Here's the list of personnel from the other sections, who are now in the 9th and will attempt to get out." In the darkness, and in a bitterly cold atmosphere contaminated with rising carbon dioxide, it seems the men were thinking again about the possibility of an escape through the hatch. They knew that the water leaking in was raising the pressure within their compartment. They knew that an ascent from 350 feet—the depth showing on their gauge—would condemn them to severe decompression sickness. Now, however, perhaps anything seemed better than staying where they were.

IV: THE MURMANSK BANKA

THE OFFICIAL NORTHERN FLEET log states with military precision that the *Rudnitsky* finally cut into the southwest corner of the military exercise area at 8:39 A.M. on Sunday, August 13, twenty-one hours after the explosions inside the *Kursk*. The tug *Altai* was already in the area, waiting for instructions.

The first task was to mark the submarine's precise position. The *Peter the Great* had found an "acoustic anomaly," but the commanders taking charge of the rescue operation still needed confirmation that they had found the *Kursk* and not the relic of a previous naval battle or the victim of a long-forgotten Arctic storm. The evidence certainly pointed to the *Kursk*. The anomaly was within the submarine's patrol zone—an area known to Russian oceanographers as the Murmansk Banka—and matched the directional estimates provided by the *Karelia*. The *Rudnitsky*'s sonar appeared to support the conclusion of the warships nearby, "pinging" an unidentified target on the seabed on a bearing of 145 degrees and at a range of about 6,600 feet. The depth was judged to be right around 350 feet, shallow water for a submarine that was more than 500 feet in length.

The rescuers had realized by this time that this was no mere mechanical failure: All of the *Kursk*'s basic emergency systems had failed. The primary evacuation method of using the escape capsule had not been attempted. There was no sign of an emergency buoy; no signal or SOS had been heard. The evidence pointed to a catastrophic malfunction, but the Fleet command urgently needed first-hand evidence of what had happened.

A thick blanket of official secrecy still surrounds the events of that Sunday morning, but it appears that a highly classified special-operations submersible was the first underwater vehicle to be deployed. The "Dronov" mini-sub operates with the Northern Fleet but is under the direct control of the General Staff in Moscow. Normally, it's engaged in covert intelligence-gathering missions, providing data to the Russian submarine flotillas on the position of America's underwater detection sensors. Now the Dronov sub was deployed as a search vehicle to bring the very first information on the disaster to the Fleet command. Exactly what data it provided is unclear, but it is likely to have recorded the first video image of the forward compartment of the *Kursk*, now disfigured beyond recognition. The pictures must have shaken Admiral Popov to the core. No submariner could look at the video pictures without recoiling in almost physical pain. The entire bow of the submarine was shattered and was now an impenetrable tangle of steel beams leading into the second compartment. The heavy casing of a torpedo-tube rear door was visible, along with fragments of the hull scattered on the seabed. The Dronov submersible also discovered that the reactor compartments and the aft of the submarine were intact, with no sign of major structural damage. If there were survivors, the only possible evacuation route was through the ninth-compartment escape tower.

The General Staff's submarine has no rescue capability, so the focus now switched to the rescue units arriving at the scene. Technicians on the *Rudnitsky* had worked throughout the nighttime passage to prepare AS-32 and Priz for their first dives. AS-32 would perform a survey of the wreck. Priz would attempt the actual rescue.

Popov stood on a walkway adjacent to the bridge of his flagship, staring out to sea and drawing heavily on a cigarette. He had smoked since his days as a young cadet but now used a cigarette holder to try to lessen his dependence on nicotine. His expression was fixed, even when he demanded fresh information from the *Rudnitsky* via VHF radio.

Two nautical miles away, the officers piloting the Priz submersible prepared to risk their lives. Commander Alexander Maisak and chief pilot Sergei Pertsev faced a truly daunting task. They would be operating a twenty-year-old submersible with such low-performance batteries that every dive would invite disaster. Ahead of them lay first a descent of 350 feet, and then a search for the *Kursk* using their sonar. Once they located the submarine, they would have to rely on Priz's crude thrusters to attempt the challenging feat of navigating over the aft escape hatch in a maneuver requiring great precision. The mission demanded more than skill and steady nerves—it required exceptional good fortune.

Pertsev vented the external tanks, which expelled the air and caused Priz to lose its buoyancy and begin its descent. Just before 5:20 P.M., nearly thirty hours after the explosions, the submersible slowly dropped out of sight below the waves.

Pertsev clung to the hope that he would be able to repeat the success of a training mission he had conducted the year before, during the exercises of August 1999. In that drill, he had taken Priz down 230 feet to a diesel submarine lying on the seabed outside of Vidyaevo, and had brought six sailors to the surface. But there was a world of difference between a carefully controlled exercise in a protected bay and a real-life disaster in the open ocean.

Alongside Priz's pilots, Sergei Butskikh was riding in the submersible's second compartment, where evacuated sailors would huddle when they were rescued. He was a submarine engineer and a specialist in the design of the Oscar II–class boats. His job was to assist in the hatch connection and to help bring the *Kursk* sailors to safety. Some of the submariners might be unconscious or badly injured, unable to make their own way up the escape tower. If necesssary, Butskikh would climb down into the wreck of the Kursk and establish the condition of survivors. It would take strong nerves.

The three officers had all eagerly volunteered for the rescue attempt. They were paid a pitiful salary, and their search-and-rescue department had been subjected to constant budget cuts, treated for years as a marginal auxiliary service. But as they began their dive, any lingering anger about their treatment was put aside. Although exhausted after three nights without sleep, they were more highly motivated than at any time in their lives.

As Maisak took Priz down, the natural light coming through the viewports faded. To try and preserve the batteries, Maisak and Pertsev used the minimum amount of power. The small, flickering sonar screen revealed just specks and flashes, picking up echoes from schools of fish. Maisak checked the heading on the gyro-compass and switched on the spotlight on the bow of Priz. The twisting shapes of Arctic cod and plankton were reflected back in the harsh light. For the submersible pilots, the descent was like driving at night through a gentle snowfall. Beyond the darting fish, the forbidding blackness of the Barents Sea stretched ahead. And somewhere out there lay the crippled submarine.

The search was slow, with Priz traveling at no more than two knots, the speed of a measured walk. Any burst of the thrusters would use up precious power. A bright, persistent splash on the flickering sonar screen provided the first clue that they were close to the *Kursk*. Staring out of the viewport, carefully slowing Priz down, initially Maisak could see nothing.

Then suddenly he glimpsed a dark mass taking shape, slightly blacker than the surrounding ocean. The submarine's acoustic tiles were providing almost perfect camouflage, but there now, standing out against the light, shone the giant propellers, the only part of the submarine not encased in the dark rubber.

Pertsev and Maisak reported the current as just over one knot, running in the direction of the body of the submarine, from bow to stern. That was bad news for the pilots. The established way to approach a disabled submarine is by maneuvering head-on into the current, which has the effect of slowing a mini-sub down and allowing more time for the precise maneuvers needed to attach to the hatch. In addition to the problem of the current, an approach from astern was hindered by the large tail of the submarine, as well as the large propellers and prominent rear stabilizers.

The rescue pilots had only ever practiced on diesel submarines, since nuclear subs are never permitted to rest on the seabed. Now for the first time in their professional lives, they realized just how difficult it was to navigate around the aft of an Oscar II. Admiral Verich was privately cursing the submarine designers. Why had they always placed such emphasis on speed and depth, weapons systems and stealth, and not on making safety and escape systems more accessible?

The only option for Maisak and Pertsev was to approach the *Kursk* from just behind her reactors, piloting the mini-sub diagonally across the current. Then they would allow the current to very slowly push Priz backward toward the aft escape hatch. Instead of fighting the current, they sought to use it to ease the rescue sub into position. At the critical moment, as they glided past the emergency buoy that had failed to release, judging their position along the hull by instinct, they used their thrusters to counteract the drift of the current, attempting to hold their position close to the hatch. For a few tantalizing moments, these desperate, improvised tactics appeared to be succeeding.

Maisak maneuvered within inches of the ninth compartment, holding position right above the hatch. Gently he brought the submersible down to dock. He struggled to fight the current and make a firm connection with the hatch, anxiously trying to hold the mini-sub steady enough.

Once in position, Maisak would open a valve to create a vacuum between his submersible and the seat of the *Kursk*'s hatch. He would then use a pump to remove the small amount of water trapped between the two hatches, allowing them to be opened. Priz would never be physically clamped to the *Kursk;* once a vacuum existed, the water pressure was easily sufficient to keep them linked together.

The only design feature on the *Kursk* that helped make this connection was a small rod just a few inches high that protruded from the center of the outer hatch, which Priz could grab and use to ensure that the final maneuver of the docking was perfect. It was a navigational aid that the submarine engineers had borrowed from the Russian space program. Indeed, some of the rescue pilots compared their work to docking with the Russian space station Mir, but they quickly added that in these circumstances it was actually far more difficult. Unlike his cosmonaut counterparts, Maisak had the water current to deal with, he could see little from his viewports, and he had no ground control to guide him in. They might be only 350 feet below the ocean surface and less than 100 miles from the Russian coast, but Maisak, Pertsev, and Butskikh had good reason to feel terrifyingly alone.

Again and again, they tried to make the seal, but they could never hold on to the protruding rod that would secure their exact position. Maisak watched the needle on the voltage gauge with growing alarm, knowing that Priz's batteries were being depleted at a frightening speed and that they wouldn't last much longer. If he drained them too much, he might struggle to get Priz back to the surface and safely to the *Rudnitsky,* but he had to push.

Could the men in the *Kursk* hear Priz's thrusters right above the hatch? If only the survivors could know that rescuers were hovering right above, so close, just one small maneuver away from a firm seal. Maisak was desperate to keep trying, but the needle gauges aboard Priz showed that the power in the batteries was too low to sustain further efforts. Their frustration can only be guessed at. They knew that the next attempt could not be made for another twelve hours, the time required to recharge the batteries.

Then just before they began the ascent, while they were inching backward away from the hatch, the mini-sub was pushed with the current faster than expected, and made shuddering contact with the *Kursk*'s upper rudder. The Priz three-man team risked not only losing their own lives but also destroying the only rescue vehicle that had a chance of evacuating the *Kursk* sailors.

With great care, Maisak regained control and delicately nursed Priz back to the surface. The dive ended at 6:30 P.M. It had lasted only one hour and ten minutes. They had risked everything and achieved nothing.

Captain Teslenko, the Northern Fleet's rescue chief, was determined to use the hours it would take to recharge Priz's power supply to some benefit, and he ordered AS-32 into the water to make the first proper survey of the *Kursk*. He wanted to add to the initial information gained by the secret Dronov mini-sub. Commanded by Captain Pavel Karaputa, AS-32 would be able to move around the entire hull, and the crew would analyze the full extent of the damage. Reports from the Northern Fleet suggest, however, that AS-32's reconnaissance effort was nothing short of a fiasco, as Karaputa even failed to find the *Kursk* for several hours. Its inferior navigation system and poor sonar left it half-blind and circling near the seabed. By the time Karaputa managed to locate the stricken submarine, the AS-32 was at the very limits of its endurance. The pilot made what Teslenko called a limited "observation pass" before being forced to return to the surface.

Frustration aboard the *Rudnitsky* was turning into anger. The stakes could scarcely have been higher, and the predicament for the rescuers could not have been more bleak. Priz was sitting on its plinths in the hold having its batteries recharged. AS-32 had been exposed as inadequate. Bester, the submersible without a mother-ship, was still ashore. Then the temporary command post on the *Rudnitsky* received another piece of bad news. The Fleet's meteorological office was reporting that the favorable, calm weather of recent days was about to change. A summer storm was expected to sweep across the Barents Sea within the next twenty-four hours.

7

I: MONDAY, AUGUST 14
Defense Command Northern Norway

AS THE SECOND DAY after the accident dawned, word that something was seriously amiss with the Northern Fleet began to reach Western military commanders. As is Russia's policy with NATO countries, they had been informed of the schedule for the Russian maneuvers. Now their intelligence services had gathered a number of signs that the war games had abruptly and inexplicably been halted. From satellite reconnaissance, NATO's naval analysts knew that the warships were remaining out at sea, either circling listlessly, as if waiting for instructions, or at anchor. None was returning to port. One of the oldest fears of Western military planners was that Russia might use a regular naval exercise to disguise preparations for a surprise attack, but that seemed an absurd explanation in this post–Cold War environment, and, besides, there was no evidence that warships or submarines were deploying toward the North Cape and the Atlantic. In fact, the opposite was true: All the ships were converging on a single spot in the midst of their own exercise.

Admiral Einar Skorgen was known simply as "Commander North Norway." His military domain stretched all the way up to the sensitive border that divides Norway and Russia high in the Arctic. Overall, he was responsible for almost a million square miles of ocean up to the Arctic icepack and a hundred thousand square miles of territory. But despite his rank and areas of responsibility, he was never informed about British and American submarine operations in the Barents Sea. The covert missions are so sensitive that even a trusted NATO commander like Skorgen is kept in the dark.

Over the past few days, Skorgen had taken only a passing professional interest in the Russian naval exercise. It was unfolding just as scheduled and seemed entirely routine. All maneuvers involving the firing of live munitions must be publicly announced, and the activity was deep within home waters. As far as Skorgen could see, the exercise threatened no one.

Skorgen was based at the military headquarters in Bodø, known by its awkward acronym DEFCOMNON (Defense Command Northern Norway). Burrowed into the middle of a granite mountain, the complex of bunkers was constructed in the darkest days of the Cold War, designed to withstand a Soviet nuclear attack. Even now, the center monitors the activities of the Russian military throughout the far northwest of Europe.

In fact, Skorgen had heard a whisper the previous day, on Sunday afternoon, that there had been a peculiar development in the Barents Sea. An officer from the Norwegian Intelligence Service visited him and explained that the Northern Fleet maneuvers had taken an unexpected twist. Russian ships were forming protective rings around a stretch of water to the northeast of Severomorsk, but the intelligence agent offered no further details and could provide no explanation. Skorgen assumed that the Russians were simply engaging in a search-and-rescue drill and thought little more about it. He had no information over that weekend from any source that suggested that the Barents had been shaken by massive twin explosions. The data had certainly been collected by SOSUS stations and seismological institutes—they simply hadn't been analyzed or fed back into the military chain of command. This failure is partly explained by a fact of disconcerting simplicity: It was an August weekend, and many NATO analysts were either away on summer vacations or were not on shift until the working week began.

Looking back, Skorgen now questions whether he was told all that was known by his own intelligence organization. Had the Norwegian spy ship the *Marjata* not been able to record the explosions? Her data are sent in real time to Oslo for analysis by naval intelligence specialists. Did General Jan Blom, the head of Norwegian intelligence, not check the data from his own spy ship after learning that the Russian summer exercise had broken up in disarray? If Norwegian intelligence was hiding something, what was it, and on whose behalf?

But early that Monday, Skorgen was alerted by one of his staff to "highly abnormal patterns" of Russian naval activity. Belatedly, U.S. satellite reconnaissance and Western signals intelligence was being analyzed. Skorgen, whose curiosity had been piqued by Sunday's strange visit from the NIS agent, decided to call a meeting of his senior officers to assess what was known. Not only were the warships concentrated in a single patch of water, there were now signs that other vessels were hastily preparing to leave Northern Fleet ports.

Skorgen needed firsthand intelligence, so he authorized a P3 reconnaissance plane to investigate. The aircraft took off from the airbase on the nearby island of Andøy and flew right to the heart of the Barents Sea exercise area, fifty minutes' flying time to the northeast. The P3's powerful cameras and sideways-looking radar transmitted real-time photographic and sonar images back to Bodø.

Aerial surveillance not only provided helpful extra information— it also served as a clever ploy that Skorgen used when conducting routine naval-intelligence work. If information came in to Bodø via a highly sensitive source such as intelligence agents or electronic sensors, Skorgen would deploy a P3 plane to the scene, making sure the Russians noticed the aircraft. He could then act on the original information without compromising the primary source.

As the data came back from the P3, Skorgen and his team determined that the Russians were either engaging in an exceptionally realistic drill or facing some kind of emergency.

On Skorgen's desk sat a unique communications link: a direct phone connection to Admiral Popov in Severomorsk, the result of some adroit diplomacy. The only person who had ever used the link was a telephone engineer who tested it every six months. This is one of the few direct military-to-military links between a NATO commander and his Russian counterpart. Both sides had pretended in public that the phone would be used to coordinate searches for lost fishermen, but Oslo and Moscow knew that the link's real value was military. The deal agreeing to the phone link was clinched in 1999, when a Russian government minister agreed to install it if the Norwegians promised to pay the bill.

Skorgen now eyed the phone uneasily, wondering whether he should call and ask the Russians what on earth had happened to their exercise. He hesitated because he knew that if he were in Popov's position, facing some kind of emergency, a well-intentioned expression of concern would be just a needless distraction.

As he pondered what to do, his thoughts were interrupted by a call from the Norwegian minister of defense. The minister thought that Skorgen should talk directly with Popov and ask him candidly what was happening in the Barents Sea. Skorgen objected, saying he wanted a better reason for making the call to the Northern Fleet Headquarters. Fine, the minister replied: offer them our assistance.

Immediately after Skorgen punched in the pre-set number, a phone rang somewhere deep in Popov's headquarters. A Russian officer who spoke excellent English answered the call.

"It's Admiral Einar Skorgen here. I would like to speak to Admiral Viacheslav Popov, please."

"That is not possible," the officer replied.

"Why not?"

"The admiral is currently at sea on board his flagship, conducting maneuvers."

"I would like to request a report on the situation in your exercise area," Skorgen continued, "and I am authorized by my government to offer assistance to you, if that is required."

"Please hold the line."

Skorgen waited as his offer was passed quickly to Popov, who was on board the *Peter the Great*.

Only a minute or so later, the staff officer came back on the line. "Admiral Popov sends his kind regards to you. The situation is under control, and we have no need for any assistance. He thanks you for the offer."

That was that. The first Western offer of help to Russia had been politely but firmly rejected.

II: Northwood Headquarters, North London

COMMODORE DAVID RUSSELL ARRIVED arrived at the Royal Navy's Northwood Headquarters that Monday morning, heading for the third-floor suite of offices where the submarine command is based. While his boss was on holiday, Russell was the acting "Flag Officer Submarines," the man in charge of Britain's attack subs and Trident nuclear deterrent. He had barely taken off his jacket and settled into his chair when one of the phones on his desk rang.

The call was from the duty officer in the adjacent bombproof bunker, where Britain collates its worldwide military-intelligence picture. The bunker is affectionately known as "the Hole" and houses the teams that communicate with Britain's nuclear submarines. The crown jewels of Britain's military secrets—the patrol patterns of the Trident submarines and the cryptology that allows signals to reach the boats—lie within these secure walls. If the order ever came from a British prime minister to launch a nuclear missile, it would be verified and transmitted from the Hole.

"Sir," the duty officer began, "there might be a problem."

"What's up?"

"I suggest we switch to secure comms."

Leaning across his desk, Russell flicked a switch that instantly encrypted the call.

"There is unexpected naval activity in the Barents Sea, sir. It's not clear what is going on. It could be part of their exercise, but there are unusual aspects to it. Communication circuits that are rarely used by the Northern Fleet are coming to life. We will keep you posted, sir. Just thought we had better let you know."

Just like Admiral Skorgen, Russell expected that the activity was just some part of the exercise, probably the Russians testing their command-and-control systems or engaging in a search-and-rescue drill.

Lying on the outer reaches of suburban London, the Joint Headquarters at Northwood is an unlikely site for one of Britain's most sensitive military bases. The garrison was built on the eve of the Second World War as the headquarters of the Royal Air Force Coastal Command. In 1952, NATO's Eastern Atlantic Command moved to Northwood. Soon afterward, it was made the Royal Navy's headquarters and home to the officers commanding Britain's fleet of submarines.

Slight in build, with an easy manner but a sharp and curious mind, Commodore Russell learned his trade under the keen eye of some of the Royal Navy's legendary submarine commanders during secret Cold War patrols. He felt more comfortable in a submarine control room than behind a desk, finding the Northwood job frustrating. You make a decision on a submarine, and within seconds you're witnessing the result; you make a decision ashore, and it gets referred to another committee.

Russell told the duty officer to give him another update as soon as fresh intelligence reached the Hole. He looked at his watch. It was 8 A.M. in London, 11 A.M. in Moscow.

III: 11:03 A.M.
Moscow

THE BEST LIES ARE WRAPPED in a blanket of truth. That Monday morning, Russia's two main information agencies issued identical news flashes that emerged simultaneously from teleprinters in Moscow's newspaper offices and government departments:

> Starting at 11:03 there are reports from the press service of the Northern Fleet about malfunctions aboard the multipurpose nuclear-powered submarine the *Kursk*. The crew, as reported by the military, is alive, and communications with them are being maintained with the help of special signals using tapping methods.

Exactly six minutes later, Russia's main television channel, RTR, broke into its normal network schedule with a separate announcement:

> The nuclear-powered submarine the *Kursk* is lying on the bed of the Barents Sea. There are no nuclear weapons on board the submarine. Unofficial queries from the Norwegian side are being made about the state of the radiation levels and about the possibility of offering assistance.

For the Russian public, shock at the news was mixed with relief that the Fleet had established communications with the crew and that the sailors were tapping messages to their rescuers. This sounded like a technical failure, certainly nothing that endangered the lives of the submariners.

But whether they fully anticipated it or not, these press releases fueled a worldwide hunger for news about what had happened to the Russian submarine. The story raised the specter of both a human tragedy and an environmental catastrophe, and within hours, the Russian authorities were dealing with not a domestic military problem but a drama that generated concern and sympathy around the globe.

The Northern Fleet command had realized that news of a submarine disaster could no longer be hidden. This was no *S-80;* there could be no thirty-six-year silence. Careers could not be pursued as if nothing had happened. Times had changed. Viewed from Severo-morsk, they had not changed for the better, but nonetheless there was no denying that the loss of a submarine had to be acknowledged in some form. The Northern Fleet had already kept news of the acci-dent from the media for forty-eight hours, and outside powers would soon be demanding an explanation. That did not mean the expla-nation need be accurate, however.

A further brief statement identified the time of the accident as Sunday. The Fleet commanders hoped to erase entirely the first twenty-four hours of the crisis from the history books. If the accident could be portrayed as having occurred on Sunday, then the Fleet commanders could claim they had found the *Kursk* immediately and would be commended for their quick response. Adding to the decep-tion, the Northern Fleet press office issued an update later that day at lunchtime:

> During maneuvers of the Northern Fleet, at the appointed time, the multipurpose submarine *Kursk* did not communicate. As a result of timely measures by the Northern Fleet command, it was possible to locate the submarine. The rescue efforts are being led by Admiral V. Popov. There is contact with the crew.

In releasing these optimistic communiqués about the state of the submarine, the Russian Navy had not counted on Frode Ringdal. The Norwegian seismologist was still puzzling over that mysterious pattern of seismic waves picked up by the Arctic Experimental Seis-mic Station in Karasjok on Saturday morning. The more Ringdal examined the data, the more it confirmed his suspicion. He knew there was no natural seismic activity in the southern Barents, so the spikes had to have been caused by some kind of detonation, and if the seismographs were accurate, it was a huge one.

The Russians are lying about Sunday, Ringdal thought to himself. The data showed that the accident happened on Saturday morning, around 11:30 A.M. He realized that the Russians were misleading the world with talk of a technical fault. After exacting analysis based on a lifetime's experience of studying seismology, he was confident that he had stumbled on the telltale pattern of artificially generated explosions and not a naturally occurring earthquake.

The study of shock waves is sometimes described by scientists as "forensic seismology" in recognition of its value as a branch of police work—for example, in identifying the time and size of terrorist explosions. Ringdal prefers to see his job in a less glamorous light. He is a scientist, not a detective, who has dedicated his career to understanding the seismology that flows from underground nuclear tests. He sees the job as a key part of arms control: If a country's nuclear-testing program can be detected, international treaties can be verified. But this time Ringdal had indeed performed detective work of the highest order. A thousand miles from the scene of the accident, in a laboratory on the outskirts of Oslo, he had the knowledge to demolish two of Russia's biggest lies: The submarine accident had not happened on Sunday, and it had certainly not been the result of a simple mechanical problem.

Shortly after reading the press reports of the accident, Ringdal called the Norwegian Ministry of Foreign Affairs and explained, in his mild and understated way, that in his scientific opinion, the Russians were not being entirely open and honest with the outside world.

As the Norwegian information seeped out into the media and was widely reported, the Russians stuck to their story that the accident had occurred on Sunday. This was the first clear sign that far from sharing information openly with concerned governments, Moscow was reverting to the time-honored tradition of obscuring military accidents in layers of lies.

Submarine-rescue professionals around the world went on alert the moment that news of the *Kursk* sinking broke. The feature of the accident that electrified them was that the submarine was at a depth of just over 350 feet. A generation of preparations and training would now pay off huge dividends, for at that depth a rescue was entirely feasible. Indeed, the sub was at such a shallow depth that the *Kursk* crew members might well be able to escape on their own. Using their survival body suits and escape hoods, the sailors surely stood a reasonable chance of ascending to the surface through an emergency escape hatch.

Fellow submariners across Russia were among those who breathed a monumental sigh of relief when they heard the news about the depth. Captain Igor Kurdin, the head of the St. Petersburg Submariners Club and a retired Delta IV commander, felt an overwhelming sense of gratitude that the *Kursk* was in shallow waters. Knowing the dreadful state of the Northern Fleet rescue forces, it struck him as an amazing stroke of good fortune: Whatever else transpired in the hours ahead, at least the sailors could make it out on their own.

Ever since submarines were first built in significant numbers, spurred on by the First World War, experts have struggled with the problem of how to save sailors trapped on the seabed. In the United States, the loss of two submarines in the 1920s, *S-51* and *S-4*, prompted renewed efforts to develop rescue technology. Dramatic proof that submarine-rescue systems were not merely of theoretical interest came in late May 1939, when the USS *Squalus* sank in 250 feet of water off New Hampshire. Commander Charles Momsen, known as the father of submarine rescue, saved thirty-three of the crewmen. He had improvised a capsule that was able to lock onto the *Squalus*'s deck hatch and was able to transfer the sailors to a surface ship. The pioneering feat ushered out the days of acceptance among submariners that if their boat sank, they died. Momsen showed that if navies combined knowledge of the issues of depth and pressure with quick thinking and the ability to improvise, then rescuing sailors from disabled submarines was eminently possible.

But only up to a point. Six decades after Momsen pulled survivors from the *Squalus,* submarine-rescue capabilities still faced severe limitations. The "crush depth" of a submarine is the point at which the water pressure outside the boat is so enormous that the hull will implode. Most of the submarines operating today have a crush depth of around 3,000 feet. If a submarine sinks in deeper water, the boat will collapse as if squeezed by a giant fist, and the crew has no chance of survival. This was the fate of both the USS *Thresher* in 1963 and the USS *Scorpion* in 1968, in which 129 and 99 men died, respectively.

Rescue systems today reflect the hull strengths of submarines. There is no point in engineering submersibles or diving bells to work below 3,000 feet when the submarine crew will have perished anyway.

The shallow part of the world's seas, the continental shelves, lie up to about 650 feet below the surface, quickly sloping off to depths of around 10,000 feet. The bad news for submariners is that the continental shelves represent less than 10 percent of the world's seas. If a submarine accident happens outside those areas and the boat sinks, rescue is not an option.

For those subs that sink in shallow enough waters, the U.S. Navy relies on a combination of systems: submarine rescue chambers and deep-submergence rescue vehicles, or DSRVs. They are designed to be carried to the scene of an accident by aircraft, ship, truck, or even another "mother" submarine. If a U.S. ship is not available, any of the world's four thousand commercial support ships can be commandeered as a "vessel of opportunity" to carry the chamber or DSRV to the accident location. A DSRV dives to the disabled submarine, locates her with onboard sonar, and attaches itself to the escape hatch, evacuating up to twenty-four sailors at a time.

Britain possesses one of the most capable submarine-rescue systems in the world in the form of the LR5 submersible, which is often described as an underwater helicopter because of its maneuverability and versatility. Weighing twenty-one tons and with a crew of two, the LR5 uses what is known as a "transfer skirt," which can be attached to a submarine's escape tower, allowing hatches to be opened and the trapped sailors to make their way into the LR5's rescue chamber.

* * *

Hearing news of the *Kursk* sinking, British and American officials puzzled over how to respond to the reports coming from Russia. They were well aware that Western rescue technology was considerably more sophisticated than that possessed by the Northern Fleet, which was in such obvious decline. But the issue of Western assistance was highly sensitive, since both London and Washington realized that they might yet be accused of either causing or provoking the disaster. Russian leaders knew perfectly well that British and American submarines engaged in intensive spy operations off the Kola Peninsula, and the Northern Fleet was bound to question the sincerity of any offer to help and, at worst, might regard the offer as an attempt at further espionage.

For the U.S. Navy, offering help was a tricky, delicate issue. The USS *Memphis* had been close to the exercise, tracking the Russian SSBN. For a short time, Navy officials were acutely concerned that the *Memphis* either was the source of the explosion or might have been involved in a collision. When a signal was received from the *Memphis* reporting that she was safe and well and transiting out of the area, the relief was palpable in the Pentagon.

American officials feared that an offer of assistance would prompt the Russians to accuse the United States of looking for military secrets or acting out of a guilty conscience. In fact, only a narrow segment of Pentagon opinion saw the accident as an intelligence-gathering opportunity. Others, including Deputy Undersecretary of Defense Dave Oliver, argued that there was a simple humanitarian principle at stake and that the United States had a moral obligation to help.

Another factor was at play inside the Pentagon, one based on a gross underestimation of the strength of Russian submarine design. Many assumed that the scale of the detonations recorded by SOSUS instruments and by the *Memphis* meant that no one could have survived. This assumption took the urgency out of the deliberations.

Since all the sailors were believed to have died in the first few minutes of the accident, the decision about a response was essentially a political calculation. U.S. Navy officials had no idea that as they were sitting around the table discussing the politics of the accident, there were survivors inside the *Kursk* in desperate need of help.

The decision was taken in Washington to make a nominal offer of help, and then to stay well clear of any rescue intervention. The Barents Sea was just too close to the primary targets of U.S. naval intelligence. Much better, it was agreed, if the Royal Navy and the Norwegians led a Western rescue effort. In any case, the Royal Navy's LR5 submersible enjoyed an important edge over the American DSRVs: It was on the right side of the Atlantic, only a few hours' flying time from Murmansk.

In London, a similar debate began about the most appropriate offer of help. Royal Navy specialists, like their U.S. counterparts, suspected that the Russians operated a substandard and antiquated submarine-rescue service. This was not a patronizing observation but, rather, recognition that underwater-rescue equipment is hugely expensive to design, build, and maintain. Even within NATO navies, it was always understood that a submarine rescue would require an international response. No one country, not even the United States, could be guaranteed to have the facilities, training, and equipment to execute a successful rescue. Western analysts knew very little about the Northern Fleet's rescue submersibles, but they suspected that the Russians would be in need of help. The question was whether they were too proud and too secretive to ask for it.

But amid the discussion of what help to offer, other British officials questioned whether the United Kingdom should respond at all. Politicians and civil servants in the Ministry of Defense and the Foreign Office took different positions. There was no precedent for the circumstances they faced. One set of diplomats argued that the best response was no response and urged ministers to wait for Russia to ask for help, pointing to Russian pride. They observed that the incident involved one of Russia's most secretive classes of submarine, and that it had taken place in an old Cold War hunting ground. These were early days for President Putin, and it might be a diplomatic blunder to embarrass him with an offer of assistance that for political reasons he couldn't accept.

The counterargument was equally plain: This was a humanitarian issue, and the Royal Navy was well placed to mount a rescue effort. What better way to highlight the new Anglo-Russian relationship than by saving Russian lives? The mission would pay spectacular diplomatic dividends—the Royal Navy plucking Russian sailors from an imminent and icy death. This was a chance in a generation. For this group of advocates, the appropriate historical reference was not so much Cold War rivalry but the alliance in the Russian Arctic during World War Two, when Royal Navy and Northern Fleet convoys worked together. Pride might stand in the way of the Russians asking for help, but they would never refuse it if offered. The advice from this camp was clear and adamant: Anticipate the unfolding crisis, mobilize resources, and deploy.

As these arguments ricocheted around London, ministers also had to sift through ambiguous legal advice. Government lawyers posed some obscure and unsettling questions. What is the position if we attempt a rescue effort but fail? Does that make the United Kingdom legally liable? What is the legal status of a British rescuer inside a Russian submarine? And from this debate emerged the sort of question lawyers love: Whose territory is a submarine that has sunk in international waters?

For Commodore David Russell, in Northwood Headquarters, the legal and diplomatic debate in the United Kingdom was overlooking one crucial point: All navies, unless at war, have a duty to help one another. This is an unshakable core value for those who go to sea, even more so for the small cadre of submariners.

Holding firm to this conviction, Russell started contingency planning the very moment he heard of the *Kursk* accident. He was politically savvy and took no action that could not be easily reversed, but he fully appreciated the urgency of the situation and knew that the mobilization of rescue resources had to begin immediately. With neither ministerial clearance from London nor a Russian request for assistance, he started the United Kingdom's Submarine Rescue Service (UKSRS) heading in the right direction. The remarkable speed of this planning is revealed by the log at Northwood Headquarters, which reads (London time):

14 August 2000

  08.05 Loss of Kursk *announced. Initial reports suggest high numbers of survivors.*

  08.10 UK Submarine Rescue Service (UKSRS) mobilized.

  10.00 Commander-in-Chief Fleet briefed that UKSRS available to assist in rescue effort.

There was an unknown irony in the role that Russell was playing, for he has a secret past: He is a veteran of submarine patrols in the Barents Sea. He has surveyed the Kola Peninsula many times, but only through the optics of an attack submarine's periscope.

Russell now confronted a challenge unlike any other he had faced, and the logistics were unfortunate in the extreme. The entire UKSRS was en route to a training exercise in Turkey, and the equipment was widely dispersed. Some parts were in transit to Portsmouth and heading in exactly the wrong direction, toward the warm waters of the Aegean; other equipment was still in storage in Faslane, Scotland, where the service is based.

Still, Russell pressed ahead. A giant aircraft would be required to fly the LR5 to the closest available port, so he quickly put in an executive order to lease an Antonov cargo plane. He didn't check whether he had authority. There wasn't time.

A successful rescue operation depended on direct communications between Northern Fleet admirals and Western rescuers. Russell paced up and down his Northwood office, every now and then paying a visit to the Hole to check on any fresh intelligence, but knew he really needed to be alongside the Russian commanders who were supervising the rescue operation. He was sure that if he could talk directly to Admiral Popov—commander-to-commander, submariner-to-submariner—they could launch a successful international rescue effort. He was convinced the crew could be saved. The *Kursk* sailors were on board the most modern submarine in the Russian Navy, with access to life-support systems that could keep them alive for many days.

The most pressing operational decision facing Russell was where to deploy the LR5. The best place geographically would be Murmansk. Ideally, it would be flown with its pilots and support technicians to the heart of the Kola Peninsula, but the LR5 support team warned Russell to be careful. The submersible needed the right "mother-ship" with the proper winch systems, power, air supply, and communications infrastructure. With no Royal Navy ship available in the area, the search was on for a suitable "vessel of opportunity" that could take the submersible to the *Kursk* site when the Russians asked for help. Russell's staff promptly ran through a computerized list of available ships and found an offshore support vessel based in northern Norway, the *Normand Pioneer,* which seemed ideal. She was in a good position for a dash to the Barents and had the right equipment to launch the LR5.

But one vital piece of the puzzle was yet to be put in place. Although the debate in London had been resolved and the acting British ambassador in Moscow had formally extended an offer of assistance early on Monday, by the end of the day, a Russian request for help had still not come.

IV: Monday evening
Moscow

THE COMMANDER-IN-CHIEF OF THE Russian Navy made his first public comments on the *Kursk* accident late on Monday. Admiral Vladimir Kuroyedov, a former head of Russia's Pacific Fleet and a close ally to President Putin, seriously dampened hopes of a quick rescue. He said that the *Kursk* was buried deep in silt and was listing heavily to port by as much as thirty degrees, adding, "There are reasons to believe there has been a big and serious collision. The situation is difficult; it is possible that not everything will turn out well." For the first time, the word *stolknovenie*—collision—had been used by a senior official. At a stroke, the political temperature of the incident was heating up, even though the statement was highly ambiguous. Kuroyedov did not say what the *Kursk* had collided with. Had she hit a Russian surface ship? The seabed? A Western submarine? The Russians had good reason to think that it might be a collision, given the history of collisions that has punctuated submarine espionage in these same waters.

At 8:16 P.M. on February 11, 1992, ninety-three nautical miles from where the *Kursk* had settled, a patrolling Sierra-class nuclear-powered Russian submarine was ascending toward periscope depth. The submarine was operating close to Severomorsk, twelve miles north of the Kola Inlet on the very edge of Russia's maritime border. The Russian captain had no idea that the USS *Baton Rouge* was directly above him. Both submarines were using only passive sonar, and the first that each knew of the other's proximity was the sound of tearing metal and a severe jolt shuddering down their hulls. The submarines both managed to limp back to their home bases, but the embarrassment in Washington was intense. The Cold War was meant to be over, and the U.S. government hoped to conceal that submarine espionage was continuing as if nothing had changed. In an unprecedented step, the Pentagon was forced to acknowledge the accident publicly.

A year later, in March 1993, the USS *Grayling* made a similar blunder, striking a Russian Delta III ballistic-missile submarine. The two incidents badly shook the U.S. Navy and led to a major effort to tighten up operating procedures and improve the training of commanding officers. Only good fortune had prevented the loss of life or the potentially disastrous environmental and political consequences of two destroyed nuclear submarines.

The *Kursk* at her pier in the Arctic port of Vidyaevo, and *(below)* with some of her crew lined up along her casing. The *Kursk* was commissioned in 1995.

Both Associated Press

LEFT: The garrison town of Vidyaevo, the home of the *Kursk* crew. Founded in 1968, the base faced steady decline throughout the 1990s.

BELOW LEFT: Russian nuclear submarines at Vidyaevo's naval docks, waiting to be defueled and scrapped.

Associated Press

BELOW: The *Kursk*'s commanding officer, Captain 1st Rank Gennady Lyachin, reporting to Northern Fleet commanders on returning from his famous patrol to the Mediterranean in late 1999.

Press Association/EPA

Captain-Lieutenant Dmitri Kolesnikov and his wife, Olga, on the upper casing of the *Kursk*. In August 2000 he took charge in the aft section following the explosions.
Press Association/EPA

Kolesnikov (*center*) with his fellow crewmen, including Rashid Ariapov (*back, far right*), Dmitri Murachev (*front left*) and Sergei Lybushkin (*back, far left*). Kolesnikov's series of notes provided a dramatic glimpse into the unfolding tragedy.

Kolesnikov's third and final note, recovered from his body and singed by the fire that roared through the ninth compartment. The end reads, "Regards to everybody, no need to be desperate. Kolesnikov."

The torpedo room of an Oscar II nuclear submarine. In an identical compartment of the *Kursk*, the disastrous chain of events of August 12, 2000, began.

The Northern Fleet's main rescue ship the *Rudnitsky* launching Priz on Thursday, August 17, 2000, after the summer storm had finally abated. This was the last Russian attempt to reach survivors.
Associated Press ITAR-TASS

The Northern Fleet's two submersibles, Priz (*left*) and AS-32, aboard the rescue ship the *Rudnitsky*. Only Priz might connect to the *Kursk*'s escape hatch and bring trapped sailors to the surface.
Associated Press ITAR-TASS

Admiral Viacheslav Popov, commander of the Northern Fleet, with his trademark cigarette holder. After a brilliant career as a submarine captain he faced his greatest test of leadership in August 2000.
Associated Press

RIGHT: Two Russian specialists examining the emergency hatch on one of the *Kursk*'s sister submarines. This upper hatch leads into an escape tower and down into the ninth compartment.
Press Association/EPA

BELOW RIGHT: The *Seaway Eagle*, an offshore diving vessel, was at the center of the British and Norwegian rescue attempt.
Press Association/EPA

BELOW: British and Norwegian saturation divers reached the hatch on Sunday, August 20, 2000, eight days after the disaster.
Popperfoto/Reuters

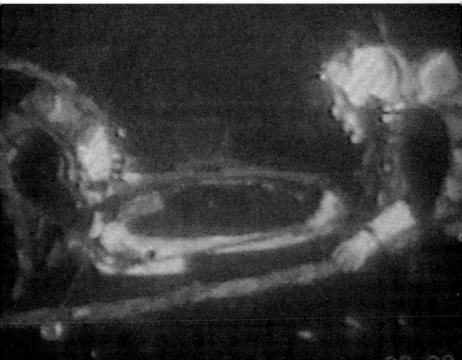

Relatives of the 118 *Kursk* submariners gathered in Vidyaevo.
Associated Press

Nadezhda Tylik, the mother of a *Kursk* officer, shouting at Russian leaders. Moments after this picture was taken, she was forcibly sedated and dragged from the meeting.
Press Association/EPA

Relatives of the *Kursk* sailors during a ceremony on the Barents Sea.
Popperfoto/Reuters

President Vladimir Putin at Vidyaevo's Officers' Club on the evening of August 22, 2000. He addressed the families of the *Kursk* crew members and endured hours of ferocious questioning.

Popperfoto/Reuters

The first bodies of the *Kursk* crew members arriving back in the Northern Fleet Headquarters of Severomorsk on October 29, 2000. On top of the front armored personnel carrier, in a red coffin, is the body of Dmitri Kolesnikov.

Press Association/EPA

The sail of the *Kursk* emerging from the water in the dry-dock near Murmansk in October 2001.

Associated Press/EPA

The *Kursk* submarine in the Arctic port o Roslyakovo after the salvage operation in October 2001. Out of the water the subm rine's size becomes apparent.

ITAR-TASS and Press Association/EPA

Britain's track record in the Barents is far from spotless too. A decade earlier, in 1981, the Royal Navy had endured a similar humiliation when its special-fit submarine HMS *Sceptre* collided with a Soviet SSBN that she was attempting to trail.

What's more, in a strange twist, technological advances are making collisions more likely. As submarines become quieter, detection ranges become shorter. Out of sight of the public, the race to construct and operate ever-quieter submarines was one of the most extraordinary and secretive technical competitions of the twentieth century, in many ways comparable to the space race. The prize is clear: If a nuclear-armed nation can build a missile submarine so quiet that she is impossible to track, the government knows it possesses an invulnerable nuclear deterrent. At a stroke, the balance of power is shifted.

For many decades, the West enjoyed a clear advantage. With better construction techniques and constantly improving "quieting" technologies, American and British SSBNs were able to leave port and virtually vanish on their top-secret patrols. This was a monumental technical accomplishment, but monumental resources had been deployed to achieve the goal.

Then, in the early 1980s, Western naval intelligence was plunged into crisis. The Soviet Victor III SSNs began emerging from their shipyards in the Baltic and the Pacific and simply disappeared. Redoubled efforts to track the new class of submarine frequently ended in failure, unless the Western boat was pursuing her Russian counterpart at much shorter range. Astonishingly, the Russians had produced a submarine so quiet that they had caught up with the West. Until the Victor IIIs took to the seas, the United States thought it held a technological lead of some twenty years in terms of the reduction of submarine noise. That advantage had suddenly been lost altogether. The Victor IIIs were followed by the Akula-class submarines, which went to sea in the mid-1980s. Now there was no avoiding the truth. The Akulas were so impressive that the Russians had not just caught up with the Americans—in some key high-tech areas, they were ahead. One congressional report concluded in 1997:

It appears that the Soviets may be ahead of us in certain technologies, such as titanium structures and control of the hydrodynamic flow around a submarine.

Another expert, the respected naval analyst Norman Polmar, reported to Congress in 1997 that this judgment underplayed the problem:

> After decades of building comparatively noisy submarines, the Soviets have now begun to build submarines that are quiet enough to present for us a major technological challenge with profound national security implications. The improved Akula is quieter than our newest attack submarines, the improved Los Angeles class. This is the first time that the Russians have submarines quieter than ours. As you know, quieting is everything in submarine warfare.

The story behind that dramatic technological advance illustrates Russia's cunning at industrial and military espionage. One significant breakthrough came in 1983 and 1984, when Norway and Japan sold sophisticated milling machines to the USSR. Soviet naval engineers were able to improve the quality of their submarine propellers as a result, although some technical advances appear to have predated the sale of the equipment. A second gift came courtesy of the Walker-Whitworth spy ring, operated by the KGB. The U.S. Navy communications specialists passed on to Moscow the details of how Soviet submarines were being tracked by SOSUS sensors on the seabed. The Russian naval engineers were quick learners. By adopting Western techniques of placing submarine machinery on rubber mounts and by isolating the outer hull, noise was greatly reduced. But the fact that both countries now had sophisticated submarines, all of them supremely quiet and trying to play their game of hide-and-seek, greatly increased the chances of collisions.

The Russians had an additional reason for believing that the loss of the *Kursk* was the result of a collision. Admiral Popov's whole strategy during the August 2000 war games was to use the routine naval exercise as a screen for the covert deployment of an SSBN. He knew the Americans would be watching and waiting, almost certainly seeking to trail his boomer to gain intelligence about her routes and hiding places under the ice. If the Americans had realized at the last moment that the exercise was a decoy, and were racing through the maneuvers to catch the disappearing SSBN, a collision was even more likely. The high-stakes game being played out by the Russian SSBN and the USS *Memphis* was the secret behind Kuroyedov's public statement that a "collision" was responsible for the *Kursk* sinking.

In addition, rumors had spread aboard the *Peter the Great* of two distinct shapes on the seabed, separated by many hundred feet, and reports from Russian defense officials indicated that an unidentified foreign vessel had communicated an SOS from the area and that wreckage with Western markings had been spotted on the ocean surface. Some Russian commanders even pointed the finger at HMS *Splendid*, a Royal Navy "special fit" regarded by the Northern Fleet as a particularly troublesome and aggressively commanded Western submarine. Superstitious Russian admirals even believed that she was a bad omen and brought bad luck wherever she patrolled. In fact, *Splendid* was thousands of miles away.

If the Russians were right, there must be *two* submarines lying crippled on the bottom of the Barents Sea. It seemed highly unlikely that a Western boat could strike the giant Oscar II and sneak away.

Some Russian officials wondered with shocked anticipation whether the West was about to acknowledge a submarine disaster of its own.

8

ON TUESDAY MORNING, forty-eight hours after the first rumors of the accident swept through Vidyaevo, the wives of the *Kursk* sailors descended on the Officers Club. They craved information, shouting questions at passing naval officers and attempting to overhear any news at all about the progress of the rescue operation. Many clung to the hope that the Navy would soon announce that a rescue had been successful and the sailors were heading ashore. The wives constantly reminded one another that their men had trained for exactly these circumstances. On hearing the television reports that crew members were tapping messages against the hull of the submarine, Olga Chernyshov felt a surge of pride. Her husband Sergei was the senior communications officer aboard the *Kursk,* and he was familiar with all the naval distress codes. She was sure Sergei was doing the tapping.

The Officers Club is a dilapidated three-story building in the heart of the garrison, used mainly for medal ceremonies or the occasional wedding celebration. Rough concrete steps lead into the main hallway, which is lined with dark red curtains and thick drapes. A rarely used piano sits on a low stage at the front of the room, while the upstairs houses a number of dank offices and meeting areas. One side of the club overlooks the town; the other has a view of the coastline.

Captain Ivan Nideev, a deputy commander in the submarine division, was assigned the unenviable task of liaising with the families. He stood at the back of the hall, surrounded by a dozen *Kursk* wives. Olga Chernyshov and Natasha Tylik were among the small crowd, pressing in on the officer and demanding answers.

"What are you doing to save our men?"

"The Fleet has said the men are knocking on the hull. Is that true?"

"How long can they last?"

"How much air do they have? I heard someone say they can last for only four more days!"

"No, that's not right," another of the women interjected. "One admiral says the crew can hold on for two weeks. Isn't that correct?"

"Why are you sitting here? Why are you not out there, helping to save my boy?"

Others demanded to know why foreign help was not being accepted. "I heard on the television that Western countries want to help. Why have we not accepted straightaway? What are we hiding?"

"Have we accepted help from Norway?"

To all these questions, Nideev replied that he understood their worries but had no fresh news from the rescue ships.

Olga listened quietly to this ferocious questioning, but suddenly she could take it no more. Her hands were trembling—with fear or anger, she wasn't sure. Shoving her way to the front of the small crowd, she shouted at Nideev, inches from his face. "Just answer us! When will the crew be evacuated? Tell us right now! When will you get them out?"

In the aftermath of earlier submarine accidents, ranging from *S-80* in the early 1960s to the *Komsomolets* disaster in 1986, Soviet commanders expected families of those killed in service to display their patriotism by grieving in private. In return, the Navy would look after them. A monument would be built; military honors would be awarded; a pension would be granted to the family. Many of the wives of the *Kursk* sailors were young and inexperienced, mostly in their early twenties, some still teenagers, and they did not share this military culture of silent sacrifice. They were children of Russia's rocky transition from Communism, and they had learned to stand up and fight for their rights.

In Vidyaevo that day, something snapped. The wives simply refused to wait in silence for officials to pass on news. They began a campaign to expose what they saw as a bungling and inadequate rescue operation, an extraordinary step to take for women who saw the Northern Fleet as their extended family. Oksana Dudko was one of the organizers. Her husband, Sergei, served in the second compartment. She told the other wives that if the Navy wouldn't save their husbands, they must do it themselves.

The families in Vidyaevo were quick learners. They remembered how Andrei Rudakov, a *Kursk* officer, had gone to court to force the Northern Fleet to pay the crew's salaries. They recalled how military pilots had won their campaign for better conditions by blocking airport runways. Even hunger strikes had, in the past, proved an effective means of forcing the admirals to back down. There was a way to succeed by working outside the military system. The Vidyaevo relatives couldn't go on strike—they were mothers and wives, not workers—and there was no time for a long campaign on behalf of the trapped men. But there was something that was within their power now that Russia had a free press. Mobilizing public opinion was the key.

Dudko and at least a dozen others retreated to their small Vidyaevo apartments and leafed through directories, dialing radio and TV stations across Russia. Irina Shubin, the wife of the *Kursk*'s deputy commander, arrived at the Murmansk railway station on her way to Vidyaevo and spoke to foreign reporters about the delays in the rescue effort. Hearing about the campaign that was gathering pace, she quickly started calling Moscow newspapers. Nadezhda Tylik rang up television stations and demanded that news programs ask why foreign assistance had not been requested. Galina Belogun's husband was a senior officer on the base who had sailed with the *Kursk* at the last moment to check on safety procedures. Galina also joined in, airing criticisms about the absence of information and the lack of urgency in a newspaper article:

> We're told the evacuation of the submarine will begin at 4 this afternoon, but what were the rescuers doing before this? There is nothing more terrifying than when you don't know anything. There is no information, only rumors. We don't know anything about the fate of the crew, although we are being told that everyone is alive.

The women were sustained by their belief that while the admirals were worried about the submarine, the country cared more for the men trapped inside.

Later that Tuesday, family members of the *Kursk*'s crew were invited to attend an official meeting at the Officers Club. A vice admiral from Moscow, Valery Kasyanov, was there; so too was Rear Admiral Mikhail Kuznetsov, the head of the Vidyaevo division, and Captain Viktor Bursyk, a widely respected officer on the base. This was the first attempt to provide official information to the families.

Kuznetsov and Bursyk began by expressing complete confidence that the men in the *Kursk* had survived the initial disaster. "Yes, they are in peril," they declared, "but they are alive, and our Fleet is doing all it can to rescue them. Have faith, and stay patient for a little longer." Kasyanov, the most senior officer, stayed entirely silent. Natasha Tylik, sitting in the front row, watched his expression intently, desperately wondering what he knew that the others did not.

The wives present at the meeting pleaded for Bursyk to be sent to the scene of the disaster. He was a professional officer and an honorable man whom they trusted. He lived among them. He might not be able to speak the full truth, but they knew he wouldn't look them in the eye and tell lies. Kasyanov agreed that Bursyk should be sent out to the rescue scene with a brief to report back to the Officers Club, and to act as a representative for the wives of the crew. The families had finally achieved a small but significant victory over the maddening forces of the military bureaucracy.

II: TUESDAY EVENING
Severomorsk Naval Headquarters

AS A MEANS OF COPING with a flood of requests for information from the press and the public now pouring in, and to counter an avalanche of speculation about what had happened to the *Kursk,* the Northern Fleet scheduled a press conference late on Tuesday. Admiral Mikhail Motsak, the chief of staff and deputy to Popov, was expected to address the reporters. But at the last moment, he pulled out on the grounds that he was too busy with the rescue operations. His place was taken by Igor Baranov, the construction director of the famed Rubin Bureau, which had designed the *Kursk.* The Bureau is regarded with something akin to awe in Russia. Home to some of the most gifted engineers in the country, this is the organization that designed the giant submarines that restored some equilibrium to the Cold War balance of power.

As the white-haired, authoritative figure of Baranov stepped forward to the podium, people across Russia listened intently. After all the speculation, here at last was a specialist with intimate knowledge of the submarine. In many ways, the *Kursk* was his ship. Surely he would not betray those who sailed in her.

Baranov could not disguise his pride in the emergency and survival systems aboard the *Kursk:* "The ship is the best in the world in terms of the life support for the sailors," he said. "We cannot know the reason for the accident or the scale of it. But in the *Kursk* there are food, water, and regeneration systems. . . . It is possible the entire crew can be saved." When pressed, he thought they might survive "five or possibly six days."

His optimism totally contradicted Admiral Kuroyedov's bleak comments twenty-four hours earlier and sent a surge of hope throughout

Russia. A Murmansk newspaper faithfully reported the tone of the press conference with the headline: CONSTRUCTOR OF THE ATOMIC SUBMARINE HOPES FOR A WONDERFUL RESULT.

A short time later, the Northern Fleet Press Service officially released the news that knocking had been heard from inside the *Kursk*. The word now used was *perestukivanie,* which means a two-way exchange of signals, implying that there was even a dialogue of sorts between the sailors and their would-be rescuers.

The twin announcements gave friends and relatives of the trapped sailors great hope: According to the Northern Fleet, the men were alive; according to Baranov, they had adequate life-support systems on board.

Baranov's optimism would not have impressed the dispirited and frustrated rescuers above the *Kursk.*

The failure of the initial dive by Priz, and the debacle of the AS-32, which had used up its power reserves circling lost on the seabed, had been bitter blows for the rescue teams. As exhausted technicians pored over manuals trying to speed up the recharging of the submersibles' batteries, the rescue pilots caught a few hours of sleep.

The next morning, Captain Maisak and his crew got their second chance. This time, Admiral Popov insisted that no time be wasted investigating the bow area of the *Kursk*—every precious minute should be used trying to dock with the hatch. The current was no better, and Maisak reported that he was again having difficulty maneuvering Priz toward the hatch. He doggedly kept at the task, continually countering the current with the thrusters, and once more finally eased the mini-sub directly over the aft hatch. A brief, desperately dispiriting message reached the *Rudnitsky* from Maisak: "I am directly over the hatch, but I cannot make a seal. Batteries showing low again."

"Can you observe any signs of life?" an officer on the mother-ship signaled back.

"No, I do not," Maisak tersely responded. In the circumstances, he did well to keep his temper. What signs of life could he possibly have seen?

With a sense of utter despair, Maisak and his crew had little time to puzzle over why they had failed to dock successfully. What were they doing wrong? Or was the hatch itself damaged, warped by the explosions? In intense frustration, Maisak brought Priz back to the surface. Once again, he had been so close.

In addition to the major Northern Fleet warships, five rescue ships had by now gathered above the submarine: the command vessel and mother-ship the *Rudnitsky,* the tugs *Altai* and *SB-523,* an engineering support vessel known as *KIL,* and a crane ship, *PK-7500.*

Just as weather forecasts had predicted, the calm seas and gentle breezes that had prevailed throughout the four-day military exercise now started building into troublesome waves and erratic gusts of strong wind. A summer storm fast approached, and the wind was reaching nearly fifty miles an hour.

Such bad weather would jeopardize the rescue effort of even the best-equipped operation, but for the Northern Fleet it would be disastrous. None of the Russian rescue ships had adequate stabilizers to manage operations in strong seas, let alone the modern technology required to work in adverse conditions. The *Rudnitsky* had a single screw, no bow or stern thrusters, and insufficient horsepower to hold position beam-on to the wind and waves.

In sharp contrast, Western rescue ships and the support vessels of the oil and gas industry use a technology known as dynamic positioning. With powerful thrusters both at the stern and the bow, these ships constantly counter the effect of wind, current, and wave action. Using satellite navigation and special beacons placed on the seabed, the ship's computers analyze whether a vessel is drifting. If the ship moves even slightly, the thrusters bring her back almost instantly. As a result, even in relatively heavy seas, these vessels can stay within three feet of a precise location, essential while conducting submersible operations.

The picture for the *Rudnitsky* could not have been more different. As the ship was increasingly buffeted by heavy swells and continually lost position, her crew began to lose their patience and their tempers.

Admiral Verich, the Russian Navy's top search-and-rescue official, had by now flown to the site, but when he arrived, the sea was too rough to allow a transfer to the *Rudnitsky*. With no helicopter deck on the ship, the admiral was forced to sit out the storm on a nearby warship, communicating with the rescuers via regular ship-to-ship VHF radio. He was deeply shaken by what he heard. Not only were the rescuers exhausted, they were enraged about the shoddy state of their equipment and the inadequacy of the mother-ship. Eighteen months later, in early 2002, when the admiral finally agreed to reflect on the rescue effort, he still shook his head in disbelief at the scene that confronted him that Tuesday amid the heavy summer seas and whistling Arctic wind. "Morale among the rescue units was very, very low," he recalled. "Extremely bad. Exceptionally low. Physically and mentally, it was extremely hard."

As the seas grew more and more tumultuous, the rescuers battled to get Priz back in the water. But the *Rudnitsky* now ran into problems with the twin derricks used for launching the rescue submersibles. They had been designed for unloading cargo alongside a pier. Out at sea, even in good weather, operating the derricks was difficult. In these deteriorating conditions, the task was virtually impossible, and they couldn't even get Priz over the side of the *Rudnitsky*. As they tried again and again, the mini-sub repeatedly crashed heavily against the hull, sending shock waves down the length of the submersible. Soaked by spray, sailors struggled desperately with ropes and pulleys to keep Priz steady, trying to compensate for the heavy roll of the ship. They knew that despite its characteristically rugged Russian engineering, Priz would not survive many more knocks. Already the gyro-compass was damaged.

Launching the submersible in these conditions was not just risky—it was suicidal. At last, Verich had to admit that he had no choice but to suspend the rescue effort until the weather relented. To make the best of the enforced delay, he ordered Bester, the most modern of the rescue submersibles, to be brought out to sea by the crane ship so that it would be ready to go as soon as the storm eased. Even though Bester's mother-ship had been decommissioned to save money, the use of a crane to launch it was worth a try. Verich could think of no other option. Help from the West was still proving politically unacceptable to Moscow. Perhaps Bester, even without the proper support, would succeed where Priz and AS-32 had so badly failed.

Meanwhile, an acrimonious conflict was brewing between the rescuers and the Northern Fleet officers watching from the surrounding warships. As the *Rudnitsky*'s technicians furiously worked on repairing and recharging Priz in the hold, the officers watching from a distance saw only the rescue ship's largely empty decks. Repeated signals from the *Peter the Great* demanded to know what was happening. Why were the rescue submersibles not in the water? Verich reacted furiously to this added pressure. "People were taking great risks, and the signals came from the Command asking, 'Don't you understand that our people are dying? Why can't you get there? Please report the status of your rescue operations.'"

The tension increased dramatically when rumors made their way to the *Rudnitsky* that the *Kursk* crew was tapping out SOS messages. Those aboard the rescue ship had heard no such sound, and some began to suspect that the news was simply being invented by Northern Fleet officers, seeking to exert even more pressure on the rescuers.

In fact, the *Rudnitsky* herself had accidentally triggered the first false report that men inside the *Kursk* were tapping out messages. As she repositioned her anchor, the ship's heavy, metal chain repeatedly banged against her hull. Several acoustic specialists on surrounding ships signaled excitedly that they could hear knocking. Wishful thinking and fatigue combined to fuel the rumors, which had spread first from ship to ship, and then ashore, and then across a transfixed country, where people's hunger for news was matched only by the misinformation that was emerging from the Northern Fleet.

III: WEDNESDAY, AUGUST 16
Defense Ministry, Moscow

SEVENTY-TWO HOURS AFTER THE ACCIDENT, and with the Northern Fleet's own rescue efforts failing miserably, offers of help from Norway and Britain still lay unanswered on the desk of Admiral Kuroyedov, the commander-in-chief of the Russian Navy. Replies were put on hold while a bitter policy debate raged on. The token gesture from the United States was dismissed out of hand, judged to be politically unacceptable. Help could not possibly be accepted from the nation that most systematically and aggressively spied on the Northern Fleet. But the British and Norwegian offers—from two countries that had historic or geographic links with Arctic Russia—split the Russian admirals down the middle.

The country's leaders had been caught badly off-guard by the crisis. In August, the political and military elite desert Moscow in overwhelming numbers and head for their plush government dachas. Most of the key Russian decision-makers were either on vacation or in the provinces. General Anatoly Kvashnin, chief of the General Staff, and the most senior uniformed officer in the Russian Armed Forces, was on holiday in Sochi, alongside his commander-in-chief, President Putin. General Leonid Ivashov, the intellectually formidable hardliner who ran the Defense Ministry's international policy, was also out of town. Known for his entrenched anti-Western views, he was on a summer tour of far-flung military bases.

Complicated internal command structures and long-festering jealousies also led to a confused picture in Moscow about what exactly was happening out in the Barents Sea. For example, Admiral Popov's situation reports from the *Peter the Great* were being sent not to the defense minister or to the General Staff but to the Navy commander, Kuroyedov. With so much at stake, including the prestige of his most powerful Fleet and his own ambitions to succeed Marshal Sergeyev, Kuroyedov carefully watched over what information was passed on.

That Tuesday, after General Kvashnin and General Ivashov had scrambled back to Moscow, the argument about whether to accept Western help reached a peak. Some senior officials argued that Russia would look callous if it rejected international assistance. Ironically, Ivashov, despite his hardline reputation, is believed to have been at the center of this group that advocated accepting foreign expertise.

Others argued that the Western offers were cynical and hypocritical gestures of naval powers whose only real interest in the Barents Sea was espionage. At the heart of this uncompromising viewpoint was the shadowy Eighth Directorate of the General Staff, a highly secretive organization inside the Defense Ministry tasked with protecting Russia's military secrets.

The *Kursk* was the most modern submarine in Russia's arsenal, and her SS-N-19 Shipwreck cruise missiles and the encryption equipment in her radio room were among the most sensitive secrets in the Navy. The idea that Western specialists should be permitted into the immediate vicinity of the submarine struck counterintelligence officials in the Eighth Directorate as not just undesirable but outrageous. They argued that the Northern Fleet was not a coast guard; the *Kursk* was not a fishing vessel. If sailors had to die in defense of Russia's secrets, so be it. Men had died in the past protecting much less. The *Kursk* was much more than a home for 118 men.

Even the name "Kursk" resonated with the traditionalists in the military. The city of Kursk in July 1943 had witnessed the climactic encounter of World War Two, the greatest tank battle in history. Fifty thousand German lives had been lost and 250,000 Russians died in what Moscow called the turning point of the war against the Nazi invaders. The battle and the city still have mythical status in Russia. To the older generation of military leaders in Moscow, who still view events through the prism of "the Great Patriotic War," the idea of losing 118 men aboard the *Kursk* to protect military secrets, while tragic and embarrassing, did not constitute a military disaster.

The inability to decide how to respond to international assistance stemmed not only from this passionate debate. There was another factor: the uncertainty among top military officials about which way their new president would view the offers of help from abroad. To them, as to ordinary Russians, Vladimir Putin remained an enigma. On the one hand, the president was a career KGB officer who was likely to be highly suspicious of Western motives and protective of military secrets; on the other hand, he might see the *Kursk* incident in political and humanitarian terms and use it to improve ties with the West. Putin's ascent to power was so rapid, and the relationship between the KGB and the military so opaque, no one in the Defense Ministry was certain which way he would veer on a national-security issue that had made headline news around the world. True to old Soviet form, Russia's ambitious generals feared displeasing Putin and waited for him to give them a lead. Meanwhile, the young and inexperienced president waited for his Navy commander and the General Staff to provide clear information.

A successful submarine rescue requires not just good equipment but lightning-fast decisions about the deployment of resources and a plan of action. In Moscow, there was paralysis.

9

I: 2 P.M. WEDNESDAY, AUGUST 16
Severomorsk Naval Headquarters

A THOUSAND MILES TO the north, in his command headquarters
in Severomorsk, Admiral Popov could vividly picture the horrors of
being trapped inside a submarine. He had come close to disaster
himself back in 1983, while commanding a ballistic nuclear sub on
exercise in the western Atlantic. The SSBN had suffered a series of
major technical failures, which culminated in both of the nuclear
reactors shutting down. Temporary repairs had saved the day, but
not before Popov had come face-to-face with the fear of going down
with his submarine.

On Wednesday, he decided he had given his own rescue specialists
enough time. Popov knew perfectly well the pitiful state of the equipment available to the rescuers aboard the *Rudnitsky*. His submariners
deserved better than this. Early that afternoon, he reached for the
dedicated telephone link to Admiral Skorgen's Norwegian headquarters in Bodø. This moment represented both a humiliating
comedown and the bravest step that Popov had ever taken as commander of the Northern Fleet. Whether or not Popov received clearance from the Kremlin for making the call is not clear. Never before
had a Russian admiral been reduced to asking a Cold War adversary
for assistance in such circumstances. Forty-eight hours had passed

since the Norwegian commander had first offered help, only to be brushed aside, but now Popov was facing the loss of the entire submarine crew, and the West represented the one real chance left.

"Hello, Admiral Skorgen. I need you to help me."

An interpreter on another handset translated from Russian into English. The simple statement stunned Skorgen.

"Admiral Popov, just tell me exactly what you need, and I will try to assist."

"I need divers. Men who can operate down to a depth of one hundred and ten meters. I need them to help us connect our rescue submersibles to the emergency hatch. That way, we can reach the survivors in the submarine. Can you help?"

The reference to survivors was electrifying after three days of silence.

"Give me some time," Skorgen replied. "Just a few hours, and I will find out and call you back."

"OK. We will wait for your call," Popov concluded.

Skorgen was convinced that the Russian commander cared deeply about his sailors and was sincere in his request. If Popov was merely playing politics—following orders from Moscow to appease Russian public opinion—he was giving a remarkably convincing performance.

The two men were hardly strangers. Skorgen and Popov had met on several occasions and been to each other's headquarters during reciprocal visits designed to break down the barriers of mistrust between the two Arctic neighbors. Norway and Russia have long viewed each other warily. Not only is Norway host to a long-running, top-secret U.S. intelligence effort—the frontier region of Finnmark bristles with intercept masts—but the Russian-Norwegian maritime border is still disputed. At first glance, the argument appears to be over wild and remote ocean, but both sides recognize that the seabed is rich in resources and that the sea-lanes are of great strategic importance. Russia's access to the Baltic and the Black Sea has been complicated by the breakup of the Soviet Union, and the Arctic routes are of increasing commercial and military importance to Moscow.

The naval-exchange visits were highly formal occasions, but Skorgen had made sure there was a chance to escape from the suffocating protocol. The previous summer, he had taken Popov to a popular Norwegian fjord, where they fished for cod and spoke about their families, jobs, and hobbies. They liked each other immediately. Popov was a raconteur who laughed heartily and spoke candidly about the problems of commanding the Northern Fleet. Skorgen detected an old-fashioned integrity.

Many senior Russian field officers, beneath the surface and away from the political maneuverings, are men who hold fast to an unspoken code of honor. The corruption endemic in the Russian military very often originates from bureaucrats in Moscow, not from officers in the field. Eighty years of Communism had failed to extinguish a tsarist-era belief that military command is a proud and dignified calling, certainly compared to the crude pursuit of political power.

In response to Popov's unprecedented request, Skorgen thought quickly. The Norwegian Navy has no deep-water divers. No military force in the world maintains a ready-to-go diving capability to that depth. Such expertise is now the preserve of private industry, in particular the companies that work in offshore oil and gas fields. The huge investment required to train divers and constantly develop and upgrade cutting-edge technology means that only those in the high-risk, high-reward business of oil and gas exploration can afford it. As a result, the commercial sector is light-years ahead of the world's navies in this field. When the U.S. Navy and the Royal Navy need welding done on their warships and don't want to bring them into dry-dock, they turn to private companies for help. The same is true for underwater emergencies. Normally, those facing a disaster at sea summon the Coast Guard or the Navy for help, but now, in a peculiar twist, the military had to ask private business to come to the rescue.

The Norwegian government urgently contacted some of the country's most prominent offshore oil and gas companies asking whether specialist divers and equipment were available. The question of cost was dismissed as of no consequence. There would be time to sort out a commercial contract later. First, they had to get the ball rolling.

Time was of the essence. The necessary equipment and expertise—the pressure chambers, specialist diving doctors, and offshore vessels—were all based around Bergen in southern Norway, close to the oil fields of the North Sea and hundreds of miles from the Barents. A rescue effort at this late stage would demand an extraordinary logistical and technical effort, first equipping civilian vessels and then dispatching them at maximum speed around the North Cape. The coordination and details of the rescue would come later.

After a series of calls between the oil companies and Norway's Southern Command, Stolt Offshore agreed to assist in any way possible. A multinational company that supports the offshore oil and gas industry, Stolt has operational headquarters at Aberdeen in Scotland and Stavanger in Norway. It is one of several companies that service and maintain the rigs, pipelines, and underwater infrastructure that support the multibillion-dollar offshore industry. Best of all for the Norwegian government, Stolt had a superbly equipped vessel, the *Seaway Eagle,* working off northern Norway that could easily be diverted to the *Kursk* site.

When Skorgen phoned Popov back to tell him that Norway could indeed mobilize a team of divers, he was concerned by how tired and dispirited Popov sounded. Skorgen felt a surge of sympathy. What private hell must Popov be going through, facing the destruction of his most prestigious submarine and the loss of the entire crew? But much as he hated to press, there was an issue that Skorgen had to address if the *Kursk* sailors were to be saved.

"Admiral Popov," he continued, "if we are to deploy to the accident site and undertake a rescue, we need much more information. We must know about your submarine-rescue systems and how your hatches and valves work. We'll need the full technical data for our experts. They cannot go into this operation blind."

Popov was silent. Skorgen was asking him to pass technical data on a Russian nuclear-powered attack submarine straight into the hands of a Western commander.

After a moment's pause, Popov agreed.

II: Wednesday Afternoon
Ministry of Defense, Moscow

ADMIRAL POPOV WAS NOT the only one in the military hierarchy willing to make a bold move. Even inside the Defense Ministry, an institution filled with highly conservative military officers, there were some reformers who glimpsed an opportunity. The younger, more progressive cadre of naval officers deeply resented the fact that their leaders appeared to regard saving the lives of the *Kursk* sailors as a secondary priority, less important than protecting national secrets.

Two of the most reform-minded admirals, Vladislav Ilyin and Oleg Pobozhy, were running a special incident cell handling the *Kursk* disaster inside Navy headquarters. On Wednesday afternoon, in a move that brazenly contradicted the hardline agenda of the Eighth Directorate, they placed a phone call to the British naval attaché in Moscow, Captain Geoff McCready, and asked what rescue technology the Royal Navy could provide.

Delighted that the Russians were finally reaching out, McCready raced across the Russian capital and was escorted to a meeting with Ilyin and Pobozhy. Several Russian experts in the design and engineering of Oscar II submarines were also gathered around the table.

From the very first exchanges at this meeting, McCready was convinced that the admirals were serious in investigating Western help. They already knew that McCready could deliver probably the most important component, the Royal Navy's LR5 rescue submersible.

But first, McCready needed every scrap of information they could give him. He couldn't help unless he knew the whole truth about the state of the submarine and the waters in which it lay.

"Is it correct there are dangerous three-knot currents around the *Kursk?*" he asked.

"There are only minor problems," Pobozhy replied, directly contradicting the false reports that the Russian Navy was giving to the press.

"What about the reports about the heavy list of the submarine?"

"She is listing at no more than eight degrees." Official reports had spoken of the *Kursk* listing at sixty degrees.

"What about visibility?"

"No problem—visibility is over ten meters."

"What about the hatch over the first compartment?"

"Utterly destroyed, along with the whole bow section," Pobozhy emphasized. "There's no way in at the forward end or through the conning tower. Our experts say the only route into the *Kursk* is through the aft escape hatch above the ninth compartment."

McCready pushed on. "We will need diagrams of the hatch." The British LR5 personnel had no experience with Russian submarine hatches. Exercises involving the British rescue team had always been NATO affairs, or had involved friendly navies. The technical issues of gaining access to a Russian sub had never even been considered, let alone rehearsed. Submarine-rescue procedures are highly complex, very often unique to each country's navy. This is not an area that can be simply improvised at a moment's notice.

Pobozhy abruptly left the room. Moments later, he came back with a rough diagram showing vertical and horizontal plans of the escape hatch above compartment nine. They then discussed the procedures necessary to operate the hatch. The admirals turned to the technicians, who took McCready through the valve lineups.

This, at last, was Russian cooperation the West needed. McCready rushed back to the British Embassy and, over a secure link, faxed copies of the hatch diagrams to London. This was not all the information needed—there would have to be cooperation at the scene on a command and a technical level—but it certainly appeared to be a breakthrough.

Quietly and urgently, behind the scenes, facing the entrenched resistance of their own ministry, Pobozhy and Ilyin were working to get the right technology down to the survivors of the *Kursk*. Whether it would arrive in time was another question.

A parallel approach to the Royal Navy came from Russian naval officers during a visit to NATO headquarters in Brussels. They asked to speak with British commanders to confirm what rescue resources were available, and they were linked by telephone conference to Commodore David Russell at Northwood Headquarters. He patiently explained the capabilities of Britain's Submarine Rescue Service and the LR5 submersible, and he chose not to tell them that he had already ordered its deployment up to the Norwegian-Russian border, far in advance of any request from Moscow.

By the end of the day, the Russians had formally asked for the LR5, and the British government authorized the deployment of their rescue team to "the limits of Norwegian territorial waters." Cautious officials in London did not want to overcommit themselves in case the political response from Moscow was overtly hostile to the movement of Western rescuers toward the Kola Peninsula.

The decision Russell had made two days earlier on Monday had been completely vindicated; instead of facing a standing start, everything was ready to go. The *Normand Pioneer* had already been chosen as the LR5's mother-ship, and the submersible and its technical staff were in the air, on board the giant Antonov-124 transporter, and heading for the Norwegian port of Trondheim.

The Russians never asked how the Royal Navy managed to reach the scene so quickly, ahead even of the Norwegians.

III: North Norwegian Sea

ONE DECK BELOW THE BRIDGE of the *Seaway Eagle*, Graham Mann prowled his quarters while his eyes flickered over a dozen video monitors. Over a walkie-talkie, he stayed in constant touch with his supervisors working in the bowels of the ship. Mann was the offshore manager of the *Eagle*, responsible for the current project, which involved laying many hundreds of feet of "risers" into the ocean for the Norwegian oil giant StatOil. Risers are the hoses and pipes that link a wellhead on the seabed to a gas or oil rig on the surface.

Mann is a veteran of these operations, a talented offshore manager blessed with the ability to improvise under pressure and think on his feet. Short but powerfully built, with cropped hair and a rest-less manner, he is a straight-talking Scot. Mann is also a driven indi-vidual, regarded as one of the most gifted offshore specialists of his generation.

Despite a gentle swell and the slap of waves against her bright yellow hull, the *Seaway Eagle* was holding steady in the water. Her dynamic positioning technology made sure she never moved more than three feet in any direction. She is essentially a platform for high-technology underwater operations: sub-sea robotics, unmanned underwater vehicles, remote welding, and specialist diving opera-tions. The vessel cuts a peculiar shape, with a distinctive double bow that was designed not for offshore work but for ocean cable laying, though by the time the Dutch shipyard had finished construction in 1996, the economic climate had changed and there was more money to be made in the oil and gas industry.

No one, save perhaps her captain, would ever say the *Seaway Eagle* is a beautiful vessel. The cranes on the decks give her an industrial feel. Her elevated helicopter deck toward the bow makes her look squat and functional. The crew quarters and workspace are like a giant box. The life rafts slung along either side of the bridge are a high-visibility orange, and her hull is painted a luminous yellow. Nonetheless, those who work in the *Eagle* talk of her with affection as a big and friendly ship with excellent facilities and a capable multi-national crew.

The *Seaway Eagle* had been on-station in the Asgard Field for the last ten days. For a vessel that was just about four years old, she had covered a lot of water in her relentless pursuit of offshore work, not just in the oil and gas fields of northern Europe, but in the South China Sea, the Persian Gulf, the Gulf of Mexico, and the seas off West Africa.

Graham Mann had first heard the name *Kursk* on a satellite televi-sion in his cabin on the *Eagle*'s officers deck when news of the acci-dent broke on Monday. All those who work in the offshore industry immediately took notice. Mann took even more interest than most:

Asgard is the farthest north of Europe's oil and gas fields, and he quickly realized that the *Seaway Eagle* was probably the closest diving-support vessel to the disaster site. Certainly the other thirty-two ships and barges in the Stolt Offshore fleet were all farther south.

Contingency planning is second nature to Mann. He likes to think through underwater problems the way others enjoy crosswords. Within minutes of hearing about the *Kursk,* he had begun to wonder if there might be a role for the *Eagle.* He looked at some charts and thought about the logistics. As an intellectual exercise, he made some quick calculations: "Our position in Asgard is 65°04'N, 06°46'E; the *Kursk*'s location is being reported as 69°40'N, 37°35'E. First, we would have to head to Tromsø to take on divers and extra kit. That's 385 nautical miles. Then, from Tromsø, around the North Cape, southeast into the Barents and to the scene of the disaster, another 404 nautical miles. . . ."

Mann had then returned to his work with the risers, but part of his mind remained elsewhere, still thinking about the *Kursk.* He allowed himself to ponder the technical challenge of reaching a submarine on the seabed with 118 crew on board: "What have I got? Remotely operated vehicles, a dive system, planners, engineers, well-equipped workshops, cranes, winches, and one of the best vessels of her class. . . . What would I need? Divers to come on board, the right mix of specialist staff, coordination with a military rescue system to bring the trapped men out alive, communications with the Russian Navy, technical data on hatches and valve systems. . . ."

All of this rumination was not wasted. Sure enough, on Wednesday evening Mann fielded a call from a senior manager at Stolt's office in Stavanger. Could Mann start planning an immediate deployment to the Barents Sea?

The *Seaway Eagle* would have to abandon the project it was engaged in for StatOil, but this was a rescue attempt, something that sends adrenaline surging through anyone connected to the sea. StatOil quickly agreed to release the *Eagle.* If a multimillion-dollar project had to be abandoned, so be it. The Norwegian government would pay Stolt, and StatOil would be compensated. The financial arrangements could be put in place later. The seafarer's code was simple and clear: Lives were in peril, and a rapid response was essential.

Mann immediately placed a few calls of his own, lining up the best people he could get for the dangerous job ahead. One of his first calls was to Pete Chapman, an ex–Royal Navy life-support supervisor with a first-class record of working around diving chambers.

"I'm putting a crew together in a hurry, Pete. Can you join us?"

"What's the job?"

"You've seen the TV reports about the *Kursk*? We're heading up there to help. We need you." Chapman said that of course he would come.

At the same time, Stolt's administrators furiously worked to track down experienced offshore divers. Many were not available, since they were already working on jobs all over the North Sea, their bodies saturated to the depth of the seabed where they were working. They would have to sit for days in decompression chambers in order to be transferred to the *Eagle*. There just wasn't time.

Tony Scott was reached just before midnight at his home in southern England. A soft-spoken and articulate forty-two-year-old, Scott has been diving since the late 1970s. He has in abundance the premier quality required for offshore diving: a calm, unflappable temperament. Even his wife says with a laugh that she's never seen him lose his cool.

"Are you available for an immediate trip off northern Norway?"

Scott had watched the news reports about the *Kursk* and immediately understood that "northern Norway" was code for the Barents Sea. Only the *Kursk* job could generate this degree of urgency. The next day was his daughter's twelfth birthday, but an attempt to save lives—that was different.

"Count me in," he told Mann.

The world of offshore divers is small—a couple hundred professionals crisscrossing a dozen resource-rich seas during the year on support ships and in diving chambers. If two divers haven't worked together, they've probably heard of each other. Stories of narrow escapes, tragic accidents, and high jinks ashore are part of their culture, and news travels between divers at lightning speed. As if to counter the isolation of the diving chamber, the hunger for information is ravenous, and the news that Stolt was putting together a rescue mission spread fast. Divers ashore started calling one another. On board support vessels out at sea, reports were passed on over intercoms and e-mails. The offshore industry's jungle drums were sounding.

The men who volunteer to work below the surface of the world's seas are not easily stereotyped. Some of the divers have worked in the armed services, often with Britain's Royal Marines, the Special Boat Squadron, or the Special Air Service. Others emerge from a mix of backgrounds—former teachers or engineers, mechanics or stockbrokers. Most are self-employed and wait at home for the call from an offshore company requesting their skills. They could be asked to work off West Africa, off South America, or in any of the seas off northern Europe. Wherever there is an offshore oil and gas industry, there are pipelines to be connected, rigs to be anchored, and valves to change. For the majority, however, the supply of work is not constant, and they have to look elsewhere to supplement their wages. One of Stolt's divers is David Cherry, who came from the Royal Navy's bomb-disposal team. A commercial diver in the summer, he's worked as a clown in the winter, entertaining children on an English skating rink. When he can't find a job with an offshore company, he does landmine-clearance work in Africa. Most divers have high-risk hobbies that allow them to release the tension that goes with the strictly controlled environment in which they work. Graham Mann's idea of relaxing ashore is to take off in his high-performance glider.

The essential requirement for a diver is that he must feel completely comfortable in the water. Some companies have attempted to train specialists, like welders or marine engineers, as divers, but it almost never works. It's easier to teach a diver a new discipline than to try to instill in an outside specialist an aptitude for diving. The divers say their skill can't be taught—it's genetic.

The business is tough and relentless. Over the course of a year, divers might have to spend a total of up to five months sitting in tiny decompression chambers, living in close proximity to their colleagues while the gases in their blood adjust to the pressures of the ocean depths. Food is passed to them through a series of pressure locks, and they breathe a mix of oxygen and helium, since nitrogen at this pressure would be toxic. The helium in their bodies distorts their voices into high-pitch squeaks and makes talking to those outside the chamber nearly impossible. There's no scope for an argument inside the chamber; there's barely enough room for four bunks. A normal dive will involve twenty-eight days in such a chamber, day and night. The only time a diver is away from the pressure-cooker environment of the chamber is when he is working underwater. The divers use the slang "going into the bin" whenever they start a month-long stint.

Many divers recognize that few outsiders really understand their profession. Their work on the seabed is done out of view of the rest of the world. Tony Scott says that more is known about astronauts than offshore divers. When his mother was gravely ill, he was in saturation at an atmospheric pressure of 160 feet on a job in the North Sea. He couldn't be decompressed in time to say goodbye before she died, and he only just made it to the funeral. His brother asked him why he hadn't been able to get to her bedside, and Scott had to explain that if he had stepped out of the chamber any sooner, he would have died himself within a couple of minutes, with a severe case of the bends.

Saturation divers are calm and self-disciplined. The average age is forty—men who joined the industry at the height of the North Sea exploration boom in the 1980s and who have gained invaluable experience since then. Their employers don't want young showmen. Those who see the business as glamorous are quickly weeded out. Their earning power is excellent if they are judged to be reliable and emotionally steady. A typical day rate is $350, rising to nearly $1,000 when they are in saturation, and in a good year a diver may earn $100,000.

These men are certainly at the sharp end—the entire ship's performance is ultimately dependent on their reliability—but everything they do is strictly controlled from the vessel above them. The gas they're breathing is constantly analyzed, the flow of hot water through their suits is monitored, and their performance underwater and behavior in the chamber are closely assessed. They need to communicate well with the supervisors and understand the technical aspects of the work, but their work is not about daring improvisation. Ultimately, it's a team game. There are two divers on the seabed and over one hundred support staff on the ship above them. The offshore vessels cost well over $1 million a week to run. The focus is on achieving their tasks in the minimum time and with the maximum efficiency.

Stolt was fortunate that Graham Mann was in charge of the *Seaway Eagle*'s operations that day. Mann's background was in salvage operations, and he had seen many more dangerous jobs than this in his day. He had left school early and taught himself about diving; as a young man, he had joined a company that specialized in recovering cargo from sunken ships. The work involved diving into the wrecks of cargo vessels or passenger liners and recovering anything of value—tin, bullion, jewels, or scrap metal. Not only was the project hazardous, but in those days the diving equipment was primitive. Mann quickly learned the value of staying calm underwater. You couldn't panic and expect to reach the surface alive.

Like everyone who worked in the world of salvage, Mann had cheated death several times. In his reflective moments, he speaks with a wry smile about a time and place that he would rather forget: May 1979, 195 feet below the surface of the South China Sea.

The *Engen Maru* was a Japanese cargo vessel that had been torpedoed by an American submarine during the Second World War. For nearly forty years, she remained an undisturbed grave on the seabed, with a cargo of tin valued at $12 million. The salvage plan was simple: to plant explosives along the top and blow off the upper deck, allowing access to the cargo holds. After the detonation, Mann was sent down to see if the deck had gone and to plan the next stage of the operation.

He stood alone along the railings on the edge of the *Engen Maru,* his umbilical snaking up to the surface, two bail-out bottles on his back. The explosions had kicked up clouds of silt, reducing visibility close to zero. Waiting for the mud to settle, listening to the sound of metal being twisted in the current, suddenly part of the ship's superstructure which had been dislodged by the blasts came crashing down and struck Mann. Stunned, he lost his balance and toppled through the jagged gash in the upper deck. Tumbling down into the cargo hold, unable to see anything around him, he risked being trapped in the falling wreckage, his umbilical cord in grave danger of being crushed or severed. The fall ended with Mann upside down and trapped in debris. He took a few quick breaths and spoke to the surface to see if his umbilical was still intact. Miraculously, it was working. Forcing himself to stay calm, Mann asked for help. The standby salvage diver was sent down and freed him from the surrounding debris.

For Mann, diving is about understanding the nature of risk and being aware in advance of what can go wrong. Like Tony Scott, he compares it to working in outer space: It is safe, but only if you have an excellent knowledge of your environment. But he had learned that day in the South China Sea that you can't predict everything. Sometimes, it's just a matter of luck.

Mann could be relied on to remember the first rule of rescue operations: Don't become a casualty yourself. In the 1970s, up to forty divers were killed in accidents every year—fatalities caused by divers getting cut to ribbons in ship thrusters, fires in dive chambers, and wrong gas mixes being pumped to the men. It was a horrendous catalog of blunders in the infant industry. The offshore industry had undergone an extraordinary safety revolution since the early days of North Sea exploration. As a result, the *Eagle* was steeped in a safety culture whose operational measures were constantly tested by highly trained men. Every ship maneuver and deck activity, every ROV and diver deployment was meticulously choreographed. Everything adhered to an agreed task plan. Rescue operations involved risks, but Mann worked sedulously to minimize them.

At 6:30 P.M. that Wednesday, Mann issued the following instruction to his supervisors: "We're abandoning the project. Reverse the operation! Bring the riser back on board!"

The *Eagle*'s captain, an amiable and capable Norwegian by the name of Dag Rasmussen, didn't even have charts for the Barents Sea, so he hastily borrowed some from a nearby supply boat. First he had to plot a course for Tromsø, where the divers and fresh equipment would be loaded, and as soon as the risers had been recovered, Rasmussen gave the order to leave the Asgard Field at the ship's maximum speed of thirteen and a half knots.

They were under way at 11:20 P.M. on Wednesday. Just over a hundred hours had passed since the explosions had rocked the Barents Sea.

Both Britain and Norway recognized that it was essential that their rescue teams work together. Already there were murmurings about a hunt for "glory and honor" as the two ships, the *Normand Pioneer* and the *Seaway Eagle,* set out to help the Russians. Some on the British side claimed that the Norwegians were using the rescue as a means of improving relations with Russia, that their humanitarian motives were tainted by political interests. In return, voices in Norway's military argued that the Royal Navy was plunging into the operation in a headlong and reckless manner certain to upset the Russians and to prove counterproductive in terms of reaching the *Kursk* survivors.

On a technical level, however, the two teams in fact complemented each other exceptionally well. The *Seaway Eagle* would be able to provide a detailed survey of the submarine, evaluate the state of the escape hatch, examine the valves, and assist a submersible attempting to dock. The Stolt divers on board regarded work at depths of around 300 feet as a "walk in the park." The whole culture of the ship, her crew, and her divers was one that relished underwater problem-solving. The more complex the issue at stake, the more rewarding the solution. On a purely technical level, they *loved* the idea of a brand-new puzzle lying at the bottom of the Barents Sea.

But the *Eagle* was not a rescue ship in any real sense. She had no facilities for bringing trapped men to the surface, and this is where the *Normand Pioneer* and the LR5 fitted into the operation. With its superior navigation and underwater endurance, the British rescue technicians were confident that LR5 would succeed where Priz had failed. Up to fifteen sailors could be evacuated at once in the LR5, crammed into the submersible's rescue chamber, and the mini-sub's battery power would be sufficient for eight trips before needing to be recharged, making a rescue of 120 survivors possible without even taking a break.

This was the preliminary plan: The *Eagle* would do the survey work and make the first contact with the *Kursk* crew by tapping on the hull; then the LR5 would swoop in and bring the sailors to the surface. Teams on both ships knew that no rescue plan withstood contact with the elements: It was certain to change once they were at the scene. The key would be flexibility and finding innovative solutions.

No less important was the establishment of a clear chain of command. With a multinational, multilingual rescue effort, the scope for miscommunication was wide. Admiral Skorgen set the rules, insisting that all Russian instructions flow through his headquarters. If the Russians had a demand or wanted to pass on information, they would tell him directly, and then he would make sure that it was relayed back out to the ships in the Barents Sea. Skorgen also asked his friend and fellow Norwegian submariner Captain Paal Svendsen to join the *Seaway Eagle* and take responsibility for coordinating the teams on the scene. If necessary, Svendsen would hold three-way summits aboard the *Eagle* at which Russian, Norwegian, and British representatives could find a way forward.

* * *

Privately, the Norwegian and British teams agreed on one additional guiding principle: This was a rescue mission—nothing more, nothing less. The sole aim was to find sailors alive and pluck them to safety. If it was established that all the *Kursk* sailors were dead, then the rescuers would pack up and go home. The Norwegian and British governments, and especially the Stolt managers, had foreseen the danger of "mission creep." Where would the Russians draw the line? Once the divers were at the hatch, might they be asked to look inside the escape tower? Once in the tower, might they be asked to search the ninth compartment, or the eighth? Might the Russians even ask Western specialists to recover corpses? Stolt was adamant that their divers would work only around the escape hatch and that any request beyond that would meet a polite but firm refusal. Working inside a submerged and wrecked nuclear submarine simply involved too much risk. The most obvious danger was that as the divers squeezed down through the escape tower, their umbilical cords might snag on jagged and twisted metal. If the multi-strand cord ruptured as a result, the diver would lose his air, communications, light, and hot-water supply—an instant death sentence. There was the added political risk that the Russians could accuse the divers of spying on the submarine.

The pressure on Stolt Offshore was intense. Their normal beat is commercially risky, physically hazardous operations, but ones with no politics attached. By definition, they worked over the horizon and beneath the waves, but this project would be in the spotlight; offshore technology would be center-stage. Stolt might be blamed if the rescue failed, and they might look like cowards if difficult conditions forced them to pull their divers out of the water.

Similar pressures troubled the British. Commodore David Russell had secured approval from the Russians to fly straight to the Kola Peninsula and join Admiral Popov at the scene while waiting for the *Normand Pioneer* with the LR5 to reach the site. When they got the word, Russell and his team raced to a military airfield near North-wood and boarded an RAF executive jet for the flight to Murmansk.

Just before he left, Royal Navy analysts handed Russell some internal research. They projected that if there were survivors and they had access to some life-support systems, the men could survive for up to seven days before being overcome by either rising carbon dioxide or a lack of oxygen. This was only an educated guess. There were just too many imponderables to be sure, such as how many sailors had survived the original accident, at what rate they were breathing down the air, and what chemical kits they were able to use to fight the CO_2. The projection of one week was both disturbing and galvanizing. The LR5 was expected to arrive in the Barents Sea late on Saturday afternoon, exactly seven days after the disaster, and very possibly at just the time the survivors ran out of air.

10

I: THURSDAY, AUGUST 17
Murmansk

WHEN THE SUBMARINE DESIGNER Igor Baranov spoke to the press that Tuesday, he had suggested that survivors in the *Kursk* would have sufficient air and life-support supplies to last "five or possibly six days." Western reports, based on seismology, had forced the Russians to concede without apology that the accident had occurred on Saturday morning, not on Sunday. Armed with this information, ordinary Russians who heard Baranov's comments made an elementary calculation: The submariners might be expected to live until Thursday, or maybe Friday.

At the time, Baranov's estimate had greatly heartened the crew's wives, but as another day passed without any positive news from the rescue scene, the families grew more and more anxious. They could not escape the horrifying image of their men living on the very edge of death, huddled in the darkness. The only comfort for the wives and mothers was the realization that the men were still together. They served together, lived together, and, if Baranov's timetable was correct, right now they were slowly beginning to die together.

But then, on Thursday morning, in a stunning shift of the official position, all those projections changed. In the widely read newspaper

Komsomolskaya Pravda, the commander-in-chief of the Navy, Admiral Kuroyedov, declared that the emergency supplies in the submarine were sufficient to keep the sailors alive for at least one more week. The trapped men, he announced, had enough air to last until Friday, August 25. Kuroyedov did not say where this new information came from or what it was based on, but the families and the Russian public assumed that he had access to the best and most reliable calculations. Surely no Russian commander would deliver such a dramatic forecast without hard evidence? The news was a shot of adrenaline injected straight into the heart of Vidyaevo. To the despairing families, it was as if their men were being plucked from the grave and given another chance of life. With another eight days to go, the rescuers would certainly be able to rescue the men from their shallow tomb.

Even as the Kuroyedov interview offered great hope, it raised troubling questions. After five days of failure, one particularly heated question was being repeatedly asked: Where was the country's top leadership? More specifically, where was the president?

The disturbing answer was that Vladimir Putin, in power for only three months, was still on holiday on the Black Sea coast, a full five days after the accident. He had spent Wednesday evening performing routine presidential duties, entertaining members of the Academy of Science, and discussing the future of Russia during a nighttime sea cruise. Despite the clamor of the public and the international attention, the Kremlin announced that Putin would not break off his vacation. Officials reassured Russians that he was receiving reports from the Defense Ministry every two hours and claimed that a presidential visit to the Kola Peninsula would only distract Navy commanders from the rescue effort.

Putin was traveling the next day to Yalta for a long-scheduled summit with leaders of the former Soviet states. When the Ukrainian hosts asked Kremlin aides whether Putin would cancel the trip because of the *Kursk* crisis, they were informed that the meeting would go ahead.

Moscow's newspapers went on the attack. In red letters, the banner headline in Thursday's *Komsomolskaya Pravda* asked, WHY DOES OUR PRESIDENT STAY SILENT? The front-page story puzzled over Putin's silence:

> For the fifth day the whole of Russia, with its heart trembling, is keeping a fearful eye on the Barents Sea drama. From the very first moment, Western leaders expressed their compassion and offered their help. Only our President stays silent. The Supreme Commander of our Armed Forces has nothing to say.

The article then pointed out that Putin had managed to find time during the crisis to appoint new Russian ambassadors to Chile and Japan.

Even worse, as young wives in the Arctic begged officials for information, Putin was enjoying the sun in the Russian Crimea, about as far away as could be imagined from the heartwrenching scenes that were now being played out across the nation's television screens. The impact on the public was traumatic.

Some in the press compared Putin's conduct to the behavior of Tsar Nicholas II during the notorious Khodynka Field incident, a tragedy in 1896 at which more than a thousand Russian peasants were trampled to death. Despite the disaster, caused by a stampede as crowds gathered to celebrate the accession of the tsar, Nicholas ordered his coronation to go ahead. Many Russians at the time questioned the judgment of their new, young ruler.

The lack of information provided to the public was so glaring that five days after the accident, not even the names of the sailors on board the *Kursk* had been released. One determined reporter set out to change that.

Vladimir Shkoda was exasperated. His Moscow editor demanded interviews with the families of the *Kursk* sailors and photographs of the children waiting for their fathers, but he was up against the crushing secrecy of the Northern Fleet. Vidyaevo was completely inaccessible to Russian journalists even at the quietest of times; now, internal security troops had placed the submarine base under virtual quarantine. Moscow might be enjoying the fruits of greater press freedom, but the military-dominated world of the Kola Peninsula still worked according to the old rules.

Every request Shkoda made for information was turned down. He felt certain that the Fleet command was hiding something. As a veteran newspaperman with a deep intuition for the people and places he covered, he distrusted the official announcements. He knew the Northern Fleet better than most. He had been born in Murmansk and had spent all of his adult life around the town. A fiercely proud northern Russian, Shkoda extolled life on the fringes of the Arctic, its purity and severity, with the shock of winter and the magical light of summer. To him, the corruption and deceit of the military was a stain on the soul of Arctic Russia.

So he set himself the goal of breaking through the layers of secrecy. Even the number of sailors on board the *Kursk* was still disputed, with accounts ranging from 112 to 130. Due to staff shortages in the Northern Fleet, ships and submarines frequently exchanged sailors and junior officers at the last moment. Even now, five days after the accident, dozens of families did not know for sure whether their husbands, brothers, or sons were on the submarine. The frantic phone calls of family members to the Fleet headquarters brought no response.

Then Shkoda saw his chance. An intermediary secretly approached him, asking if he was interested in buying the list of the crew, with the names of everyone on board the *Kursk* as well as their hometowns. The price would be 18,000 rubles, about $600. The original source of the information was a very senior officer in the Fleet headquarters. If Shkoda could make it to Severomorsk, and follow strict instructions to preserve the officer's anonymity, he could have the list. Shkoda knew the document would be emotionally and politically explosive. The revelation of the names would cause some families heartbreak, but others would discover that their loved ones had not been transferred to the *Kursk* after all and were safe at sea in other ships or submarines.

Severomorsk, like Vidyaevo, is a base closed to outsiders, guarded by military police, but the size of the town and the volume of traffic mean that it is much easier to pass through the roadblocks. Two local reporters working for Shkoda had naval passes, one a legitimate document, the other forged. As instructed, they waited by a bus stop on a deserted back street in the town. After a few minutes, a thick envelope was thrown out of a fast-moving car as it drove past. They never saw the face of the driver.

Komsomolskaya Pravda published their scoop the next day under the headline SOLD FOR 18,000 RUBLES. The Navy, unsurprisingly, ordered an immediate inquiry into what it called the theft of a secret document. For Shkoda, publishing the list was a small but satisfying act of revenge against this crass military culture that, as he put it, valued machines more than men.

II: SOUTHERN BARENTS SEA

AS THE STORM LASHED the rescue ships through all of Tuesday and Wednesday, no further attempt to launch the Priz submersible had been possible. To make matters worse for Admiral Verich, his plan to bring the Navy's other rescue mini-sub to the scene was proving disastrously ill-timed. In heavy seas, Bester stood no chance of being launched off the exposed deck of the crane ship that brought it to the scene. Far from being a suitable mother-ship, the crane ship was nothing more than a self-propelled barge, designed for use in the inlets, ports, and bays surrounding the Kola Peninsula. She was utterly ill-suited to work in the open ocean. That she was even being used was a sign of the desperation of the rescue operation.

There were now *three* types of submersibles on the scene—Priz, Bester and AS-32—and none was able to deploy into the ocean, let alone make it down to the survivors.

Older rescuers observing the fiasco mourned the failure to keep the Lenok India–class rescue submarines intact. Two of these special submarines were built in the late 1970s, each carrying two mini-submersibles on their hulls and containing a diver decompression system inside. The great advantage of Lenok was that an evacuation could be done submarine-to-submarine, a transfer of survivors that did not depend on surface weather. But these submarines had gone the same way as most of the Fleet's noncombat ships: They were sold for scrap in the mid-1990s. Keeping a Lenok submarine in service would have involved annual running costs of 60 million rubles, about $2 million. The Navy didn't have a fraction of that money.

As Northern Fleet officers watched the débâcle from the bridges of the *Peter the Great* and the *Admiral Chabanenko,* their anger began to spill over. Verich says one staff officer, whom he refuses to name, stared straight at him and shouted, "Admiral, you are a disgrace to your uniform and your Navy!"

On Thursday, when the storm finally abated sufficiently to allow submersible operations to be resumed, the rescuers regrouped on the deck of the *Rudnitsky.* Both Priz and Bester had undergone makeshift repairs and were being hurriedly readied for dives. Several more experienced pilots had also arrived, including Captain Andrei Sholokhov. He joined Sergei Pertsev and Alexander Maisak as the team that would take Priz down. Alexander Kalugin and Dmitri Podkopaev would pilot Bester.

There was something undeniably heroic about the work of the Russian submersible pilots during this period. Their bravery was all the greater because of the grossly inferior rescue equipment they were working with. All around them, out on the warships and back in Severomorsk and Moscow, officers were trying to duck responsibility, worrying about their careers, and blaming others for the rescue fiasco.

The rescue pilots were different. They felt a huge weight of responsibility. This was what they had trained for all their professional lives. They were the only hope for survivors, and they begged Captain Teslenko and Admiral Verich to select them for the next dive.

Andrei Sholokhov had rushed to the Barents Sea as soon as he heard about the *Kursk* accident. He had spent five years as Priz's chief pilot before retiring in early 2000. Widely regarded as the most capable and experienced submersible pilot in Russia, Sholokhov knew that his place was at the heart of the rescue operation. He was a patriot with a deep affection for the ordinary sailors of the Northern Fleet, men who endured such shocking conditions to serve their country. He also had the experience and self-confidence to believe that if any man could pull off an against-the-odds rescue, it was him.

Late on Thursday, Sholokhov got his chance. Priz was again winched off its plinths and gingerly raised out of the hold. A photograph of this moment, taken from the *Admiral Chabanenko* warship, shows the thirty-five-foot-long, sixteen-year-old submersible as it was being lowered awkwardly over the port side of the *Rudnitsky*. The bold orange-and-white stripes of Priz stand out against the battle-gray paint of its mother-ship, and the mini-sub seemed strangely vulnerable as it was prepared for what amounted to the most dramatic dive in submarine-rescue history.

Sholokhov was joined by Pertsev, as copilot. If there were two Russian specialists who could succeed, these were the men. Calm and experienced, schooled in the tough, under-resourced world of the Russian Navy, they brought to the task a fierce determination to reach the ninth compartment and bring possible survivors to the surface. Even as they focused on the technical challenge ahead, they were well aware that they carried the hopes of Russia with them.

After the forty-eight-hour suspension of rescue operations due to the weather, it was a huge relief for Sholokhov to be finally in the pilot's seat. On the surface, visibility was two miles, and the wind was gusting from the northeast. In a few minutes, they would be below the waves, and neither would matter.

At 4:40 P.M., Priz was free of the last tethers. The actual dive began thirty-five minutes later. Sholokhov had learned from his colleagues' previous efforts that preserving battery power was crucial, and he switched off unnecessary lighting inside the submersible's cabin. Only a red glow illuminated the instruments. The most economical way to descend was to use no thrusters at all, just to let Priz slowly sink toward the seabed under its own weight. Every use of the vertical, horizontal, or forward thrusters reduced the time that Priz could stay underwater, creating a devil's bargain between navigational precision and endurance. The technical manuals suggested that Priz could operate for six or seven hours before the batteries needed to be recharged, but in reality they usually lasted only half that time.

Sholokhov was well aware that every maneuver he made took a toll on the batteries, and as the mini-sub edged toward the body of the *Kursk*, communications with the surface were kept to an absolute minimum. He absorbed the information from the instrument panel and kept to the routine he knew from previous training exercises. He tried not to dwell on the knowledge that if there were sailors trapped in the aft compartment, then his piloting skills were the best, and very possibly the only, chance of reaching them before it was too late.

As the dark hull loomed into view, the submarine at first seemed like a giant shadow on the seabed. Only the white-painted circle around the hatch reflected the beam from their bow light and provided any sense of orientation. This was their target, but inching the rescue sub to that point was immensely tricky. Sholokhov chose the same approach as Captain Maisak had used four days earlier during Priz's first dive to the *Kursk*, opting to avoid the hazards of coming in behind the large rudders, and instead maneuvering diagonally across the upper casing. The troublesome current, flowing at just over a knot, was still running from the bow to the stern. Sholokhov was using his inefficient side thrusters to guide Priz into place.

Finally, with Pertsev struggling next to him to see their exact position, Sholokhov attempted to set Priz down over the hatch. At this point, they were extraordinarily close to docking, perhaps only a few feet out of position. Sholokhov used the thrusters to move a little forward and try again. He was determined to do better. The *Kursk* sailors lay too close to betray them now. Sholokhov had trained his entire career for this moment.

Again and again, he brought Priz in, the gentle thud ringing through the mini-sub as it dropped onto the giant hull. On two occasions, the maneuver was so good that Sholokhov and Pertsev managed to attach Priz to the little rod protruding from the hatch. But even so, on neither occasion could they make a proper seal. Priz was momentarily resting over the hatch, but when they opened the valve, no vacuum was created to clamp the mini-sub in position. The same questions kept running through Sholokhov's mind. Was something wrong with the hatch mechanism? Had it been damaged or distorted by the explosions?

Eight times he landed Priz onto the face of the escape hatch. On the final attempt, Sholokhov held position for nearly twenty minutes, an incredible feat of skill and stamina. The mental effort, the dexterity and finesse required at the control levers, the physical discomfort of working in the cramped, darkened submersible—this was in the finest traditions of Russian heroism and ingenuity.

But something always prevented them from securely mating to the cofferdam, the mechanism above the escape hatch that enabled docking to take place. Sholokhov felt certain that the reason was damage to the *Kursk*'s hatch, possibly caused by the shock waves that traveled down the submarine after the giant explosions. He had no way of judging whether the hull had distorted around the hatch, but it seemed the most likely explanation.

All too soon, the voltmeter battery gauges showed that Priz's power was nearly spent. The last maneuver Sholokhov made was to slide forward just above the upper hull of the *Kursk*, past the emergency buoy that had failed to release. The conning tower loomed straight ahead of them, with its raised periscope and masts. To ascend, he pumped out some ballast and floated up, vertically, the black hull of the *Kursk* directly below them, a scar on the seabed.

Sholokhov and Pertsev had pushed to the very limit of the mini-sub's capability, trying every maneuver they could think of. The failure was devastating.

* * *

The Russians still had some last-ditch options. Bester was next in line, with Captain Dmitri Podkopaev as the chief pilot. After its wretched passage out to sea aboard the crane ship *PK-7500*, Bester had been taken away and launched in a protected bay forty miles to the south to wait out the storm. Then the submersible had been towed back out to the disaster site. As it was pulled through heavy seas by a tug-boat, battered by the wind and waves, some of its key instruments were damaged, including the gyro-compass.

Once Bester was launched, within moments of slipping below the surface, Podkopaev faced an emergency. The mini-sub's second compartment, designed to hold the evacuated submariners, was leaking, and Bester rapidly dropped toward the seabed in an uncontrolled dive. Only at the last moment, frantically pumping ballast out, did the pilots manage to stabilize the sub. Without even locating the *Kursk*, Podkopaev brought Bester back to the surface, and it emerged in severe distress. Wallowing low in the water, with the second compartment partially flooded, the sub was on the verge of sinking. Frantic shouts and orders rang out as rescuers realized what was happening and, just before the mini-sub slipped below the surface again, one of the crane operators on the *Rudnitsky* managed to grab it and bring the vessel safely alongside. The *Kursk* rescue effort was in grave danger of magnifying the disaster. The loss of a mini-sub, and the death of its crew, was a real possibility.

Now all the rescuers could do was wait once again for Priz's batteries to recharge.

That Thursday evening, it appeared to many of the exhausted rescue professionals on the *Mikhail Rudnitsky* that their effort was being sabotaged by the disastrous performance of the mini-subs, and in particular the batteries that powered them. The troubled story of the batteries used by Russia's rescue submersibles is a microcosm of the crisis that faced the Northern Fleet in the 1990s.

For many decades, a small company called Balt-electric, based in

St. Petersburg, had produced specialized batteries for the Navy's rescue submersibles. After the breakup of the Soviet Union, excited by the prospect of being free to choose their own product ranges, the factory managers saw no value in continuing to produce these extremely specialized batteries. The Russian Navy didn't have the money to pay for them anyway. There were Navy officials who recognized the problem, but the Defense Ministry was barred by law from investing in private companies. When Admiral Verich asked Balt-electric how much it would cost to buy four new submersible batteries, the plant manager priced them at $1 million—an impossible sum for the impoverished Navy.

No one in Moscow's ministries cared. In the early 1990s, amid tumultuous political change, debates about batteries on mini-submersibles seemed irrelevant.

III: BODØ HEADQUARTERS, NORTHERN NORWAY

TWENTY-FOUR HOURS AFTER NORWAY had requested technical data on the *Kursk*'s hatch mechanism, Admiral Popov delivered on his promise. On Thursday, a Northern Fleet staff officer turned up unannounced at the Norwegian consulate in Murmansk, clutching a thick brown envelope. To ensure the security of the information, the envelope was immediately driven by a Norwegian diplomat across the border and out of Russia. At the Norwegian border town of Kirkenes, the package was opened, and the pages and diagrams were faxed to Admiral Skorgen at his headquarters in Bodø.

The Norwegian admiral could not contain his excitement. This transfer of data was strong evidence that there were still survivors in the *Kursk*. Popov was taking a great political risk with this material, and there would be no point in passing the information to the West if he believed that the sailors were all dead.

As he studied the pages with his technical advisers, however, Skorgen's heart sank. The rescue specialists and divers needed the precise procedures for operating the hatch as well as the lineups for the valves. Instead, Popov had sent over several pages showing an Oscar II escape tower from different angles. The accompanying text could barely be deciphered. Russian phrases were scribbled illegibly in the margins. These were rough hand drawings, not the technical diagrams required. Inadequate as an original, they looked even worse after being faxed. This was no better than the information obtained by the British naval attaché, Geoff McCready, in Moscow earlier in the week.

Skorgen reached for the direct line to the Northern Fleet and asked to speak to Popov again. For the first time, to try to break out of the formality of their previous exchanges and to soften his message, he decided to talk to him on first-name terms. The conversation remains etched in Skorgen's mind.

"Viacheslav, it's Einar Skorgen here in Bodø. I have a problem."

"OK, what's the issue?"

"I have received the data from your headquarters showing the *Kursk*'s escape hatch. Let me be honest with you, Viacheslav. It's inadequate. It's no good at all."

Popov was silent. Skorgen could hear him breathing heavily. Ten seconds passed, and Popov said nothing.

Finally, the Northern Fleet commander sighed deeply. "Einar, I understand you. I know that you cannot operate like this."

"This is my proposal," Skorgen quickly said. "We need your experts to talk directly to ours. The people who need the data are aboard the *Seaway Eagle*. The ship is heading for a supply stop to pick up divers and equipment, and then she'll be sailing to the Barents Sea. Fly your team of technicians to Norway, and I will take them on a helicopter straight to the *Eagle*."

"It is best if I give you the information when your ship arrives at the scene."

"No, Viacheslav, that is not going to work. We need the technical data right now so that our specialists can plan the rescue and put divers down to the hatch as soon as they arrive."

"OK," Popov relented, "but I will have to call you back."

But before they hung up, Skorgen addressed one more issue with Popov, an especially sensitive one. Five days had passed since the explosions, and Skorgen wanted to make sure the Russians were not cooperating as a way of protecting themselves against Russian or world opinion.

"Viacheslav, we must also understand that this is a rescue mission. Whether we save fifty people or a single individual, it doesn't matter. We are acting in good faith."

"I understand that," Popov replied. "The Northern Fleet is not in the business of wasting people's time and effort."

So Popov did believe that survivors could still be saved. Skorgen checked once more on the progress of the *Seaway Eagle*. She was due to arrive at Tromsø early the next morning, where the divers would join the vessel. From there, the ship would take another thirty hours to make her passage around the North Cape and reach the scene of the disaster.

To satisfy Skorgen's demand for quality information, Admiral Verich was ordered to leave the rescue site and join the *Seaway Eagle*. The Russians wanted him on board watching the Norwegians, and making sure the Western specialists had the right amount of information—enough, but not too much. They also needed to be certain that the Stolt divers and their underwater cameras did not get close to the *Kursk*'s secrets inside the forward compartments or near the shattered bow.

Then a truly bizarre turn of events threatened all the goodwill that Skorgen and Popov had established.

At the Severomorsk naval airfield, a pair of Russian Ilyushin-38 long-range anti-submarine aircraft belonging to the Northern Fleet's aviation regiment took off and headed out to sea. At first they flew on a westerly bearing toward the North Cape, but to the alarm of the radar controllers monitoring NATO's northern airspace, the planes then turned abruptly south, tracking along the Norwegian coast. The Ilyushins were flying low and slow, crisscrossing the sea, far beyond their normal pattern of surveillance operations. At headquarters in Bodø, the Norwegians were stunned. Northern Fleet aircraft hadn't deployed this far down the Norwegian coast since the Cold War. The timing shocked Skorgen: The Russians were engaging in aggressive flights at precisely the time he was mobilizing Norwegian rescue forces to help the Russian Navy.

F-16 fighter jets were scrambled to identify and monitor the Russian planes. The NATO pilots reported that the Russian planes appeared to be engaging in a serious submarine hunt, dropping sonar buoys from their bomb bays into the water and working their way across the ocean in a methodical pattern.

Astonished that the Ilyushins were now virtually at his doorstep, Skorgen once again picked up the phone to speak to Popov.

"Admiral, would you like to explain what your planes are doing off my coast?"

The Northern Fleet commander was unfazed. "Admiral Skorgen, let me be quite clear what we are doing. My intelligence services inform me that a foreign submarine was the source of the accident. They tell me the *Kursk* was hit in a collision with a Western submarine. What are we doing now? We are searching for that submarine."

Skorgen was incredulous that nearly a week after the *Kursk* accident, the Russians had suddenly decided to search Norwegian waters for a foreign submarine. "Admiral Popov," Skorgen responded, "I don't believe it was a collision. You should remember that if there had been such an accident with the *Kursk*, you should be looking for the second submarine next to your submarine, not down here along my coast." Although Skorgen was not privy to the highly secretive movements of British and U.S. nuclear boats, he was a submariner himself and felt certain that if anything had struck the *Kursk*, the largest attack submarine in the world, it would not have escaped undamaged.

Popov was unapologetic. "I can only repeat what I've already said: This is the information I have from my intelligence services. This is what I believe."

Though the Russians may have seemed wildly off the mark to be hunting a sub along the Norwegian coast, they were, in truth, very close to successfully tracking the submarine that had been spying on their exercise.

Several hours after the heated exchange between Skorgen and Popov, the distinctive profile of an American Los Angeles–class attack submarine glided toward a pier at the Haakonsvern submarine base in southern Norway. The USS *Memphis* was finally returning from her Northern Run after eight weeks at sea. The sailors clambered out, relishing the sea air, and amid the activity another group of men carefully unloaded equipment and moved boxes into vehicles parked at the quayside. They were the spooks who had recorded the vast amounts of electronic and acoustic information over the last few weeks. Guarding the data every step of the way, they would fly it back to the United States on a military plane.

The *Memphis* had left the southern Barents Sea at the end of her patrol, the day after hearing the buildup of emergency-signals traffic. Only this sudden, frantic burst in communications had allowed Captain Mark Breor to reach the conclusion that he had "witnessed" the destruction of a Russian submarine on that fateful Saturday. There was no value in staying around—Breor knew that the presence of a U.S. submarine in the vicinity of a Northern Fleet disaster could be the cause of a major diplomatic incident. The USS *Toledo,* another Los Angeles–class submarine, which was due to take over from the *Memphis*'s Barents Sea patrol, was also ordered to leave the area. The commander of the U.S. submarine fleet in the Atlantic, Admiral John Grossenbacher, knew that it was vital to give the accident site a very wide berth.

The *Memphis*'s arrival at the Norwegian base five days after the *Kursk* accident was reported in local newspapers. It was, in fact, a scheduled stop that had been part of her plans for many months. Haakonsvern is a regular stop for American submarines, allowing commanders to unload acoustic and electronic data, and a place for the spooks riding on the boats to disembark and fly home, saving themselves the long, tedious transit across the Atlantic.

In Russia, the docking of the *Memphis* in Norway was seized on as ammunition for those who believed an American submarine had collided with the *Kursk*. The Russian government formally requested permission to inspect the *Memphis*'s hull, to look for signs of structural damage, but the Americans refused. From the U.S. Navy's perspective, that would set a very dangerous precedent.

As soon as the *Memphis*'s data arrived in the United States, it was sent to highly specialized naval facilities in Virginia and Maryland for meticulous and prolonged technical analysis. The audio recording of the *Kursk*'s destruction shocked those who heard the tape; they immediately recognized that they were listening to a submarine's death throes.

The tape begins with the unmistakable sound of static, generated by the active sonar transmissions from the numerous surface ships in the area. Then, suddenly, there is a high-pitched audio spike as the first explosion occurs. For the next two minutes and fifteen seconds, the tape reverts to the active transmissions and other background sea noise, and then, the shocking indication of a second and much more powerful detonation, which totally saturates the receivers, blanking them out. The mass detonation of the *Kursk*'s torpedo warheads is under way.

The naval analysts understood only too well what the sound spikes represented for the sailors and officers aboard the *Kursk*—the destruction of the hull, the fire and explosion blowing backward into the heart of the submarine, the terror and shock, the instant realization that the submarine was facing a catastrophe.

Even during the darkest days of the Cold War, there was a strange affinity between the American and Russian submarine communities. The gamesmanship and bravado under the surface of the Barents Sea turned it into a unique theater of superpower competition. Amid the rivalry, there was always the glimmer of mutual respect. American and Russian sub commanders knew they faced the same conditions and the same hazards. They were both doing their duty with the same profound sense of serving their countries. In this gentleman's war, there was even scope for admiring the enemy.

In the late 1980s, watching intently the performance of the Northern Fleet submarines, British and American naval analysts suddenly noticed a single boat of exceptional quality. Out of the scores of submarines that were active, this one stood out. What made her better than the rest was difficult to define, except that she appeared to have a captain of extraordinary skill and natural aptitude. The Russian submarine in question was a Victor III–class boat with the pennant number PL 667, but the identity of her captain remains a secret. As a small token of respect for this unseen adversary, British submarine commanders gave the Russian officer the nickname "The Prince of Darkness." He had an uncanny ability to avoid detection by Western attack submarines, and every time his boat was spotted she was being superbly handled.

In a game in which British and U.S. submarine commanders believe they have a decisive edge, here was a worthy competitor, a captain on whom they would never set eyes but whom they believed matched their own levels of training and tactical awareness. His performance became the subject of fascinated scrutiny, and his absence was immediately felt when he left active service sometime in 1989.

This kinship and mutual respect among submariners was never more acutely felt than during this week in August 2000, as the international rescue effort to save the *Kursk* crew gathered belated momentum.

II

I: 8:30 A.M., FRIDAY, AUGUST 18
Tromsø, Norway

STEAMING AT FULL SPEED, the *Seaway Eagle* reached Tromsø harbor just nine hours after she had left the Asgard Field. Now the frenzied work began to transform her from an offshore support ship to a fully equipped diving vessel. The extraordinary level of readiness in the port and the motivation of the workers struck all who witnessed it. The cranes started lifting and landing equipment even before the *Eagle*'s ropes were secure. The dock workers were eager for the challenge, and the port authorities committed every available resource.

The Norwegian military treated the mobilization of the *Eagle* like a national emergency. The air force notified Stolt that fighter jets were available: If needed, divers or other key staff would travel in the navigator's seat. Over 120 tons of equipment gathered from across northern Europe was already waiting on the dock. Streaming up the gangway were members of the Norwegian Radiation Protection Board with their monitors. Dive-support teams also boarded, with their helium-and-oxygen gas mixes, enough to sustain four separate teams of saturation divers. Russian and Norwegian translators arrived.

As the ship's two cranes worked at maximum capacity to load the stores, the British divers slipped on board unnoticed by the press gathered at the dockside. Their Norwegian counterparts, however, were mobbed like celebrities. Men who normally work hundreds of feet below the surface of the ocean and in tiny decompression chambers found themselves fêted as heroes. Some in the *Eagle* looked on aghast as the Norwegian divers gave interviews on the quayside. All the dive supervisors wanted to do was to get under way.

Despite twenty years of diving, this was Tony Scott's first time with the *Seaway Eagle*. He brought his usual kit: working clothes, diving knives, tools, and logbooks. Despite the rumors circulating about the mission ahead, Scott had his own calm and methodical way of dealing with the uncertainty in front of him. He simply didn't listen to the talk, keeping to himself and waiting instead for the briefing. He knew very well that only once they were at the site and could do their own pre-dive surveys would the real picture emerge. Concentrating on the job ahead, he went straight to the ship's bell-hangar, where the diving bells are stored, and began preparing them with the freshly loaded equipment.

At exactly midday, just three and a half hours after arriving, the ropes were pulled in. The red, leatherbound logbook notes that at 12:02 P.M. the ship "moved off the dock." Normally reconfiguring the *Seaway Eagle* for a saturation-diving operation took a whole day. The work at Tromsø was a stunning achievement.

The speed of the mobilization could not have been achieved without making some safety compromises. Under Norwegian and British regulations, any diving operation on this scale requires what is called a hyperbaric lifeboat, which contains a life-support system for divers that operates independently of the mother-ship. If the *Eagle* caught fire or began to sink, the rest of the crew could escape to the standard lifeboats on deck, but the divers in their chambers would be trapped. If they chose to flee the chambers, they would die from the bends. A hyperbaric lifeboat would allow them to escape while remaining under pressure. But loading and checking a hyperbaric lifeboat is time-consuming business. To avoid this major delay, Stolt had asked the Norwegian Maritime Safety Board for permission to operate without the special lifeboat. The exemption was granted on condition that a hyperbaric system would be moved to a nearby port at the first opportunity.

Stolt knew the risk involved all too well—the industry had learned about it the hard way four years earlier, when a vessel in the Far East was caught in a tropical storm and began sinking. The ship had no hyperbaric lifeboat, and the divers on board, who were living in pressure chambers secured to the deck, could not be decompressed in time. Realizing that their bodies had not yet adapted to the surface pressure, the divers simply sat in their chambers knowing they would go down with the ship. They wrote farewell letters to their families, strapping the notes to their bodies so that search teams would find them later.

To assist Graham Mann in the coordination of the rescue operation, Stolt agreed to place another highly experienced offshore manager inside the Norwegian military headquarters. The move made sure that throughout the coming days, Skorgen had instant access to someone who knew the diving capabilities of the *Seaway Eagle* and who could help troubleshoot technical problems as they arose. The man chosen for this role was Bob Rose, a Scottish diver and mechanical engineer.

Rose and Mann had been colleagues and friendly rivals for as long as anyone could remember, competing against each other for the industry's most challenging and rewarding jobs. During the *Eagle*'s short stop, they had held a brief meeting to map out what they would do and, more importantly, what they would *not* do. They suspected that they would come under pressure to use their cameras and equipment for more than rescue purposes. The *Eagle*'s sophisticated ROVs (Remotely Operated Vehicles) were equipped with highly specialized low-light underwater cameras, and Western intelligence agencies would regard this as too good an opportunity to miss. Mann and Rose were adamant that they would not be pressured into any activity that might be interpreted as Western espionage.

As the *Eagle* got under way, Captain Dag Rasmussen plotted a course on the ship's borrowed charts that would place them over the *Kursk* by Saturday evening, a voyage of about thirty-six hours. They would arrive almost exactly one week after the accident. As the *Eagle* navigated rapidly through the islands in strikingly clear weather, even the old hands on board believed that the Russians would order the rescue mission to be aborted. One of the supervisors, Mark Nankivell, remembered his experience in 1986 working on a diving ship off Brazil. When the *Challenger* space shuttle exploded shortly after launch, NASA asked for the assistance of the ship to recover the remains of the astronauts, but the mission was canceled when the U.S. military said the situation was too sensitive for civilian divers. Nankivell guessed that the same would happen now.

As they steamed north, Mann and his team despaired of getting reliable information from the Russians. Instead, they pieced together data from the Internet and combined them with their own educated guesses. On one website, they found a diagram of the layout of an Oscar II submarine, and from that they made their own deductions about how Russian engineers would have designed the hatches.

The one fact that the Russians had consistently reported was the depth of the *Kursk*, which was said to be lying on the seabed about 350 feet below the surface. Ocean charts for the area confirmed that depth. This was excellent news. In many parts of the world, offshore diving operations are conducted at almost twice that depth. In the North Sea, dives to 600 feet are considered easily achievable. In rare cases, 1,000-foot dives are conducted, although this is regarded as the very limit of human physiology, so deep that divers report a strange and debilitating combination of psychological and physical symptoms, including extreme fatigue and lethargy.

Mann suspected that much of the rest of the information the Russians had made public was false. In particular, the talk of poor visibility around the submarine seemed highly implausible. A lifetime of experience in diving and underwater construction projects told Mann that conditions could not possibly be that bad. He had worked in similar water before, off Labrador and in the north Norwegian Sea, in extremely clear conditions. He knew that when a site on the seabed is far enough from the coastline to avoid discharges from factories and rivers, there is simply no reason for poor visibility. Also, the divers who in 1981 had retrieved ten tons of gold from HMS *Edinburgh,* a British warship torpedoed in the Barents Sea in May 1942, had enjoyed excellent visibility. The only place where Mann could remember dreadful conditions at such a depth was close to the mouth of the River Congo, and that was due to the vast amount of natural debris and silt that the river carries out to sea after snaking through the African jungle for nearly a thousand miles.

The reports about underwater currents exceeding three knots also sounded like nonsense. Mann suspected this report was fabricated to explain the Russian failure to dock with the *Kursk*'s escape hatch. He hoped he was right, because even the most advanced submersibles in the world, including the LR5, could not maneuver in such fast-flowing water. Divers would fare no better: They can operate only in underwater currents of one and a half knots or less. Above one knot, and the divers would have a massive struggle on their hands just to stay in position long enough to do any useful work.

Mann was tired of the speculation and the secondhand news. He craved sets of tide tables, seabed charts, drawings of the *Kursk,* schematic diagrams of the rear hatch, and knowledge of the underwater currents, valve systems, and pressure readings. Two decks below him in the heart of the ship, the *Eagle*'s young field engineer, Matt Kirk, was trying to draw up a task plan, a technical assessment of the project ahead and a clear step-by-step guide as to how the job would be tackled. But he really needed to hear from the Russians first. What had they attempted? What was the real situation down there over the ninth hatch? How could he plan the *Seaway Eagle*'s rescue effort when he knew so little of what the Russians had learned?

The *Eagle* was making good progress in near-perfect weather, following the Norwegian coast. Just after midnight, twelve hours after the vessel departed Tromsø, they made the passage around the tip of the North Cape, famous to mariners for its midnight sun and stark beauty. As a brief darkness fell over the gentle sea in the early hours, the *Eagle*'s captain, Rasmussen, swung his ship onto a southeasterly course of 095 degrees.

Graham Mann on board the *Seaway Eagle* and Bob Rose in the Bodø HQ were determined to stamp their authority on the mission. The rules they had set were non-negotiable. They needed space for their team, and they insisted on a minimum exclusion zone of 1,640 feet around the *Seaway Eagle*. Under no circumstances was any ship or aircraft to enter that zone without Mann's permission. They feared that, otherwise, Russia's naval and air assets would be circling around, getting in the way and endangering the diving operation. A Russian warship racing through the rescue area risked tangling with divers and bells in the water below. They also insisted on a detailed risk assessment, with all personnel in the *Eagle* being adequately briefed on the potential hazards, especially the divers. The *Kursk* crew, after all, was not just trapped inside a hull. Alongside the sailors were two nuclear reactors and multiple weapons systems, some of which were almost certainly damaged. Torpedoes, missiles, toxic gases, jagged metal, and loose debris all lay in wait.

As the *Eagle*, her lights ablaze, steamed along at her maximum speed, her bridge and deck areas were scenes of constant activity. The crew was hard at work preparing for diving operations over the hull of the *Kursk*.

Offshore specialists are not sentimental people. They didn't give a damn about improving diplomatic relations with Moscow. This mission had nothing to do with politics. The Northern Fleet High Command evoked no sympathy. No one cared for the prestige of the admirals or the pride of the Russian Navy. The team was determined to do everything in their power to help the Russian sailors, but if they stepped on toes in the process, so be it.

The fourteen divers on board were split up into four teams, each with three divers, with two divers held in reserve in case someone was injured or fell ill. All fourteen men—ten British, four Norwegians—were asked to sign special accident-waiver forms, agreeing to dive without the hyperbaric lifeboat and not to hold Stolt responsible for radiation injuries.

In the mess room, the divers gathered for a briefing from the nuclear specialists. Each man operating over the escape hatch would have his own personal Geiger counter, and the ROVs would constantly monitor radiation levels in the water. The Norwegian Navy surgeon-commander also briefed them about the psychological stresses they would face in the operation. The divers might confront corpses trapped in the escape tower; they would certainly be working close to potentially unstable weapons systems. Every diver was asked individually if he was prepared physically and emotionally to work on the *Kursk*. Pulling out of the dive would not be regarded as a sign of weakness, they were all told. All agreed to continue.

Many of the divers had dealt with body recoveries. Ali Clark, a former Royal Navy diver, had recovered the body parts of a sailor who had been torn apart by the propellers of a nuclear submarine off Scotland. These were men not easily scared underwater.

Some of the divers tried to get a few hours' sleep in anticipation of a round-the-clock push. Tony Scott was uncharacteristically restless—he had been selected as Diver One and would be the first man to reach the *Kursk*. He didn't relish the task ahead, but he was certain he could cope with the challenge. Despite his reputation as a diver who never lost his cool, his mind worked overtime that night as he thought about dropping out of the diving bell and swimming over to the submarine. Once on the job, he was sure his confidence would return. Waiting and thinking was always the most difficult part of any operation.

II: FRIDAY AFTERNOON
Vidyaevo Naval Base

THE BASE WAS NORMALLY QUIET during the summer exercises, half abandoned while the sailors were out at sea and their families took their August holidays. But by Friday, Vidyaevo's population was swollen with anxious parents and wives of the *Kursk* sailors arriving from all over Russia. The Northern Fleet moored the large hospital ship the *Svir* in the docks to provide extra accommodation.

Natasha Tylik sat at home, mesmerized but appalled by the wildly contradictory information coming from the television. Vidyaevo received just two TV channels, the state-run RTR network and the independent station NTV, and every time Tylik switched between them, another retired naval officer was speculating about whether the *Kursk* sailors were alive or dead. Even when she found the energy to visit the Officers Club, Natasha encountered only recycled rumors. The trusted naval officer Viktor Bursyk, who had assumed the role of the families' representative, had returned from the rescue scene with no fresh news at all.

Admiral Kuroyedov's suggestion the day before that the submarine crew could survive another week had thrown Natasha an emotional lifeline. She had endured her darkest day on Thursday, deciding that Sergei was dead. Staying at home, she had wept bitterly, screaming at the television, throwing herself against the walls of the tiny apartment until neighbors called for help. Now, with Kuroyedov's statement that afternoon, her mood had swung from despair to renewed hope. His words had had such a powerful impact that on Friday morning Natasha sat with the television sound turned down and the apartment door open so she could hear Sergei's footsteps when he bounded up the outside staircase. At any moment, she expected him to race into the apartment, laughing about his miraculous escape.

During the early afternoon, nervous word spread that leaders from Moscow were on their way to Vidyaevo to talk to the families. Heading the team was Russia's deputy prime minister, Ilya Klebanov, the newly

appointed head of the Kursk Commission of Inquiry. He was joined
by the governor of the Murmansk region, Yuri Yevdokimov, and the
governor of the city of Kursk, Alexander Rutskoi. Klebanov knew he
would be the lightning rod for the families' distress, and he must have
guessed it would be a difficult and emotional evening. But nothing in
his political life could have prepared him for the hours ahead.

Even before he made it to the main hall, the wives had surrounded
him. This was not frustration he was facing but fury. A cameraman
caught the shocked look on his face as questions rained down on
him. "Why are you here, not out there on the sea saving our men?"
one woman shouted. Others were weeping and swearing at him.

"How could it happen? Why are they not rescued yet?"

"Why did you delay before asking for the help of foreigners?"

"Don't you care about our men?"

As Klebanov took refuge in a corridor, the mother-in-law of a
Kursk sailor pursued him. She lunged toward him, grabbing his tie.
"Go there and save them yourself!" she shouted. "You are such
scum . . . scum!"

After taking a few minutes to regain his composure, the deputy
prime minister reached the lectern in the main hall of the Officers
Club. Dressed in a casual shirt and dark blue sweater, he hesitated as
he absorbed the disturbing scene in front of him. Many of those in
the front rows were openly weeping; others gazed straight at him,
faces drawn after so many nights without rest. Before Klebanov could
open his mouth to speak, the mother of Sergei Sadilenko, one of the
Kursk's senior engineers, approached the platform and started hitting him, her arms flailing, before she was dragged away by naval
officers and security guards.

For the second time that evening, Klebanov paused to collect his
thoughts. He began by explaining that the rescuers were doing all
they could at the scene. He listed the ships that were out there: the
flagship the *Peter the Great,* the cruiser the *Admiral Chabanenko,* the
rescue vessel the *Mikhail Rudnitsky,* the carrier the *Admiral Kuznetsov.*
He named the naval commanders in charge of the operation: Popov,

Motsak, Verich, and Yuri Boyarkin (the head of the Northern Fleet's military training department). Such lists of ships and names struck many in the audience as reminiscent of old Soviet propaganda, designed to impress the ignorant. Statistics were meaningless. The question was not how many ships and admirals were at the scene but what their chances of success were. "The situation is still unclear," Klebanov continued, "but we are trying everything within our power to save your men and bring them safely to the surface."

The Tylik family was sitting near the front, straining to hear Klebanov's softly spoken words. Natasha's mother-in-law, Nadezhda, who had spent the first day of the crisis convinced that the *Kursk* was unsinkable and that nothing could have happened to her son, now realized that many of the official statements contradicted one another. She is a short woman, strong-willed and determined. Nadezhda stood up in silence, her hands trembling, unable to suppress her grief and anger. She began shouting at Klebanov.

"Why did I raise my son? For what? You probably don't have children of your own, so you don't understand. You don't understand anything. You eat so well, and now you're just sitting here—and our boys have nothing. This is no way to live. I cannot say anything else. I'm so fed up with all this chaos. I've had enough!"

Klebanov looked deeply uncomfortable. Alongside him, Yevdokimov sat with his eyes cast down; Rutskoi rested his head in his hands. Nadezhda's words stunned the hall. Some sat in astonishment and embarrassment. But many more respected that this was a mother fighting for her son and urged her on.

She looked at Nikolai next to her. "My husband served for twenty-five years. For what? What was it all for? Tell me, for what? Just for me to bury my son? I'll never forgive you for this! Tear off your medals and shoulder boards!" she shouted. "Do it right now, right here, you son of a bitch!"

As she shouted and screamed abuse at Klebanov, Nadezhda failed to notice that a woman in a light-colored jacket was approaching from behind, holding a syringe. A naval officer tried to smother

Nadezhda's tirade with an embrace, while the nurse plunged the needle into Nadezhda's thigh.

She never saw the injection coming—she was too emotionally charged even to feel the jab through her clothing—but Nadezhda's body seized, her shouts stuck in her throat, her cries became a contorted whisper, and the muscles in her legs tightened. As she collapsed, the officer started to ease her out of the row of seats, half-dragging, half-carrying her out of the hall.

Several days later, video images of Nadezhda Tylik being forcibly sedated reached the outside world, shocking many viewers in the West. The scene chillingly recalled a time in the Soviet Union when medicine, like psychiatry, was used as a means of political control.

III: 11:30 A.M., SATURDAY, AUGUST 19
The Barents Sea

PRECISELY ONE WEEK AFTER the explosions sent the *Kursk* crashing to the seabed, the *Seaway Eagle* crossed the ill-defined line that separates the Norwegian and the Barents seas. The crew expected the Northern Fleet to be eagerly awaiting their arrival, but, strangely, there was no acknowledgment over the VHF radio from the Russians as they approached the *Kursk* site, only an ominous silence.

Aboard the *Eagle,* an animated debate began about the prospects for success. The history of seafaring is filled with accounts of people surviving against the odds. The consensus of opinion was that if the *Kursk* sailors had access to emergency equipment and possessed the necessary collective strength and training to stay calm, there remained a real chance that some of them were still huddled together near the escape hatch, awaiting evacuation. Just in terms of the physiology of breathing, there was a strong possibility there were survivors. The cavernous aft compartments of the *Kursk* contained large quantities of air. The ninth section was 19,420 cubic feet; the eighth compartment was nearly twice that size. If the survivors were breathing at a regular rate, using up about half a quart of oxygen a minute, they could keep going for days. With no detailed accounts of the damage to the sub, they could only speculate about how many sailors might still be awaiting help. The harsh reality remained that the fewer men still surviving, the more prospects they had of staying alive long enough to be rescued.

Even before he arrived, Graham Mann had a clear philosophy for the work that lay ahead. "Until I know for certain that the sailors are dead," he declared, "I will work on the assumption they are alive."

With her head start and slightly faster speed, the *Normand Pioneer,* carrying the precious LR5 strapped to her deck, was an hour ahead of the Stolt divers. But the Royal Navy effort was recovering from a severe blow. Commodore David Russell and his small team of advisers had been given initial authority to fly to Murmansk directly from their British base. The expectation was that they would be taken to the scene to work alongside Russian commanders and that together they would coordinate the multinational rescue operation. But when the Royal Air Force executive jet touched down at Bodø in Norway on Wednesday to refuel before the final leg to Murmansk, a telex was delivered to the aircraft: Permission to fly into Russia had been rescinded. The message concluded with the phrase, "It is no longer convenient to receive a British delegation."

Russell and his team were appalled. This wasn't about *convenience*—this was about saving people's lives. They weren't a *delegation*—they were professional submariners on a rescue mission. After the high hopes nurtured on the flight from the United Kingdom, the sense of exhilaration at doing something positive at last, the Russian move seemed beyond comprehension, not only clumsy but callous toward their own lost sailors.

In Moscow, the decision to halt Russell's flight appears to have been made by hardliners in the Defense Ministry who drew a distinction between accepting Western help and allowing Royal Navy officers to operate from Russian territory. A compromise was born. The foreign rescuers would be permitted to reach the accident site by sea, staying in international waters, but mustn't leave a "footprint" on the Kola Peninsula.

After the Russians had refused to let him fly straight to Murmansk, Russell had chosen to join the ship as she made her passage around the North Cape.

The Royal Navy submersible pilots, like the civilian divers on the *Eagle,* were astonished that so little was known about the condition of the *Kursk,* when the Russian rescuers had been inspecting the wreck for nearly a week. In an early situation report filed from the ship during her journey north, the rescuers sent a signal pleading for information to their own headquarters.

Are there Russian codes for hull-taps? When was the last tapping heard? Has any guaranteed tapping been heard? Could it have been systems settling? Is there any guarantee it was human-generated? What is the normal configuration of the escape system? How are the hatches left?

There had been little direct communication between the *Seaway Eagle* and the *Normand Pioneer,* but some details of how they planned to combine their resources had been discussed. Now as the two ships neared the disaster scene, Captain Paal Svendsen, the Norwegian responsible for coordinating the teams, decided to hold a summit meeting aboard the *Eagle.* Russian and British naval rescuers flew out to the ship. Svendsen hoped that the Northern Fleet would finally provide the necessary technical data. His ambition was to have an action plan firmly in place by the time they arrived.

This was a critical gathering, the first time the rescue specialists from all three nations would gather around the same table, the perfect opportunity to brainstorm the problems and formulate a detailed rescue plan. The key players—Admiral Verich, Commodore Russell, Captain Svendsen, and Graham Mann—were finally together. Only Admiral Popov was missing, still coordinating the Russian effort.

Under bright fluorescent lighting, the Russians lined one side of a crowded pine table in the *Eagle*'s cramped conference room, and the Royal Navy officers and Norwegian liaison staff found seats wherever they could. The throb of the engines at maximum power could be felt as the vessel surged eastward. The *Seaway Eagle* staff, who had come straight off the ship's decks to attend the meeting, were wearing their oil-smeared, high-visibility orange overalls; others were in jeans and casual shirts. The Russians sat stiffly in naval uniform, in a striking clash of cultures.

Mann sat at the head of the table. Engineer Matt Kirk also attended. His job was to draw up a formal task plan that would choreograph the entire rescue effort. Kirk now waited for the Russians to give him the extra information he so badly needed.

The meeting took an awkward turn right away. For a record of those attending, a blank piece of paper was passed around the table for people to sign. The Russians froze, looking at Verich in embarrassment and uncertainty. Mann watched in disbelief. If the Russians were reluctant even to write down their names without Verich's consent, they were unlikely to have the authority to make fast decisions about more important matters. Finally, they agreed to reveal their identities.

Even more troubling, Verich then embarked on a formal speech, thanking the Western specialists for helping in Russia's hour of need. Verich's interpreter laboriously translated the comments into English as his fellow officers nodded solemnly, but the admiral had badly misjudged the mood from the outset. The Western specialists were stunned by this ridiculous protocol. They expected only hard facts about the state of the sub and the latest information about possible survivors.

Mann lost his patience, interrupting Verich. "Admiral, surely speed is of the essence? So let me explain what we can achieve with our equipment and our divers. And then you must be clear about what you want us to do."

He then briefed Verich, carefully outlining what could be done and what was not possible. He explained the value of first putting down the ROVs to survey the wreck, and then described how divers would be capable of assessing possible damage to the escape hatch. They could also tap signals through the hull to the survivors and listen for a response.

Verich listened, shaking his head. "No. We are looking for the diving bell to land on the submarine," he insisted, "and for the divers to gain entry to the *Kursk* to confirm that it is fully flooded."

Mann and his team were shocked. How could he know that the aft compartments of the *Kursk* might be flooded? The only way to check whether water had leaked into the stern of the sub was by assessing the pressure differential at 350 feet between the ocean and the inside of the *Kursk,* and the Russians had never suggested this had been properly established. What were they all doing here if the Russians believed that the sub was flooded? Had all their work been devoted only to service an elaborate subterfuge? Besides, even Verich's rescue proposal was absurd. What did he mean, "land on the submarine"? Verich appeared to have little idea about Western diving technology; the bell couldn't "land" on the submarine. Rather, it would act as a high-tech elevator taking a team of three divers down to the depth of the *Kursk,* at which point two of the men would swim over to the hatch, the third remaining in the bell to oversee safety. And the Stolt team certainly would not consider opening the hatch. If they did what Verich wanted and the aft of the *Kursk* was still dry, the submarine would be flooded in the process and they would drown the sailors they were trying to save.

Remarkably, the Russians also announced that their own rescue efforts would continue, using their submersibles, for another twenty-four hours. Only at midday on Sunday would a decision be made about whether the Western teams would be allowed to begin operations.

In bewilderment, Russell implored Verich to understand that it was imperative the LR5 be deployed as soon as they arrived. They simply couldn't wait for another day to pass. Perhaps Verich was acting on out-of-date information about Western submersibles. "Admiral," Russell pointed out, "the Royal Navy rescue vehicle has been significantly improved in recent months. It has much better navigation and docking capabilities. I urge you to approve LR5's use at the first opportunity. You're also welcome to visit the *Normand Pioneer* to see the submersible for yourself."

Verich declined the offer, saying he had to get back to his own rescue ships. He then left the Western rescuers in stunned confusion. In an immediate signal filed back to Northwood, Russell wrote a signal that hinted at the frustration he now felt:

> The Russians informed us that there was nothing to add to the mass media reports about the *Kursk*. At no time did Admiral Verich address employment of LR5, which he discounted and was not even prepared to try.

Verich had certainly given a technically illiterate performance, but he was no fool. He had his reasons for stalling. The bitter struggle at the top of the Russian government over the role of the foreign rescuers had continued all of this time, even as the president was becoming directly involved.

Many of the Fleet officers were prepared to accept Western help, but many commanders in Moscow continued to believe the country's twin priorities were to protect Russia's naval secrets and avoid national humiliation. The debate was splitting the armed forces, polarizing opinion and inflaming passions. The newspaper *Sevodnya* captured the politicized and belligerent mood of the military hardliners when it quoted an official as saying, "Even if one sailor is saved from a Russian submarine with the help of foreigners, for the admirals this will be a political catastrophe."

At 8:27 P.M. on Saturday, in the cold blue light of the Arctic evening, the *Seaway Eagle* finally arrived at the disaster site. The specialists were prepared, the equipment readied, and the adrenaline flowing, but the Russians still hadn't approved a plan. After the nine-hundred-nautical-mile journey, Graham Mann and his crew now waited for instructions from the Northern Fleet commanders.

12

I: SATURDAY NIGHT
Southern Barents Sea

FROM HIS VANTAGE POINT on the *Eagle*'s bridge, Graham Mann scanned the wreck site, baffled. Ahead of him lay an empty stretch of water. Russian warships patrolled the perimeter, but there was no sign at all of a rescue effort. He had expected to see rescue ships supporting frantic submersible operations. The Northern Fleet had signaled the *Seaway Eagle* to move nine nautical miles to the west of the disaster scene; the *Normand Pioneer* was instructed to stay at an anchorage even farther away, at a distance of fourteen and a half nautical miles. Officially, they were told, the Fleet needed to "clear the area" ahead of more of their own submersible operations.

More than two hours after the Western vessels had arrived on site, with darkness descending, no more word had come from the Russians until, at last, a small boat could be seen heading toward the *Eagle* from the warship *Admiral Chabanenko*. The boat pulled up at 10:40 P.M. to the port side of the *Eagle,* and a pilot ladder was lowered. Admiral Verich was coming back on board, this time to take charge of the next phase of the rescue operation.

Walking unsteadily behind Verich was a squat, tough-looking Russian officer, visibly exhausted, with heavily bloodshot eyes. The diving specialists in the *Eagle* eyed this man with extreme curiosity. He was one of the crew from the Priz submersible, and evident on his bruised and puffy face were the classic symptoms of "the squeeze," caused when a diver endures a rapid rise of pressure while underwater. The sudden pressure sucks a diving mask violently onto the face, rupturing blood vessels around the eyes. These telltale marks were a sobering reminder that the Russian crews had been desperately engaged in a week-long life-and-death struggle.

Since the three-nation summit a few hours earlier, Mann had been thinking through his options. His first aim was to deploy both unmanned ROVs to assess the conditions. The larger vehicle, known as SCV 006, or Zero Six for short, was a highly capable underwater robot, weighing two tons and powered by six thrusters. Costing nearly $1 million, it had a full range of instruments, a sonar with a range of three hundred yards, and two sophisticated low-light cameras. The other ROV was called Sea Owl, a much smaller "flying eyeball" that could shoot close-up video. Mann was also contemplating a bolder move. If the Russian Priz submersible couldn't dock with the *Kursk* under its own power, perhaps he could attach the mini-sub to one of the *Eagle*'s cranes and lower it directly onto the escape hatch. The *Eagle* could be maneuvered until she was in precisely the right position over the ninth compartment. Essentially, the Russian submersible would be handled like a specialized diving bell. This had never been tried before, but now was the time for innovative solutions, and Mann's mind was racing, trying to think of fresh options to place before the Russians.

Suddenly moving into high gear, Mann decided to put two diving teams into saturation. A total of six men would enter the compression chambers and be "blown down" to 350 feet, and they would stay at this pressure for the duration of the mission. The eight other divers would be kept on standby. Dive Team One would comprise Tony Scott, Paal Dinessen, and Jim Mallen; Dive Team Two would be Ali Clark, John Hvalve, and Stuart Bain. A political logic lay behind Mann's selection: Both teams included British and Norwegian divers. They were also experienced, calm men Mann could trust.

With Verich back on board, Mann convened another meeting with the Russian delegation. Again, he wanted no protocol or formality but fast, clear decisions. He asked Verich for permission to start ROV survey operations immediately and to put divers into the water to perform a visual inspection of the aft escape hatch. His six divers were ready to be transferred into the diving bell for the journey down to the submarine. The request should have been a formality.

Verich shook his head. "I cannot permit your cameras to conduct a full survey of the submarine. They must stay at the aft of the *Kursk* and never forward of the emergency buoy positioned between the seventh and eighth section." This was ludicrous. "If I am putting men into the water," Mann angrily insisted, "I need to conduct a survey of the whole area. This is an elementary safety precaution."

The idea of being limited to assessing one small area of the huge wreck was unacceptable. The conning tower of an Oscar II—the sail or fin, as it's known to modern-day submariners—rears high above the hull, a colossal structure. If diving operations were to proceed safely, with a bell in the water over the *Kursk,* Mann had to know its exact measurements and location. The propellers were also a serious hazard and needed to be properly examined and mapped. In addition, Mann was worried about weapons or jagged debris that might be lying on the seabed. In the offshore business, a survey of the ocean floor is absolutely routine, a basic first step to ensure that the divers' umbilical cords stay clear of wreckage.

Working through a translator, the discussion dragged on. To the Stolt team, the survey was a matter of safety; to the Russians it was an issue of national security. Gesturing at plans of an Oscar II submarine that he had downloaded off the Internet and printed, Mann also pointed out that the emergency buoy was a risk. If it suddenly released, it could strike the divers or the bell, or even become entangled in the thrusters of the *Eagle* herself.

Verich glanced at the Internet plans and waved away Mann's concerns. "There's no buoy in that position on the hull of the *Kursk.* Don't worry about it."

Engineer Matt Kirk observed the night-long battle of wills between

Mann and Verich. He struggled to concentrate, his mind constantly straying, thinking about the scene a few miles away and 350 feet down. He tried to imagine the situation for the men inside the *Kursk*, the best part of eight days after the accident. Could some still be alive down there, trapped and terrified in the stern of the submarine, presumably enduring freezing and pitch-black conditions? He struggled to reconcile the desperate urgency of the sailors' predicament with the ill-tempered bargaining going on around the table.

With nothing agreed, Mann made a final appeal to Verich. "Admiral, we're all trying to achieve the same goal. We're all humans. We all want to try to bring people out of the *Kursk* alive. Let's work together. Let's agree on a way forward right now."

Verich asked to review Mann's plans yet again.

"Believe me, Admiral, we know what we are doing. To us, this is not difficult. We operate at this depth as a matter of routine and deal with valves and hatches all the time in sub-sea construction work. We want to get on with our job. We are diving professionals; we do this for a living."

Those around the table were now slumped in their seats, physically and emotionally exhausted. Outside, visible through the conference room's two portholes, dawn was beginning to break. The ominous silhouettes of warships at anchor emerged out of the darkness.

Mann fought to control his temper. He had the distinct feeling that Verich was still playing for time, throwing up obstacles, finding reasons for saying no. He wasn't much interested in the politics of the disaster—he preferred to leave it to others to puzzle over Russian motives—but in all his years at sea he had never encountered a mentality like it.

Suddenly, after those in the room had almost given up hope of any progress, Verich leaned forward and stared intently at Mann. He was smiling for the first time. His translated words cut through the fatigue, with a jolt of surprise.

"OK, let's do it. Let's go ahead."

The dive was on.

Kirk sat in his small, windowless office in the bowels of the ship. Somehow he now had to come up with a feasible, step-by-step guide to the diving operation that Verich would approve, even though he had still not received from the Russians the kind of data he normally needed. Determined to push ahead, he started typing:

> *Project:* Kursk *diver intervention*
> *Work site: Barents Sea, Russia*
> *Task Plan: 01*
> *Date: 20.08.00*
> *Task Objective:*
> *1. ROV survey with SCV 006 of stern escape hatch*
> *2. Diver check for signs of life on board submarine*
> *3. Diver close visual inspection of hatch, sealing ring and trunking*
> *4. Equalize pressure in escape trunking*
> *5. Open escape hatch*

Kirk kept the plan simple. The less information he put down on paper, the less the Russians could argue over. Once the divers were down at the *Kursk,* the plan could be adapted, depending on what they discovered. This was not yet a plan to rescue survivors—without the Royal Navy's submersible, no Russian sailors were going to be brought to the surface, and Verich had still not approved the use of the LR5—but at least it achieved Mann's main goal of getting Western technology down to the *Kursk* so that they could try to make contact with survivors. Once divers reached the hatch, their first step would be to knock out a signal on the hull of the sub to which any survivors would hopefully respond. Trying to anticipate the issues ahead, Kirk made a checklist of some of the likely hazards:

> * *confirm status of armaments on sub and possibility of detonation*
> * *check for radiation levels*
> * *check potential entrapment areas e.g. propellers*

He drafted "Task Plan Number One" in just forty-five minutes and presented it to Verich and Mann for approval. Just after 4 A.M. on Sunday, Verich scrawled his signature on the document. Verich had won the battle to make sure that none of the *Eagle*'s high-tech monitoring equipment ventured forward of the reactor compartment; Mann had won the struggle to get the rescue mission under way.

The *Eagle* had been kept in the holding area for a total of seven hours and fifty-nine minutes. A third of a day, precious time, had been wasted for no reason.

II: 4:26 A.M., SUNDAY, AUGUST 20
69°36'59"N, 37°34'26"E

LESS THAN THIRTY MINUTES after the deal was signed with Verich, the *Seaway Eagle* left her holding position and sailed the nine nautical miles to the waters precisely above the submarine. Captain Rasmussen maneuvered the vessel until she was exactly 328 feet behind the *Kursk*'s stern. No one wanted the ship sitting directly above the torpedo compartment. The vessel's thrusters and computers were tested to make sure they were all working for the diving operations ahead. For an indefinite period, the ship would hold her position, despite wind, waves, and currents. In fact, the conditions were nearly perfect. The ship log noted that the ocean was in "sea state 2," with wavelets less than two feet high.

At 8:10 A.M., the ROV SCV 006, Zero Six, was slowly lowered into the water. A "pilot" operated the ROV from a control room in the ship, using a fiber-optic-linked joystick. The young Norwegian "flying" the machine took it down to a depth of about 300 feet, just 75 feet above the seabed, and then kept the ROV in an almost stationary hover as its sonar searched for the vast steel hulk of the *Kursk*. At twice the size of a jumbo jet and longer than a soccer field, the submarine would present the dive team with many problems, but finding her was not anticipated to be one of them.

Incredibly, the ROV detected nothing. The sonar received absolutely no signal. The *Kursk* had apparently vanished. There was confusion aboard the *Eagle*. The Russians had passed on the precise coordinates. She couldn't just go missing.

The ROV pilot quickly checked his instruments while the dive supervisors stared over his shoulder. The video display from the special low-light camera on Zero Six revealed nothing. Then, after several minutes of flying the ROV in different search patterns, a faint signal "pinged" back. Zero Six had found its target. The confusion turned to amazement as the men realized that the acoustic tiles on the outer hull of the *Kursk* were so effective that they had been absorbing the ROV's active sonar signals. Only the huge twin bronze propellers, standing high in the water like seven-bladed Turkish knives, betrayed the lurking mass of the submarine.

On board the *Eagle*, riggers, deck foremen, and mechanics alike crowded around the video monitors in fascination, as Zero Six glided effortlessly toward the submarine. The divers also watched on small screens inside their pressure chambers as the *Kursk*'s image emerged from the gloom. No one who saw the *Kursk* that day was left untouched by the sheer scale of the submarine, the immensity of her design and the ambition of her engineering.

The exact position could now be verified and logged: She lay at 69°36'59"N, 37°34'26"E. Her bow was pointing in a direction of between 285° and 290°, and the hull was lying on the seabed at 8° bow down, with virtually no list. The Russians, by contrast, had initially spoken of the *Kursk* resting at an angle of 25° with a list of 60° to port.

The radiation monitors registered zero. Inside the submarine, the conditions might be very different, but there appeared to be no external leaking from the two nuclear reactors. The pictures showed that there was also no visible structural damage to the outer hull around the ninth compartment. There did appear to be some cracking to the starboard side of the escape hatch, but the divers would be able to examine that in more detail. The specialists aboard the *Eagle* could now see for themselves that much of the information the Russians had given them was indeed pure fiction. The reports about the three-knot current and poor visibility bore no resemblance to the reality around the *Kursk*.

On the bridge, Mark Nankivell, one of the dive supervisors, hunched forward over his monitor, staring at the stream of pictures coming from the ROV. To his expert eye, the hatch and its immediate surroundings looked in excellent condition, but over his shoulder Admiral Verich started shouting excitedly, pointing out a crack along the outer tiling. He told a Russian cameraman on board the *Eagle* to zoom in on this part of the picture. Nankivell glanced at Verich in surprise. The crack Verich had spotted was of no consequence, just a poor join between the acoustic tiles surrounding the hatch. Then Nankivell realized why this insignificant crack mattered so much. If the Russians could say that the hatch was damaged or distorted, they could explain why their own rescue attempts had failed. Verich *needed* a fault in the hatch mechanism. How else to explain seven days of missed opportunities?

Inside the dive chamber, Tony Scott, Paal Dinessen, and Jim Mallen lay on their bunks, waiting for news. The chamber system is a thick green-steel capsule positioned deep in the *Eagle*'s hold. Immediately next to it is the control room, where the life-support technicians keep a twenty-four-hour eye on the gauges that monitor the chamber's atmosphere. The divers are cut off from the outside world while they breathe a mix of gases known as Heliox—95 percent helium and 5 percent oxygen. Food and drinks are passed through an equipment "lock" to allow the chamber to stay isolated from the atmospheric pressure outside.

Saturation divers have a knack for killing time in these claustrophobic conditions. Many are able to sleep over prolonged periods to try to escape the boredom, but the men of Dive Team One were all wide awake. Scott was listening to his Walkman to calm his nerves. The others were flicking through magazines.

Just after 9 A.M. on Sunday, they were notified by the life-support technicians that the next stage of the task plan, the inspection of the ninth hatch, would shortly begin. Scott ordered his usual breakfast of toast and cereal, which was passed through the lock and into the chamber, and started his steady preparations. Routine is everything for the divers. They stick to well-rehearsed preparations honed over years of working on oil and gas projects, never rushing and always cross-checking. When established patterns are broken, accidents happen.

Matt Kirk's task plan was passed to the divers through the locks, and they studied his approximate drawings of the submarine's dimensions and the hatch mechanism. From the divers' perspective, things looked encouraging: The ROV survey had revealed excellent visibility, minimal current, and zero radiation.

Jim Mallen was acting as the bellman, and he now began his pre-dive routine, entering the bell and reconnecting the electrical fittings. He also checked the valve positions and communications. During the dive, he would stay inside the bell, monitoring the progress of the other two, ready to intervene at any moment. Control of the dive and all instructions would be managed by the supervisors on board the *Eagle*. Each man's helmet had a camera attached to it, which beamed live pictures back to Dive Control. Everyone would be able to monitor exactly what the two men outside the bell were doing and seeing.

The technology and equipment around the divers has, again, largely been developed by companies supporting the offshore industry. Working in cold waters raises particular challenges, and the process of breathing helium compounds those problems because helium conducts heat away from the body seven times faster than air. Keeping the divers warm is a vital part of all underwater operations, since both icy seas and the helium mix accelerate heat drain. The solution is simple but revolutionary: As the divers work, warm water is delivered between the layers of their suits. The men wear what they call a "woolly bear"—a thick one-piece fleece—or multiple layers of soft normal clothing. Over that they wear their neoprene "hot-water suit" with its network of pipes that feed warm water over their arms, legs, chest, and back. The water pumped down the umbilical is kept at 109 degrees Fahrenheit, and, having circulated, exits at the ankles and wrists. Essentially, the diver is cocooned in a hot-water bath.

Once Mallen had completed his checks, Scott and Dinessen moved through to the transfer chamber to put on their clothing and harnesses. At 10:55 A.M., the aft bell was gingerly lowered through the moon-pool—the carefully engineered hole in the hull of a ship through which a diving bell can safely be lowered directly into the ocean. There was no disguising the anxiety and excitement inside the bell. Pretending this was just another job wasn't working. This was different. Dive Team One was on its way down to a crippled Russian nuclear submarine.

Mallen helped Scott put on his heavy diving helmet and the bail-out bottle, the twin set of reserve gas canisters he carried on his back. The bell was pressurized to a depth of 335 feet. Once they reached that depth, the pressure inside and outside would equalize, and the door on the bottom of the bell could be eased open.

The dive supervisors stopped the bell 50 feet to port of the *Kursk*'s casing. They didn't want it directly over the hatch, knowing that any gases escaping from the submarine would ascend vertically and could contaminate the carefully controlled atmosphere in the bell. Once again, they were sticking to offshore safety rules: A diving bell should never sit directly above a hazardous work area.

The *Eagle*'s "black box" videotapes recorded every part of the operation, the dialogue between the supervisors and the divers as well as the technical data. These tapes form the basis of the account that follows. The dive began at 11:06 A.M., when Scott left the bell and dropped out into the open ocean.

III: AT THE NINTH HATCH

SCOTT CALMLY CONFIRMED TO Dive Control that he was outside the confines of the bell.

"Diver One in the water," he reported via his umbilical.

"Diver One in the water," the dive supervisor, Mark Nankivell, repeated in confirmation.

Scott stood on the frame below the bell until Dinessen joined him, staring out to starboard and slightly below him to see what awaited. He couldn't make out the black hull at that distance and found it impossible to gain any perspective. The Sea Owl ROV, the small "eye" that was monitoring the operation, hovered close to the hull and used its light as a powerful underwater torch to show the way.

Staring back at Scott like a bright beacon was the white ring that encircled the emergency hatch. He was hugely relieved. The hatch was an ideal target to swim toward. As for the rest of the *Kursk*, he could see nothing. With Dinessen paying out the umbilical cord, the swim was easy. A few kicks of his fins, and Scott was safely away from the bell and heading for the hatch.

When he reached the hull, he touched the acoustic tiles of the *Kursk*, for the first time directly encountering the amazing size of the submarine. He expected to find the casing of the hull to be slightly curved, but Scott found himself staring at a huge expanse of flat steel. Neither the propellers at the stern nor the tower ahead of him was visible. The dark hull simply tapered off into the blackness of the ocean. It was nearly impossible to believe that a disaster had engulfed the submarine. From his vantage point, there appeared to be nothing wrong with the *Kursk*. There was no visible damage, no ruptured metal or twisted steel.

He connected a rope, known as a "swim line," between the hatch and the bell to make it easier to transit to and from the submarine, and peered down at the Geiger counter he was carrying.

"Zero reading on the Geiger counter," he reported back.

"You're going to do some tapping," Nankivell instructed Scott.

Tapping out a code on the hull of a submarine may seem a primitive technique for making contact with trapped men, but it is effective. Sound travels exceptionally well underwater. Any heavy knocks on the outer hull would be clearly heard by survivors. The Russians had given exact instructions on where the tapping should be done and what code should be used. The spot chosen was a recessed area called the lifting-pad eye, immediately in front of the hatch and welded directly onto the pressure hull. The emergency code was four sets of four taps—sixteen strikes against the hull in total.

"I'll wait for Paal to come over and then start tapping," Scott said.

"No," Nankivell replied. "Leave Paal on the bell."

"I am going to tap on the lifting-pad eye."

"Yes, copy. Four taps, four times."

Scott pulled the hammer from the webbing around his harness, fighting against the water resistance in slow motion. He struck the hull four times in succession, then again, and again, and again. "Performed with some vigor," the official log dryly noted. Tiny flakes of paint floated away with each strike.

Scott leaned forward so that his diving helmet was resting on the edge of the hatch, metal on metal. Any noise or vibration from within the *Kursk* would be more easily detected that way. In this position, Scott wouldn't just hear a cry for help—he would actually *feel* it. To all those watching on the video monitors, Scott seemed almost to be bowing his head in prayer, willing a response.

Then Scott inhaled deeply and held his breath. He didn't want the rasping of helium being sucked down his umbilical cord to obscure the slightest sound from the submarine. Scott wasn't sure what would frighten him more: no response or a reply from deep within the *Kursk*. He tried to picture the scene on the other side of the hull. Was it a flooded compartment with floating corpses, or were there men still alive in there, their hopes soaring as they realized that divers had finally arrived?

For an interminable few seconds, there was absolute silence. If the survivors were too weak to knock back, Scott thought, perhaps they would find the strength to drop a tool. He continued to listen carefully, his heart pumping hard. Dinessen stood above him on the rim of the diving bell. Dive Control briefly switched off communications to the divers to cut out any static in their helmets, and Sea Owl's thrusters were slowed to lessen noise in the surrounding ocean.

Then Scott hammered the code again. Four quick strikes, four times in succession, against ice-cold steel. "Don't tap any more. Just listen," Nankivell urged.

In the *Eagle*'s Dive Control, no one moved a muscle. The eyes of the supervisors, the Russians, and life-support technicians were glued to the monitors and instruments. Any sound from inside the *Kursk,* however faint, would send a shock wave through the crew and trigger an intensive new phase of the rescue mission.

But from the giant hull came only silence. No response, however, did *not* mean no life. There were several scenarios that could explain why survivors were not acknowledging Scott's hammering: They might be unconscious; they might be too weak to tap back; they might be trapped under debris or machinery. The statistics of atmosphere and breathing were well known to the offshore divers: Normally, air is 21 percent of the atmosphere; if it is "breathed down" to 18 percent, mental abilities deteriorate; at 16 percent unconsciousness will occur; and only when the air is reduced to about 12 percent of the atmosphere will most people begin to die. The sailors could be somewhere in this horrific twilight world, unable to respond but still alive. There was another possibility, too, one that reflected the psychological horrors of being trapped inside a disabled submarine for eight days: The sailors might be suffering mental breakdowns, unable to comprehend the message of hope they were hearing.

After sixty seconds, Scott tried a third time. Again, nothing. Hoping against hope, he tried one more time, banging out his message.

"No response, then?" Nankivell asked.

"No response," Scott replied. Even with the helium-induced distortion to his voice, his disappointment could not be disguised.

From the edge of the diving bell, Dinessen spoke up. "I can help him listen."

"OK, off you go," authorized Nankivell.

"When Paal gets here, I'll have another go," Scott insisted. He simply refused to give up hope.

13

I: SUNDAY AFTERNOON
Barents Sea

THE OMINOUS SILENCE THAT followed the divers' tapping was deeply disheartening for those in the *Seaway Eagle*. There was no question that the heavy thud of the hammer would have resonated deep within the *Kursk,* so if there were survivors trapped in the stern compartment, there was some unknown reason they weren't responding. Graham Mann, for one, was not yet prepared to accept that the silence meant that all the sailors were dead; it was circumstantial evidence that no one was left alive, but it was certainly not proof.

Above all, Mann needed to find out if the ninth compartment was flooded. Verich appeared to believe that it was, but the Norwegian and British specialists were not so sure. The Russians, after all, could have their own reasons for wanting to end the week-long rescue effort, which was now playing as a major international embarrassment for the Northern Fleet. Besides, the video from the ROVs and the hard evidence from the *Eagle* divers revealed that the outside of the aft of the *Kursk* appeared to be in almost pristine condition.

But the problem was this: Any attempt to open the hatch into the submarine to assess the conditions inside would immediately flood the compartment. If there were unconscious survivors, they would be drowned. Far from being saviors, the *Eagle* team could end up unwittingly killing the very men they were trying to rescue. This knowledge made Mann determined to proceed cautiously.

The technical riddle facing Mann was in fact even more complicated: There were *two* hatches that needed to be opened. The top hatch opened outward and led from the ocean into the escape tower. The second hatch was at the bottom of that tower, and it swung inward, down into the compartment itself.

Puzzling over the conundrum, the experts came up with a two-step plan for gaining access to the submarine. The first stage involved finding out if the escape tower was flooded; the second part would be to establish the state of the lower hatch and the compartment itself.

If the escape tower was filled with water, this would be an indication that the interior of the sub was also flooded, although it was still conceivable that water had seeped through damaged valves around the hull but not penetrated the lower hatch. In addition, if the tower was flooded, it would be exceptionally difficult for the LR5 to dock with the hatch. The pressure would be equal on both sides of the hatch, and no vacuum could be created to keep the submersible in place. Furthermore, a flooded tower would make it almost impossible for rescuers to get down through the column of water and open the lower hatch into the *Kursk*'s ninth compartment. Mann decided to cope with that predicament when and if it arose.

The engineers in the *Eagle* devised a technically simple method of assessing whether the escape tower was flooded. The brilliance of the plan lay in the fact that they wouldn't need to open the hatch to gain the information. Instead, they would use the hatch's equalization valve, or e-valve, to reveal the state of the tower. The e-valve has a special purpose for submariners facing an emergency. To escape from a sub, a sailor first opens the lower hatch and clambers up a ladder and into the escape tower. But the upper hatch is being held down by the massive weight of water. The way to circumvent that problem, and escape to the surface, is to flood the escape tower until the pressure inside and outside are the same, allowing the upper hatch to be pushed open. That is the role played by the e-valve. By opening the valve tap from the inside, the sailor can allow outside seawater to pour into the tower and equalize the pressure while he breathes from his own air canister.

Thinking through the process in reverse, the engineers aboard the *Eagle* realized that opening the e-valve from the outside would tell them whether the escape tower was filled with water. If they opened the valve just a little and water was sucked into the tower, it meant there was a pressure differential and it must be dry. But if opening the e-valve did not trigger a flow of water into the sub, it meant the pressure was already equal on both sides of the upper hatch. That could only be the result of the tower already being flooded.

Before performing this procedure, the divers were instructed to inspect the outer hatch to make sure it wasn't damaged. The huge shock waves that had raced down the hull of the submarine during the explosions could easily have distorted the hatch. Scott and Dinessen were asked to perform what's known as a "CVI," a close visual inspection. Scott scrutinized the area around the hatch, running his hands over it. Through his mask, he could clearly see some narrow gouges and scratching on the outer rim of the cover, but overall the hatch appeared to be in excellent shape.

"So there's no obvious damage?" Nankivell asked.

"No distortions," Scott confirmed.

The two divers then turned their attention to the narrow gap in the tiles running up to the hatch, the crack that had been spotted with such excitement by Admiral Verich. Sure enough, this wasn't damage at all but simply a poor join between two of the acoustic tiles, as Nankivell had suspected. Scott used his diving knife to make sure, wedging it between the tiles. The rubber matting had slightly separated, but nothing more. "Not metal fatigue, just a rubber crack," Nankivell agreed from above.

Visual distortions, however, are common underwater, especially through the thick glass of a diving helmet. A straight metal bar across the hatch was the best way to establish if there was buckling. "Let's get the straightedge and put it across," Nankivell told Scott.

Meanwhile, Dinessen was studying and measuring the scratches on the hatch. "Thirty-five millimeters long, ten millimeters wide, and maybe one millimeter deep," he reported. The only other damage was to a little steel rod protruding from the structure that appeared badly bent and twisted to one side. Unknown to Dinessen or Scott, this was the small rod that Priz pilot Andrei Sholokhov had descended onto during his dramatic bid to seal with the hatch three days earlier. The scratches were the result of the repeated attempts by the Russians to maneuver over the ninth compartment.

After confirming with the straightedge that the hatch was not distorted, Scott was instructed to go ahead and open the equalization valve fractionally, to study the water flow. To help analyze the flow, divers normally use dye. This time they used milk. Scott carefully squeezed some of the liquid into the water around the valve inlet.

This was the procedure that would reveal whether the escape tower was flooded. There was no risk of accidentally flooding the compartment—the e-valve was a "needle" design that required eleven rotations to be fully opened. It could be quickly closed if the milky water was being sucked through the valve.

At this critical point of the technical investigation of the hatch, the crew of the *Seaway Eagle* entered into one of the strangest episodes of the *Kursk* drama.

The Russian specialists aboard the *Eagle* told the divers that the e-valve opened counterclockwise, stressing that if it was turned the wrong way, the valve could break, effectively transforming the *Kursk* into a sealed tomb and ending any rescue hopes. Scott tried at first to open the valve by hand; then he used a wrench. The valve hardly budged. Scott assessed at most it had moved just one-sixteenth of a turn. As he strained at the valve, he constantly reminded himself that if there was any suction of water into the hatch, he should stop immediately, for that would mean the escape tower was dry. The small white cloud of milk showed no directional flow, just slowly spreading outward.

He realized he needed some extra leverage in order to apply more force to the valve and, after a brief discussion with the divers and careful study of the Sea Owl video, a tool was quickly welded in the *Eagle*'s workshop to fit the valve. Within minutes, the tool was being lowered down to the hatch using the aft crane, into the hands of Scott. Verich was astonished at how quickly the *Eagle* engineers had moved from seeing a problem to improvising a solution, and he nodded his congratulations.

Now Scott was able to put a lot more leverage into turning the valve. But when he tried again, it moved only a fraction more.

"It's solid?" dive supervisor Graham Legg asked from Dive Control.

"It moved a little bit," Scott reported.

"Any flow, you close," Legg reminded Scott. He was deeply worried about flooding the submarine compartment. He also recognized that they needed to put their heads together about why the e-valve wouldn't open. "OK, lads, stop what you're doing. We need to think about it." The divers sat on the *Kursk*'s casing, awaiting further instructions.

One horrible possibility now struck all those puzzling over the situation: Perhaps the valve was already wide open. But if so, who had opened it? A possible answer hit the dive supervisors like a high-voltage shock. Had the *Kursk* sailors themselves opened the valve in an attempt to reach the surface? Had they flooded the tower as the first stage of opening the hatch and escaping? Was it even possible that some survivors had actually left the *Kursk,* only to perish on the surface? This train of thought led to immediate safety concerns.

If the valve had been opened and no one had escaped, there must be a submariner trapped in the tower. Graham Legg and Garry Ball in Dive Control realized that if the upper hatch was now opened, the body of a *Kursk* sailor, presumably wearing a lifejacket, would surge to the surface. As the lid swung open, a corpse might strike a diver working directly over the hatch. If the dead sailor was fully dressed for an emergency ascent, he would shoot out of the hatch with considerable velocity at that depth. A lifejacket alone has forty-four pounds of buoyancy. For Scott and Dinessen, who were right there above the hatch, this possibility posed a macabre hazard.

Not wanting to alarm the divers with this scenario, Legg radioed down to Scott and Dinessen again. "OK, don't do anything. Just relax for the time being."

Legg was a veteran of undersea disasters and had considerable experience working with corpses trapped underwater. He felt that the divers should be warned about what lay ahead, including the risk that if they tried to grab the body as it shot out of the tower, it might start to disintegrate in their grip. Ball disagreed, believing that too much ghoulish detail might spook the divers.

Down below, Scott reached his own conclusion. "You could have someone trapped in there," he warned the supervisors.

"Yes, if you think about it, you're right," Legg replied. "I don't have to explain. You're on hold for the time being."

All of a sudden, they faced the prospect of confronting their first body, not neatly contained in the ninth compartment, as they had expected, but ready to explode from the hatch. Treating the dead with sensitivity was a priority. With so much video footage being filmed, both from the divers' helmets and the ROVs, any pictures of an escaping corpse might eventually be leaked to the press and could cause deep distress to the families of the submariners.

Tony Scott was not worried about how a corpse might look, or what might happen if he grabbed it, but he did feel real anxiety about the possibility of a body either striking him around his helmet or getting caught up in his umbilical cord. "We're going to need a bag or something," he suggested. He knew he wouldn't be able to hold a corpse with positive buoyancy at that depth. Scott needed something with which to catch and trap the body.

Above the divers, workers aboard the *Eagle* began searching for a suitable means of trapping a corpse. Finally, the deck foreman realized that the heavy, open-meshed safety netting normally hung below the gangway when the ship is at a dock would be perfect for the job.

All the while, technicians in the *Eagle* continued to debate whether or not the valve was really open. Maybe it was simply jammed. Or maybe, just possibly, the Russians were wrong about the way in which it opened. They had said counterclockwise, and it seemed impossible that the Northern Fleet specialists could get a detail as basic as that incorrect. But just in case, Legg once again checked with the translators: Were the Russian technicians absolutely certain that the valve opened counterclockwise? The answer came back: yes, counterclockwise to open, clockwise to close. The reverse would risk breaking it.

A short while later, armed with the netting, Tony Scott resumed his effort to turn the e-valve.

"It's solid—very, very hard," he informed Dive Control again. "Can I have permission to turn it the other way?"

The supervisors looked at one another and around Dive Control. The Russians weren't anywhere near. They wouldn't be at all happy, but this was Scott's chance.

"OK, Tony, why not turn it in a clockwise direction?" Legg ventured.

Seconds later there was a shout of excitement from Scott. "It's moved straightaway," he reported.

Incredibly, the Russians either didn't know which way the valve turned or they had lied. All the worry over whether a body might be trapped in the tower had been without cause. Since the valve had actually been closed, no escape attempt had apparently been made.

Scott turned the valve little by little, checking constantly for water flow into the escape tower, but even after four rotations, he detected only the slightest flow toward the hatch. The tower must surely be flooded.

The situation was now perplexing, even for the technically gifted engineers aboard the *Eagle*. With the escape tower flooded, and the pressure equalized, the upper hatch door should swing open. But it stayed stubbornly and mysteriously closed, suggesting that there was still a pressure differential between the tower and the ocean. To add some pulling power, the divers tied a lifting bag to the upper hatch and inflated it to apply 550 pounds of buoyancy. The hatch still didn't budge.

Despite Admiral Verich's dismissive view of the LR5 submersible, one bold Russian officer stepped forward to try and push things ahead. Oleg Burtsev, a three-star admiral and commander of the First Submarine Flotilla, visited the *Normand Pioneer* to assess the Royal Navy's rescue equipment. Openly contradicting what Verich had said aboard the *Eagle*, he requested that the mini-sub be deployed as soon as possible. He even offered to fly an Oscar II submarine engineer to the *Pioneer* to discuss technical matters with the Royal Navy team. The *Kursk* served in his flotilla, Gennady Lyachin was his friend, and the crew was his responsibility. Burtsev appeared haggard, at times close to tears, openly disillusioned with how Moscow was handling the crisis.

Russell felt that at last he had built up a personal rapport with a Russian admiral. In his next situation report, he noted:

> Atmosphere with Admiral Burtsev was businesslike and extremely warm throughout. There appears to be considerable confusion about what the Russian plan is and who is in charge of it. Nevertheless, Burtsev is clearly a man who is well motivated and liable to get things moving.

But Russell was wrong about Burtsev's ability to overcome the political constraints being imposed on the Northern Fleet. As soon as he left the *Pioneer*, the Russian admiral was overruled by hardliners in Moscow, who continued to believe that hopes for an espionage coup were shaping Western motives.

Looking on in frustration and feeling the strain of the mounting pressure from the Defense Ministry to resolve the *Kursk* crisis one way or the other, Verich demanded that Mann simply rip off the top hatch using the *Eagle*'s cranes. Mann angrily brushed aside Verich's request. Even if the escape tower was flooded, he reminded Verich that there was still the lower hatch to consider. There was a remote chance that the ninth compartment might be dry, and Mann was adamant he would not bow to political pressure.

Verich then ordered Mann to leave the equalization valve open from now on, even when the divers were not working at the submarine. It was not a request, it was an instruction, and Verich did not expect to be contradicted.

He had underestimated Mann. As soon as Verich walked away, the offshore manager quietly phoned Graham Legg and Garry Ball in Dive Control.

"The Russians have asked us to leave the e-valve open," he told them. "I am instructing you to ignore that. Make certain the valve is shut before the divers return to the surface."

He took no pleasure in defying the orders of the Russian Navy's search-and-rescue chief, but there are times to follow your client's wishes and, just occasionally, times to follow your conscience.

A launch headed the short distance from the *Peter the Great* cruiser toward the *Seaway Eagle*. Verich was visibly agitated at the prospect of a top military officer arriving who would outrank and possibly overrule him.

Admiral Viacheslav Popov, commander-in-chief of the Northern Fleet, stepped aboard, surrounded by a group of staff officers. There was a cordial exchange of greetings and a firm handshake as Mann and Popov were introduced. They sized each other up; they could scarcely have been more different characters. When Popov was commanding Soviet nuclear submarines on Cold War patrols, Mann was spending his youth treasure-hunting in the South China Sea. Popov was deeply loyal and patriotic; Mann had no time for rank or hierarchy. Both were savvy and had made a living working under the surface of the world's oceans, but in terms of values, background, and outlook, they had nothing in common. Mann also recognized wryly that this was not exactly a meeting of balanced forces. Popov had direct authority over tens of thousands of men and command of dozens of warships; Mann had under him about fifty men—the divers and their support team—and command of no ships, not even the one they were standing on.

Popov wasted no time. To Mann's astonishment, Popov launched into an immediate attack on the *Seaway Eagle* team, asserting that the Stolt divers were psychologically ill-suited to the operation. Mann stared at Popov in disbelief. How dare he make that accusation? Yes, there had been concern about corpses, but only from the standpoint of the safety of Scott and Dinessen. His team included some of the most experienced and emotionally stable men in the business.

Believing for a moment that the translation must be mistaken, Mann turned to the interpreter. "Please ask the admiral to repeat what he just said." Popov's concerns were repeated exactly as before. Verich had obviously reported to Popov that the Stolt divers were frightened. Few things irritated Mann more than his men being patronized, especially by a fleet that had so badly mishandled the rescue operation and had distributed an array of false and misleading information.

Controlling his tone, careful not to raise his voice but looking Popov squarely in the face, Mann framed his response. "Admiral, understand this. My men have worked under the sea all their lives. They have worked on many disasters. They have seen bodies that have been submerged for a day, a week, even a year. They retrieved the dead from the Piper Alpha oil-rig disaster. They pulled corpses from the Alexander Keiland platform that sank with over a hundred lives off Norway. Quite frankly, they have seen sights far worse than those they will encounter here."

Popov stared back at Mann, then switched his gaze to Verich, who visibly blanched. The Russian commander shrugged. "But your technicians are not adequately trained to work on this submarine. They do not understand the hatch mechanisms. They are not technically aware of our systems."

This was too much for Mann. He spoke through gritted teeth.

"Admiral Popov, your officers misled us about which way to turn the valve. They provided us with no adequate diagrams or technical sketches. I promise you this: When we finally get the accurate information from your engineers, we will get this job done."

The *Seaway Eagle* and the *Peter the Great* were at anchor no more than two nautical miles apart, but after the misunderstandings that had built up, they might as well have been in different oceans. Popov was taken aback by Mann's candid manner and open criticism. He expected deference to his rank and expressions of sympathy from the Westerners; instead, he found himself face-to-face with a gritty professional who judged people purely by their performance and who made it quite clear to Popov that the Russians had fallen far, far short of the mark.

The Northern Fleet commander collected his thoughts. Then he decided to offer the *Seaway Eagle* team a concession, a gesture of goodwill. They wanted to know about the hatch mechanism of an Oscar II submarine—well, let them see one for themselves. The decision was certain to upset people in naval headquarters in Moscow, especially the hardliners, but he could handle that. Popov turned to Mann and told him to get two of his divers ready for a trip ashore. One of the *Kursk*'s sister submarines, the *Oryol,* was in dry dock in Severomorsk, seventy miles to the southwest. "Your men can visit the boat and look at it for themselves," Popov told Mann.

Mann was stunned. Popov was offering to let two Westerners inside one of the Russian military's most sensitive bases to inspect one of their most advanced nuclear submarines. Determined to act before Popov could change his mind, he phoned down to Dive Control and told Mark Nankivell and Garry Ball to pack their bags right away. Within minutes, they had assembled some basic kit: overalls, hard hats, measuring equipment, and a change of clothes. The two dive supervisors were taken to the *Peter the Great* by Norwegian helicopter, and from then on they were in the hands of the Northern Fleet. The two men, both British, walked from the stern of the Russian warship and waited for a Russian chopper to take them ashore.

Popov, having just returned from the *Seaway Eagle* on his own launch, emerged to greet them and promised them full access to the aft compartment of the *Oryol* submarine.

"Will we be able to operate the hatch to see how it works?" Ball asked.

"Yes, absolutely," Popov replied.

"Can we look at the internal hatch mechanism?"

"No problem."

"Can we open the inner hatch too?"

"Of course."

"Can we take photographs, so we can show the specialists on board the *Seaway Eagle*?"

"Yes."

"Will we be able to speak to Russian naval engineers and the crew members ashore who are familiar with the ninth compartment?"

"Certainly."

The journey to Severomorsk took Ball and Nankivell over the low coastal hills of the Kola Peninsula. Out of the window, as they swept past, Ball glimpsed the side of a mountain with a set of giant doors built into it and a convoy of military vehicles lined up outside. The two supervisors were venturing into a place that few Westerners had seen before. After an hour-long flight, they arrived at the military airfield at Severomorsk, to be met by a group of staff officers who escorted them through the town's checkpoints and down to the docks.

The naval headquarters was eerily quiet. The familiar sounds of a busy port—the noise of pierside generators and onboard machinery and the shouts of dockworkers—were absent. The listing hulks and rusting hulls of long-abandoned ships haunted the piers. Out in the bay were moored the abandoned wrecks of the submersible mother-ships that the Fleet now needed so badly.

Ball and Nankivell strode out ahead, down a long pontoon bridge, eager to inspect the submarine and report back to Mann. They felt strangely uneasy, approaching a top-secret dock, their bags packed with a digital camera and measuring devices. Nankivell and Ball hoped they were not walking into a trap and wouldn't find themselves being accused of espionage.

At the end of the pontoon lay the floating dry dock. A huge construction, bigger than any such facility they had set eyes on before, the dock housed two warships and a submarine, all sitting on keel-blocks, freshly painted.

They had expected the *Oryol* to be big, but they were still amazed by the size of the submarine out of the water.

Nankivell and Ball followed a group of senior officers down the casing of the outer hull until they were standing over the hatch system. Ball crouched down to examine the mechanism, determined to understand its secrets. The bright, stainless-steel surface stood out against the background of the dull acoustic tiling around it. Watched by the *Oryol*'s commanding officer, Ball opened the hatch while Nankivell took notes and photographs. They confirmed what their divers had learned the hard way, that the e-valve opened clockwise.

Ball and Nankivell spent an hour working on board the *Oryol*, sketching the hatch mechanisms. They also examined the internal pipework in case they needed to cut their way into the *Kursk*. Descending the ladder through the escape tower and seeing the small space of the compartment's upper deck, Ball realized that if there were dozens of survivors, they would be packed like sardines below the hatch, or else forced to stand in the narrow passageways around the machinery.

Before they left, the *Oryol*'s chief engineer quietly passed on another vital piece of information: Whenever the Oscar IIs are stationary, water leaks into the ninth compartment through the stern glands around the propeller shafts. When the submarine is secured alongside a pier, a clamp has to be fitted to stop the leak, but at a pressure of 350 feet, the flow of water would be impossible to plug from the inside. Ball was shocked by the implication: If the escape compartment of the *Kursk* leaked, not only would trapped sailors face the hazard of flooding, but their bodies would be subjected to rising pressure too.

No wonder the crew hadn't escaped from the *Kursk*. Their bodies would quickly have become saturated at that pressure, and any attempt to reach the surface on their own would have triggered an agonizing and fatal attack of the bends. For the first time, it began to make sense to the Western rescuers why no one had tried to make it out of the *Kursk* but, rather, had chosen to wait for outside help.

II: 8:30 P.M., SUNDAY, AUGUST 20
Aboard the Seaway Eagle

GRAHAM MANN AND HIS TEAMS were still puzzled over the state of the escape tower. They could not reconcile the contradictory evidence: On the one hand, the fact that there was no flow of water through the e-valve suggested that the tower was flooded; on the other, the hatch wouldn't open, suggesting a pressure differential and the possibility that it might be dry. This technical riddle left Mann with a strong desire to resolve the issue, by persuading the Russians to agree to the deployment of the LR5. The Royal Navy submersible would be of value only if the escape tower was dry—but that possibility still existed.

By late evening on Sunday, a final crisis summit began, once again in the crowded conference room on the officers' deck of the *Seaway Eagle*. It was the last throw of the dice.

Looking directly at Verich, Mann made his position crystal clear. Given the continuing confusion over whether the escape tower and aft of the submarine was flooded, the LR5 should now be allowed to attempt to dock with the ninth escape hatch. He urged Verich to authorize its immediate use. The official Royal Navy log of the meeting noted the admiral's response:

> Admiral Verich expressed gratitude to the UK and Norway for their help. He said he rated the LR5 highly but he believed that the slow flow rate around the hatch meant the submarine was full of water and there was now no chance of life. He wished the upper lid and lower lid to be opened to make the situation clear.

A few minutes later, a call came through for Verich from Admiral Popov. He took it outside the conference room. When he returned to his seat, he appeared chastened. Popov had ordered him to reverse his position and allow the deployment of the LR5. The rift within the Russian military was finally on full display in front of the Westerners: The search-and-rescue chief was demanding that Mann rip off the hatch with a crane, while the Northern Fleet commander was now authorizing the use of a foreign rescue submersible. One Russian admiral was behaving as if he knew there were no survivors; the other was acting in a way that hinted he had not given up all hope.

For the third time in five days, Popov was taking a considerable political risk, reaching out to the Western rescuers in defiance of hardliners in Moscow. On Wednesday, he had telephoned Admiral Skorgen to ask for foreign help; on Saturday, he had allowed Western specialists to visit the *Oryol;* and now Popov was sanctioning an attempt by the LR5 to dock with the *Kursk*. Within the constraints of his position, despite having to get clearance from Moscow, Popov was persisting in doing his best to save his submarine crew.

Delighted by Popov's unexpected change of heart, the Royal Navy officers eagerly pressed ahead. They agreed that the LR5 operation would begin at noon the next day. On Monday, August 21, a full nine days after the accident, the final attempt would be made to rescue survivors.

Over the last twenty-four hours, the Russian admiralty had allowed the *Normand Pioneer* to edge nearer to the accident site, but no closer than five nautical miles. Furthermore, there appeared to be a deliberate and obstructive effort to prevent the LR5 technicians from getting the submersible ready for a dive. On Sunday morning, just as the Stolt diving operation was beginning, the Royal Navy had requested authority to put LR5 into the water for an "integrity check," to make sure the vehicle was still watertight after the long journey from Scotland. Even though it would have remained tethered to the *Pioneer* throughout the test, permission was refused.

Admiral Burtsev's visit to the ship and his promise to permit the LR5 to be deployed down to the *Kursk* had come to nothing. The intense frustration felt by Commodore Russell and the LR5 pilots was increased by the knowledge that whatever the Stolt divers did, the only way sailors might come out of the *Kursk* alive was inside the Royal Navy submersible.

As the Russian, British, and Norwegian specialists had debated whether the escape tower was flooded, the best submarine-rescue equipment in the world was languishing unused just a few nautical miles away.

Then, shortly after dawn on Monday, when no one was watching closely, the top hatch, still being pulled upward by a 550-pound buoyancy bag, swung open. There were no divers around the stern of the *Kursk* at the time, and even the ROVs had been pulled out of the water for maintenance and were back on the *Eagle*'s deck. During low tide that morning, the pressure bearing down on the hatch had been reduced just enough to make the difference. Despite all the prolonged analysis and high-tech equipment, the timeless intervention of nature had done the trick, allowing the pressure to equalize and the upper escape hatch to swing open. The buoyancy bag was sufficient to open the door upward against its own weight.

At the bottom of the tower, the lower hatch was now visible, the last closed doorway into the submarine. Deep in his soul, Graham Mann had to admit that no one was coming out alive from the submarine. Crucially, he spotted that small quantities of gas were pulsing out from under the lower hatch. The engineers on the *Eagle* had come across this phenomenon before: The pulsing was the result of the pressure being virtually equal on both sides of the hatch, but as the waves passed overhead on the ocean surface, they slightly changed the pressure differential, causing the door to open and close a tiny amount, allowing gas to escape.

Mann consulted a tide table for the Barents Sea and quickly realized that the trapped air inside the submarine was simply expanding and contracting as the tide was rising and falling, providing further evidence that the compartment was internally flooded. There was no dissent aboard the ship about the next step. The evidence, although circumstantial, seemed overwhelming. Nine days after the accident, in the absence of any internal sounds, with the escape tower flooded, with bubbles escaping around the lower hatch, the moment of truth was reached.

The Dive Control supervisors, who normally show a tough exterior and thrive on rough humor, were silent and distressed. Over their shoulders, Admiral Verich and his staff officers watched the screens. No one said a word.

There was now no reason not to go ahead and open the lower hatch for final confirmation. They had to recognize there was no one left alive. Welders in the *Eagle*'s workshop manufactured a tool that would allow the lower hatch to be opened remotely, by one of the ROVs.

At 10:30 A.M., with the ROV adding just a small amount of extra pushing power, the lower hatch dropped open. Mann and his team stared at the video monitors, knowing what this moment represented. As the hatch fell downward, swinging into the compartment, the final, slim hopes of a rescue vanished.

Then, to the surprise of many, large pockets of gas belched violently out of the compartment. A gushing stream of bubbles was escaping; to those watching, the submarine appeared to be exhaling her final great breath.

The volume of air that emerged momentarily horrified many of the workers aboard the *Seaway Eagle*. Had they just done what they had been trying so hard to avoid and accidentally flooded a dry compartment? They had expected a small air pocket, but not this torrent of gas lasting for several minutes.

Mann knew that the images were a cruel illusion. There were always going to be large quantities of air inside the submarine: Since the moment of the accident, the air trapped inside had nowhere to

go. The slow flooding through the stern glands had simply compressed the 19,420 cubic feet of air into a smaller and smaller area
at the top of the compartment. The sight of the giant bubbles coming from the hatch may have been deeply disturbing, but it was not
"breathable" air that could have supported life; it was a poisoned,
low-oxygen, high-carbon-dioxide brew.

There was a shocking finality to the scene now before them. They
could do nothing more. The hatches were open, the ninth compartment was flooded, and the crew of the *Kursk* was lost.

A debate began in the *Eagle* about whether a diver should attempt to
slip down the escape tower and try to bring out some of the bodies.
Among the divers themselves, there was a widespread feeling that the
recovery of some of the corpses would bring a sense of closure to the
families waiting ashore for their loved ones. Knowing that Stolt's
managers would likely resist the move, only discreet preparatory
steps were taken. The divers were asked if they were prepared to
enter the ninth compartment, and they expressed willingness if the
task was adequately prepared. There was no way that they could
squeeze down the tower with their bail-out bottles, so a special hose
was improvised. But when Mann spoke to his onshore team about the
wisdom of the move, they expressly forbade him. The message to
Mann could not have been clearer: "This was a rescue mission, not a
recovery operation. You were there to save lives, not retrieve corpses.
The divers are absolutely forbidden from entering the wreck of the
submarine."

There was still, however, a burning curiosity to glimpse the inside
of the submarine. A few hours after the bottom hatch opened, Stolt
divers used a long pole to lower a small video camera down the
escape tower and into the ninth compartment. The pictures were
watched live throughout the ship. These were the first images from
inside the *Kursk*, and the supervisors braced themselves to see the
horrors that lay within the flooded compartment.

The pictures were marred by dreadful visibility. The camera appeared to be looking through a dense, dark mist. The supervisors had expected debris but not this thick fog of particles dancing through the water. The camera was slowly and carefully maneuvered around the ninth compartment until the lens came within a few inches of an internal bulkhead. The specialists in Dive Control immediately spotted a startling feature: The wall was blackened, the paintwork cracked and blistered.

They had seen this before, in a dozen different underwater locations, and they all shared a common feature: *fire.*

The poor visibility now made sense. The haze in the water was millions of floating carbon particles, a by-product of fire.

The rescuers had pictured the crew members of the *Kursk* dying from either flooding or from carbon-dioxide poisoning. Now there was a new possibility: Perhaps they died not in icy water but from the extreme heat of a flash fire. There was no way of knowing at this stage whether the fire had broken out before or after the crew members had died. That was the kind of detail that could only come from postmortems on the bodies.

The camera then captured another fleeting, shocking image: Out of the dark water, a ghostlike glimpse of a blue overall flashed by, a body floating face down. Neutrally buoyant, the corpse eerily drifted past the lens.

The Stolt divers took a gas sample from inside the *Kursk,* just before they left the scene. They extracted a small amount of the gas that remained trapped in an air pocket in the top layer of the ninth compartment and analyzed its chemical composition. The content of the carbon monoxide was registered at 2.3 percent, a lethal level in a very short period of time. The oxygen was reduced to 6.1 percent, a level insufficient to support life.

Had the sailors drowned? Had they died from carbon-dioxide poisoning? How had the men of the aft compartments lost their battle to survive? These questions would be answered by a highly secretive investigation by the Russian Navy. The conclusions have still not

been officially released, though at the end of August 2002 parts of
the report were leaked to the Russian newspaper *Rossiskaya Gazeta*.
The details from the report square well with accounts I was given by
some of those closest to the probe. Those accounts provide a harrowing picture of the last hours of the *Kursk* sailors.

But before that probe began, Vladimir Putin knew he had to deal
with the politics of the disaster. Assailed for his lack of leadership, the
president agreed with his advisers that he had no choice. He would
fly to the Kola Peninsula, visit the forlorn and grieving base at
Vidyaevo, and speak to the families directly.

14

I: 8 P.M., TUESDAY, AUGUST 22
Vidyaevo Naval Base

TEN DAYS AFTER THE ·*KURSK* sank, the gates and checkpoints leading to Vidyaevo opened for an approaching cavalcade. The cars barely slowed as they roared down the potted road and through the rich late-summer forests of dwarf birch trees.

Dressed in a dark suit and black open-necked shirt, surrounded by bodyguards, even President Putin's physical appearance added drama to the bleak surroundings. Inside the dilapidated base, he first paid his respects to Irina Lyachin, the wife of the *Kursk*'s captain. Putin showed no reaction to the peeling paint and the visible decay as he entered the apartment block where she lived.

An ordeal lay ahead for him—for several hundred relatives were by now crammed into the Officers Club in the heart of the town, waiting to confront the nation's president.

Although the opening of the hatches of the ninth compartment had represented the end of the rescue effort, very few of the families had completely given up hope. They clung to the belief that amid the haze of official lies, their loved ones were still alive. Some of the wives of the crew serving in the forward compartments, however, recognized they were facing widowhood. Natasha Tylik knew there was little chance left for Sergei, but there were many mothers and wives of crew members in the middle and aft compartments who were convinced there were still survivors in the *Kursk*. There had been so much deceit—why should they believe the admirals now? The aft compartment was flooded, but perhaps the men had taken refuge in the larger sixth, seventh, or eighth compartments? Naval officers at the base tried to explain that only the ninth compartment had an escape hatch, so the rescuers had no choice but to end their efforts.

What infuriated the relatives most was the news that the very next day, Wednesday, August 23, had been declared a national day of mourning. No one had consulted them. Some of the wives were shaking with rage at the idea of Russian officials "burying" the crew members before there was conclusive evidence that every compartment was flooded. The women saw the decision to have a day of mourning as a crude attempt by the Navy to abruptly end the crisis, even if it meant abandoning survivors.

Inside the hall, the mood was a potent mix of grief and anger. Relatives had been told that the president would appear at 4 P.M. He arrived four hours late. All journalists had been evicted from the hall, but the security guards failed to spot Andrei Kolesnikov, a reporter from the newspaper *Kommersant,* who had passed himself off as a relative and taken a seat. Hidden underneath his coat was a tape recorder.

Putin walked briskly to the front. He took a deep breath, and for a moment even the sobs and choked cries seemed to abate.

"We planned to hold a meeting at the Navy Headquarters in Severomorsk," Putin began, "but I decided first to meet you here . . ."

"We can't hear you!" a voice shouted from the back of the hall.

"Well, I will speak louder. I would like to talk to you about the situation. It is a terrible tragedy. Words of condolences and apologies have been offered to you, and I add my voice to that."

"Tell us why the rescue operations were stopped when the hatch was opened to the ninth compartment," a woman called out. "What about the seventh and eighth sections—maybe there is no water there?"

"I put the same question to the experts," Putin replied. "I called them every three or four hours, and I wanted to phone them every few minutes, but I was worried about distracting them from their work . . ."

"Why didn't you ask for foreign help immediately? Why?"

"The Northern Fleet had all the rescue facilities we needed. I was called by the Defense Minister Marshal Sergeyev on the thirteenth of August at 7 in the morning—"

There was a small gasp from the hall. A man shouted out bitterly, "The submarine is lost on Saturday, and you were called on Sunday?"

"The submarine was lost at 11 P.M. on Saturday, and the search was started then. It was found at 4:30 A.M. The minister of defense called me at 7 in the morning and reported, 'Something has gone wrong in training—contact with the submarine has been lost, and we have found it on the seabed. Rescue operations are under way.' My first question was, 'How about the reactor? What can we do to save people? Do you need extra resources?' The answer was clear. The military officials considered that they had all the facilities they need—"

Putin was interrupted by a low, angry murmur that rolled through the hall. "Wait, I must finish my answer. Foreign assistance was suggested on the fifteenth, and Admiral Kuroyedov agreed to it."

There were more shouts from the restive crowd. The relatives knew perfectly well that the Fleet did not have the necessary rescue facilities and that the admirals had delayed the arrival of the Western rescuers. Putin moved from defense to attack.

"The television tells lies. It lies. It lies. It lies. There are people on the television who like to speak about all this, but they've been trying to destroy the Army and the Navy for ten years. Their purpose is to discredit and ruin the armed forces. They have stolen money for years—"

There were more cries from the body of the hall. "Everyone is deceiving us."

A woman at the front was sobbing out loud. "Where is my son? Where is my son?"

Another mother joined her. "How long must I wait for my son?" A third woman spoke up. "I have no more money . . ."

The president pounced on this opportunity to shift the discussion away from the failed rescue and toward money and compensation.

"A woman asked me earlier," he said, "if it is possible to receive her husband's salary for the next ten years as compensation. I think it would be fair if we take such action. The country would not become poorer. We'll take the average salary of an officer and give that amount to each family for the next ten years. We are ready to do this as soon as possible."

It was a masterly stroke, for this was an issue on which Putin could actually deliver. He also knew that amid the humiliating poverty of the Northern Fleet bases, money was a pressing issue for the widows and mothers of the submariners.

"But do you know what an officer's salary is?" Putin was asked.

"Yes, I was told . . ." He fumbled through some papers.

"What's a lieutenant's pay?"

"No, I do not know, but the average salary is three thousand rubles."

There were further jeers from the floor.

"What about a captain's salary?"

"Six thousand rubles," Putin guessed.

"How much? What are you talking about?" Cries echoed around the room. None of the officers in the Northern Fleet received such pay. "These are Norwegian salaries, not Russian ones!"

"Please, I can't hear anything." Putin threw his notes down onto the table and looked across at Admiral Kuroyedov, who stared in embarrassment at the floor.

"My husband's salary is two and a half thousand rubles. Is that enough? It's shameful!"

"Do you know our homes are not heated? There's not even hot water."

"Maybe it's not true, but I am reading what I have," Putin retorted. "A lieutenant-captain earns four thousand eight hundred."

"Yes, but that includes allowances they earn on long voyages, and no such payments have been paid in three years. Your information is wrong."

The mother of Mamed Gadjiev, the civilian torpedo engineer, then spoke up. "My son is aboard the submarine. He is a civilian specialist, with a wife and two daughters, and yet the compensation will only go to the families of the servicemen in the submarine."

Putin didn't even hesitate. "I agree. Your son will be treated like a crewmember."

A man called out, "And what about the widows? Will they be provided with housing?"

"I suggest the following solution: For the wives of the crew, we'll acquire apartments, in the Moscow and St. Petersburg area."

"So my son has died for the cost of an apartment!"

"I am ready to answer for anything that has happened over the last hundred days, since I've been president," Putin replied. "As for the past fifteen years, I will sit down and put your questions to others."

Lyudmila Safonov and her friend Irina were both in the audience. They had been living with their boyfriends, who were among the crew of the *Kursk*, but neither couple had yet married. What was their status? What would they be entitled to? Where would they now live? Putin urged both young women to talk to Irina Lyachin, the widow of the *Kursk*'s commander, who would arrange for them to be looked after.

Natasha Tylik was sitting in the third row, listening to the exchanges between President Putin and the audience, but she felt curiously detached. It seemed so irrelevant compared to the fate of Sergei and the other sailors. As Natasha watched the Russian leader, his words tumbling out, his body language alternately defensive and aggressive, she felt nothing for him. He was just a politician trying to save his skin.

The angry debate in the hall moved on to the question of whether to try to salvage the submarine and recover the bodies of the sailors.

One old man stood up. "I am sorry to interrupt you, but what are these hundred men for Russia? You must raise the submarine and rescue those poor boys who died."

"I give my word of honor that we will do our best to raise the submarine."

"Is it true that tomorrow will be declared a day of mourning throughout Russia?"

"It is true," replied Putin.

There were more shouts from throughout the hall. The idea of official mourning was a threshold that the families were not yet prepared to cross.

"Why has mourning been declared already? For whom? Raise the submarine, and if everyone is dead, declare it then."

"But we know there is a hole in the bow, nearly two meters across," Putin remarked, looking at his notes. "We know that a part of the crew must have perished. The mourning is for them."

"It is not yet time to declare mourning!" Several people were on their feet, shouting at the president. "Cancel the national ceremonies!"

Putin tried to retreat. "We can cancel the mourning music. But in Moscow, it is past 11 P.M.—that means in the East, on our Pacific coast, the national mourning has already begun. How can we cancel it now? But I'll tell television stations of your request, and they can stop the transmission of any ceremonies related to the death of your loved ones."

"But do you understand that each family is here with just one thought? To take their son or husband from the submarine and bury him in their hometown?"

"Yes, I know that."

"Well, how long must we wait? Two months, three months? My town of Zaporozhye is waiting. Even if just a zinc coffin is delivered with what is left of him—"

"Operations will continue, and we will try and raise the *Kursk*."

"But I have another question: Why have you arrived up here in the north only now?"

Why had the president failed to break off his holiday? Why had it taken him ten days to travel to the Northern Fleet to see the situation for himself? He sensed that he was vulnerable, and these were the hardest questions for Putin to answer.

"From the very beginning, I had to decide whether I should fly up here or not. I asked military officials, 'Can I help there?' They said firmly to me, 'No, even the talk alone of you coming will raise people's concerns. All operations would stop for several days.' Do you know how many people would come with me? How many aides and officials?"

"You should put the officials in jail," shouted a woman, standing up in the front row.

"They deceived you, Mr. President." Some of Putin's bodyguards closed in on the woman, forcing her to sit down again, but the president shouted at them. "Don't make her sit down! Let her speak. You can get up. Speak your mind."

There was a chorus of shouts in support of the woman. "She is right. We have all been deceived!"

Perhaps no Russian president had ever confronted such anger. Mikhail Gorbachev had seen angry crowds in his time, but never as volatile as this. The people in this room were not peasants but the relatives of elite nuclear submariners. This was the military family turning on itself.

Putin defended the Fleet admirals. "We cannot say they deceived us. They told us the truth: that rescue facilities were available. But the systems failed to operate."

"No. They lied to us!"

An old sailor stood up. "They knew the search-and-rescue facilities were in ruins. There was an accident in Kamchatka in 1983 in just thirty meters of water, and the Fleet could do nothing. And these officials told you that they had all the resources they needed. They deceived the president. For such an action, they should be stripped of their ranks and honors!"

"They said they had the rescue vehicles—"

"Yes, but from the 1950s!"

"And the Fleet command will, as usual, bear no responsibility," another man shouted bitterly.

"Just a second," Putin responded. "They acted according to regulations. When they saw their means were ineffective, they tried to use others. That's all."

"For years, they have abandoned the rescue services. It took us eight days of fumbling with the hatch. The foreigners came and did it in eight hours. What are your thoughts about that? Did our command not realize during eight days that they were failing? Or were they aware and simply kept telling us lies?" The young woman broke down, sobbing, her voice gone.

Another man took up where she had left off. "The Norwegians managed to get inside within hours. Damn it, why all this secrecy? To accept help or not to—why was it so secret?"

"The Norwegians arrived on the fifth day," Putin replied. In the heat of the discussion he was forgetting that they had in fact arrived after seven days. "They gained access the next day. The Norwegian government doesn't have such divers either—they had to use divers from a commercial firm. It is for the commission to investigate in detail, technically, why our rescue vehicles failed to latch on to the submarine—whether it was because the hatch was damaged or because the vessel flooded."

"And what about the foreigners?"

"They didn't try to dock. They worked manually, in a simple way, using the methods of our grandparents. They made a wrench—"

"Oh God!" A woman was addressing the hall from the crowd. "And we couldn't even do *that* . . ."

But the anger had begun to dissipate. The encounter, which had lasted several hours, had perhaps served its purpose. There was a collective sense of emotional exhaustion. Few of the grieving families had slept more than a few hours in recent nights, and it was now past midnight. Minds that had clung to hope were recognizing that their worlds had changed forever. There would be no rescue ships coming back into harbor with survivors. Their men were dead.

Another man stood up and declared unexpectedly, "Mr. President, I would like to thank you for being here, together with us today."

A woman added her voice. "I am also thankful, but I want to ask you to apologize to the widows and the mothers."

Putin grasped the opportunity. "I think that's how we began our talk at the very beginning. I started with an apology."

Before he left, Putin surveyed the huddles of bereaved families, the widows, the small children asleep next to their mothers. In human terms, he had won them over. He had lanced their anger. In political terms, the meeting was a triumph. He had displayed a mastery of information worthy of his former career in the KGB.

Andrei Kolesnikov, the journalist who had sneaked in past Putin's guards and recorded these angry exchanges, overheard an exhausted presidential aide turn to a Kremlin colleague and declare, "It's a victory!"

There are some who say that this meeting in Vidyaevo was Vladimir Putin's public baptism of fire, a searing experience the like of which he had never known before. But in fact, there was a little-known confrontation with an equally angry crowd earlier in his career. The president has mentioned the incident only to a handful of friends.

It had happened eleven years earlier, in 1989, amid the ferment that was East Germany as the Berlin Wall fell. Crowds of people were directing their pent-up anger at the Stasi secret police. In Dresden, a furious mob headed for the Russian Trade Center, well known as the local headquarters of the Soviet KGB. Inside the building was the senior intelligence officer—Vladimir Putin. Having been warned that the crowd was heading for their offices, Putin and his KGB colleagues started burning documents. Tensions ran high as they tried to destroy decades of secret paperwork. Putin even phoned Moscow for advice. There was a Russian regiment stationed just thirty miles outside Dresden that could have intervened, but the KGB in Moscow would not sanction military force to save its East German stations.

Putin and his colleagues had just five submachine guns between them. Outside, the crowd was threatening to storm the building. Putin chose to emerge from the office and address the crowd. He spoke for an hour in fluent German, protesting the innocence of the Russians inside, insisting that they were trade officials, not KGB agents. It must have taken strong nerves, for as he was saying this, his colleagues were still furiously burning and shredding documents only a few floors above him.

Eventually the crowd cooled down and dispersed. Putin has called it the greatest test of his life. He had bluffed the crowd, gained some extra time, quite possibly saved his career. Eleven years later, he did the same—not in East Germany but high in the Russian Arctic, on an emotionally volcanic night in Vidyaevo.

II: SOUTHERN BARENTS SEA

THE APOLOGY WAS SIMPLE and heartfelt, and it had a profound effect on the millions of Russians who watched the gesture on television. Admiral Viacheslav Popov stood on the deck of the *Peter the Great* and spoke straight to the camera. He looked drawn and exhausted. "We did everything in our power, and more than that. Three thousand sailors of the Northern Fleet were trying to rescue the ship and her crew. Circumstances overwhelmed us. This is the shared fate for submariners—on such a boat, everyone lives or everyone dies. Grief is embracing us. But life must go on. Continue to bring up your children and your sons."

Popov was now crying. He removed his soft naval cap, gripping it, twisting it in his hands, and for a few moments fought to control his emotions.

"Forgive me for not saving your men."

He hesitated, as if wanting to make another comment, but then stepped away, out of the view of the camera.

A short time later, Popov received a final call from the Norwegian military headquarters in Bodø. Admiral Skorgen was shocked by the difference in the Russian's voice. For the first time, the Northern Fleet commander sounded like an old, sick man. There was no bite in his voice, no emotion, not even anger. Skorgen likened the experience to talking to a dead man.

"I'm desperately sorry that the accident has ended like this, for both you and the Northern Fleet." Skorgen could think of nothing else to say. This was not the time for grand statements.

Popov tried to talk about the timing of the departure of the *Seaway Eagle,* but the conversation drifted. He appeared too tired to concentrate. He did, however, manage to express satisfaction that in the end there had been an international rescue effort. "Perhaps we can take some comfort in that, and learn some lessons."

Skorgen agreed. The Norwegian admiral felt a deep sympathy for Popov, and his mind skipped back four months to when the two men had gone fishing together in the Norwegian fjord. There's a photograph of Popov on the fishing boat in a bright red windbreaker, grinning. Skorgen remembers looking at him even then and thinking about how they were children of different systems. They were neighbors, fellow submariners, who shared the same corner of northwest Europe—yet there existed so much distrust.

Skorgen brought himself back to the present. "Viacheslav, I'm sorry. I wish it could have been different."

"I do too. Goodbye, Einar."

"Goodbye."

As the Western rescuers waited for a decision about the timing of their departure, a signal was received on board the *Normand Pioneer.* Commodore David Russell was invited to attend a meeting on the *Peter the Great* with the commander-in-chief of the Russian Navy, Admiral Kuroyedov. Russell accepted immediately. It afforded a once-in-a-lifetime view of the Northern Fleet flagship, and, more important, he would meet the top admirals. After the intense frustrations of the last few days, Russell was desperate to understand what drove the Russian decision-making. Did they really care more for the secrets of the *Kursk* than for the lives of their sailors? Why had they refused to allow the deployment of the LR5?

A helicopter was sent to bring Russell to the flagship. He could not fail to be impressed by the reception line waiting to meet him. There was Admiral Popov, commander of the Northern Fleet, Admiral Kuroyedov, commander of the Russian Navy, and Ilya Klebanov, Russia's deputy prime minister.

There were salutes and handshakes, but no smiles. The mood was subdued and somber. Kuroyedov clasped Russell's hand and held it, giving a short speech. "Welcome aboard. I wanted to thank you personally for your offer of help. This is a tragic day for the Russian Navy and for the Russian people. There is heartfelt gratitude from our government for the British rescue effort."

Russell nodded in sympathy, but it was impossible not to think about the wasted opportunities: the lost hours before Russia acknowledged the accident, the decision to put the *Eagle* and the *Pioneer* into a holding area, the initial refusal to allow the LR5 to attempt a rescue.

Months later, Captain Simon Lister, a Royal Navy officer acting as Russell's interpreter and now the British naval attaché in Moscow, recalled the scene: "The meeting was a high-voltage encounter. There were so many emotions in the room—suspicion, grief, gratitude. Popov seemed so tired, and it was impossible to imagine a more dreadful position for him in terms of his pride. He had been unable to save a single one of his sailors from the best submarine in the Fleet. And now a British commander had turned up on his flagship."

In contrast, Kuroyedov cut a superbly polished figure, handling the meeting with ease and dignity. The admiration that Russell and Lister felt for the Russian Navy commander was ironic—unknown to them, a week earlier Kuroyedov had argued against accepting Western help.

The Russian Navy commander was on the brink of opening a bottle of vodka when he had second thoughts. He turned to the group and declared that while normally they would toast their foreign visitors, it would not be appropriate at so tragic a time. A few of the officers eyed the unopened bottle with longing.

The Russians went on to ask whether they could hire the LR5 in the future and discussed whether the world's navies should establish a truly global submarine-rescue service. Russell even found himself being quizzed about what he thought had happened to the *Kursk*. Even in their questions, they were revealing much. Popov emerged from his gloomy silence to ask what emergency procedure the Royal Navy would adopt if a fire broke out in the torpedo compartment. "Do you surface?" he asked. "And what's the assessment of the stability of your warheads?"

Russell explained that in wartime sailors would fight a fire while still submerged, but if detection was not an issue, then any submarine in trouble would immediately attempt to surface. There was no talk about whether a British or American submarine had been in the exercise area. Russell felt that the admirals knew it hadn't been a collision. They would scarcely invite a Royal Navy commander to lunch if they thought a Western submarine was responsible for the disaster. Ilya Klebanov, who was heading the investigation, mentioned the possibility of a Second World War mine, but he did so with little conviction. He also complained about the intolerable pressure placed on the rescue effort by the families in Vidyaevo. "They are such a problem, sitting there and demanding information . . ."

The group departed in awkward circumstances. Popov, sullen and shaken, escorted Russell to the stern of the *Peter the Great* only to find that the helicopter pilot had gone missing. The two men stood on the deck of the cruiser, staring out over the Barents Sea in silence.

These were the waters in which Russell had spent so many secret patrols aboard HMS *Superb* and HMS *Sceptre*. And now here he was alongside the commander of the Northern Fleet on a cool, sunny August afternoon, staring out over the Barents Sea, a few nautical miles from the wreck of the *Kursk*.

Popov gave formal clearance for the two Western rescue ships to head home.

The *Seaway Eagle* headed for the Norwegian port of Kirkenes. Graham Mann and his team had done what they could, but there was still a quiet, reflective mood aboard and a profound sense of regret that their efforts had not paid dividends. Tony Scott and the five other divers were still living in their chambers as their bodies were carefully decompressed back up to surface pressure. In less than a week, they would emerge and breathe fresh air once again.

As the Norwegian vessel passed through the crowd of Russian ships, the *Eagle*'s captain sounded the horn in one long blast, a farewell to the Northern Fleet. There was no response from the warships.

The *Normand Pioneer* also left for Norway, but not before a parting exchange of signals with the *Peter the Great:*

COMMODORE RUSSELL: On behalf of the First Sea Lord, all members of the Royal Navy, and all those on board the *Normand Pioneer* and myself, please pass on our deepest sympathies to all those associated with the submarine *Kursk* and in particular on this day, their families. We have all worked well together during these last few days in tragic circumstances. With Admiral Popov's permission I will depart now and leave the area. We go with a heavy heart and hope we will meet soon under happier circumstances.

ADMIRAL POPOV: Thank you for your sincerity at this moment, which is tragic for us all. In your honor and as a mark of our thanks, the warship *Admiral Chabanenko* will accompany you from the area.

As the *Normand Pioneer* began steaming west, back toward the Northern Cape, Russell looked to the port side and saw the Russian anti-submarine ship catching them at an impressive thirty knots. As she passed, the Russian crew "manned and cheered ship," the naval custom in which the entire ship's company gathers on the deck and roars their gratitude to another vessel.

Russell looked up at the powerful warship and surveyed the line of

Russian sailors, their naval caps held aloft, their cheers reaching across the water. In a lifetime of naval command, he had never glimpsed a more poignant tribute. He could only shake his head in wonder at the contradictions presented by the Northern Fleet: so much suspicion and duplicity and yet, at the very end, a striking gesture of dignity and friendship across the Barents Sea.

15

I: OCTOBER 2000
Severomorsk, Northern Fleet Headquarters

THE SPECIALISTS OF THE *Seaway Eagle* had been the first to glimpse the fate of the twenty-three sailors in the aft compartments. Their camera footage revealed that a fire had raced through the ninth compartment, but the real breakthrough in terms of the forensic investigation was achieved only when the first bodies were retrieved from the wreck in October.

Admiral Gennady Verich was placed in charge of the recovery operation. After the rescue débâcle in August, there was no hiding the need for foreign expertise, but divers would still not be able to enter the submarine through the narrow ninth compartment escape tower. In their bulky suits, trailing umbilical cables and safety gear, such a maneuver would be too perilous. The *Kursk* would have to be cut open.

The underwater expertise of the offshore industry would again provide the solution to the Russians' problems. This time it would be not Stolt but the company's chief rival, the U.S. energy giant Halliburton. Special equipment was needed, including high-pressure water jets that used diamond emulsion to cut through the thick pressure hull, as well as a substantial support operation above the divers.

But whatever technical assistance was accepted from the West, it was politically unthinkable that foreign divers would be allowed inside the *Kursk*. The task of scouring Russia for the specialist divers willing to work inside a flooded, pitch-black, and corpse-filled submarine fell to Verich.

In the end, one diver was chosen from the Baltic Fleet and another from the Black Sea Fleet, and the ten others were selected from two secretive naval organizations that operate near St. Petersburg: the 328th Rescue Division and Institute Number 40. Both serve the Ministry of Defense in the area of underwater special operations, and in the absence of adequate Russian diving ships, neither had played a role in the original rescue attempts.

Captain Vladimir Salutin was among the divers chosen. He had served as a member of Russia's naval special forces, starting his career clearing old Second World War mines from the Black Sea. This was dangerous work that required stamina and steady nerves. At thirty-seven, he was already well used to seeing death at close quarters, having recovered bodies from a number of sunken fishing vessels as well as from helicopters and planes that had crashed into the sea.

The elite team was flown straight to the Northern Fleet Head-quarters at Severomorsk, where they were plunged into study of the *Kursk,* analyzing diagrams and charts detailing the construction and layout of the submarine.

The divers then moved from the classroom to the *Oryol*. The officers of this Oscar II submarine advised them where the *Kursk* sailors might have taken refuge after the explosions. They also practiced taking alternative routes to the captain's personal safe, where code-books and other secret documents were held. Then they blindfolded themselves and walked the passageways, negotiating their way by touch through hatches and down ladders.

From Severomorsk, the Russian divers flew back to St. Petersburg and the Military Medical Academy, where they toured the academy's huge morgues to study fatal injuries. They were shown men who had perished in fires, in car crashes, and from drowning, and they were asked to look closely at bodies in advanced states of decomposition.

The support operation comprised a mix of British and Norwegian divers based on the giant offshore platform *Regalia,* which was moved into the Barents Sea. The foreign specialists performed the under-water construction work, cutting openings in carefully selected posi-tions through the *Kursk*'s double hulls, while the Russian divers prepared for their delicate mission. The scope for confusion and entangled cables meant that only one diver at a time would be allowed to work inside the submarine. The second Russian would wait on the outer casing, while a Western diver remained inside the diving bell, ready to act as a rescuer at a moment's notice.

Warrant Officer Sergei Shmygin was the first man to enter the tomb of the submarine, maneuvering his way cautiously down through one of the holes cut into the seventh compartment. His powerful halogen lamp barely penetrated water that was ink-black with oil and floating particles. To help his coordination inside the submarine, Shmygin was wearing boots instead of fins. He also wore a white plastic covering over his normal diving gear, to be removed and discarded after he emerged from the submarine, to ensure that no contaminants were taken into the diving bell. A long, wide hose was used to try to suck out some of the stale water from inside the submarine and to eliminate some of the floating waste from the decomposing bodies. It also helped to remove some of the chemicals and debris that obscured the view.

A blue-and-white-striped mattress floated by Shmygin. Like the bodies, many of the non-metal items inside the *Kursk* had gained neu-tral buoyancy and were drifting around the compartments. Shmygin was armed with a six-foot-long pole, with a small hook on the end, but he found no bodies during his first six-hour shift.

In fact, no corpses were found in compartments seven or eight. Over the next few days, the focus of the divers shifted to the crucial ninth compartment, where it was assumed the sailors had gathered. The Russian divers immediately saw the evidence of an intense fire, with machinery and equipment heavily charred. The first body was found floating largely intact, its legs covered in thick green clothing, its torso naked. The divers attached a rope to the waist and, using the pole, eased the body through to the seventh compartment and up into the open sea. The *Kursk* had reluctantly given up the first of her sailors.

Soon afterward, a second crewmember was found, severely burnt only along his upper body. Outside the submarine, a large, latticed steel container, painted a high-visibility yellow, was lowered from the *Regalia.* As each body was gingerly removed from the ninth compartment, it was placed inside and taken to the surface.

Directly underneath the hatch where Tony Scott had hammered, six bodies were recovered. One of them, Seaman Roman Kubikov, was lying just below the escape tower. Other corpses were visible farther aft, down the narrow passageway, wedged so deeply that the divers could not retrieve them, despite struggling for hours with their specially improvised pole. Eventually, they were forced to give up. One body that Vladimir Salutin touched simply disintegrated in his hands, limbs falling away in the water.

After they had explored the seventh, eighth, and ninth compartments, the divers were ordered to move down to the fourth. In this area, which included the private cabin of Captain Lyachin, in conditions of the greatest secrecy, divers spent three hours unloading files and documents from a single locker.

They then moved forward, toward the heart of the explosion, to compartment three, and attempted to approach the most sensitive area of the submarine, the radio room. Trying to enter through the hole that had been cut through the double hull, it was immediately apparent that what confronted the divers here was an entirely new proposition. "It was something horrible," one of them reported. "We couldn't even swing our legs through the hole. It was full of broken parts, metal and plastic." The machinery and equipment were so chaotically entangled that the divers gave up.

At 1:15 A.M. on October 26, the meshed-steel sleigh containing the first corpses emerged from the depths of the sea and was swung onto the vast, open deck space of the *Regalia.* The powerful floodlights gave the platform an eerie look amid the heavy swell and darkness of the Barents Sea. Winter was unmistakably arriving. The first two bodies were quickly carried the short distance to a large shipping container that had been converted into a temporary morgue. White drapes ensured that the bodies were not glimpsed by any of the *Regalia*'s curious Norwegian workers.

Standing expectantly inside the container, the size of a small room, were two naval pathologists and Colonel-Lieutenant Sergei Chernishov, who served in the office of the prosecutor-general. There was also a staff member with a small video camera, recording the investigation for the military archives.

The first body examined was partially burnt around the head and chest and heavily smeared with a mix of oil and soot. The hands had turned ivory-white after their long immersion in water. The examiners spent some time looking at the inner blue overall that had the sailor's barely decipherable naval number on it, which would help identify him.

The second corpse soon became the focus of the examiners' interest. The upper body was severely burnt, and much of the flesh had peeled away in the area around the neck and head. But there were still recognizable features, and the lower body was in remarkably good shape. As the pathologists examined the body, they spoke aloud so that their moment-by-moment thoughts and impressions were captured on tape.

"There appears to be some kind of package on the body."

"Take a look," Chernishov encouraged.

The tight bundle, the size of a man's wallet, heavily covered in oil, was bound by waterproof wrapping that was stained almost black. The little packet was squeezed into a breast pocket of the singed overalls.

"The front surface is solid. I am now removing it from the clothing. Everything is saturated, we're finding . . . I'm not opening it, I'm afraid to break it into pieces."

"Go ahead and open it," Chernishov authorized.

"It appears to be some writing, some letter." The excitement in the investigator's voice was impossible to disguise.

Newsprint and paper survive surprisingly well underwater. As many salvage divers have discovered, documents and labels on packaging are often legible after being submerged for decades, so long as they have been undisturbed. Even letters recovered from First and Second World War wrecks have been readable.

Wearing white surgical gloves, the investigators gingerly separated the note from the wrapping. It was written on a page from a logbook, both horizontal and vertical lines covering the page. The note was folded into four, and the writing was obscured by moist oil marks, but it was still just legible. The note had survived immersion. The name at the end of it jumped out, visible even on the video footage.

Kolesnikov.

The body on the table was that of Captain-Lieutenant Dmitri Kolesnikov, commander of the *Kursk*'s seventh compartment.

On one side of the note was written the list of twenty-three survivors with the time 13.34 at the top. The pathologists gently turned the note over. At the top, above the last words that Kolesnikov had written after the *Kursk* was plunged into darkness, were five lines written earlier to his wife:

> *Olichka, I love you.*
> *Don't suffer too much. My regards to*
> *GV and regards to mine.*
> *Mitya.*
> 12.08.2000. 1545.

GV were the initials for Galina Vasiliena, his mother-in-law; Mitya was his own nickname, the Russian diminutive for Dmitri.

The last lines written at the end of the message has been scrawled in the dark:

> *It's dark here to write, but I'll try by feel. It seems like there are no chances, 10–20%. Let's hope that at least someone will read this. Here's the list of personnel from the other sections, who are now in the 9th and will attempt to get out. Regards to everybody, no need to be desperate. Kolesnikov.*

For the first time, here was incontrovertible proof that sailors had survived the initial explosions. Dozens of Russian specialists were now called in to examine in minute detail every aspect of the bodies, clothing, and notes. One laboratory revealed that the type of oil that was smeared over some of the corpses came from a lubricant used only in the stern glands leading from the propeller shafts. The water had leaked into the ninth compartment through the shaft seals and brought the oil with it. This was confirmation that the submarine had slowly flooded over several days, increasing the pressure within the compartment.

Everywhere the Russian investigators turned, there were fresh clues to what had happened in the ninth compartment, allowing them to piece together the terrifying final days of life in the aft of the destroyed submarine.

Most of the bodies were clothed not just in their normal dark-blue working overalls but in a second layer of thick green insulation fabric. These were the emergency suits issued to submariners to ward off hypothermia.

Despite the strength of the twin blasts that rocked the *Kursk* at 11:28 and 11:30 on Saturday, August 12, the sailors in the aft compartments had survived with surprising ease. None of the twenty-three crewmembers listed in Kolesnikov's first note had sustained serious impact injuries such as broken bones or severe bruising.

Following the explosions in the torpedo room, it appears, the survivors dressed in their thermal suits and opened their emergency superoxide chemical cartridges to generate additional oxygen and fight the rising carbon dioxide. Video from inside the ninth compartment shows numerous used cartridges lying discarded on the upper deck.

Kolesnikov's final note highlights the terrible moment when the ninth compartment was plunged into darkness. Still, the men had known exactly what was happening around them. They could hear the slow flooding through the propeller shafts. They were also cogent enough to analyze its significance: realizing the risk was not only of drowning but of steadily increasing pressure that ended any hope of reaching the surface alive.

We know that the sailors confronted this devastating predicament squarely because of another note, written at an unknown time. This one was found on the body of Captain-Lieutenant Rashid Ariapov, the commander of the sixth compartment:

> *In the 9th compartment, there are 23 sailors. We feel bad, weakened by carbon dioxide. . . . Pressure is increasing in the compartment. If we head for the surface we won't survive the compression. We won't last more than a day.*

For many months, this letter deeply puzzled investigators because the handwriting was not Ariapov's. The contents were kept secret. Eventually, experts decided that it had been written by Captain-Lieutenant Sergei Sadilenko, commander of the eighth compartment, and that for unknown reasons he had handed it to his good friend Ariapov to keep safely on his behalf. The letter was partially released by Deputy Prime Minister Ilya Klebanov.

Prevented from escaping by the rising pressure, the only remaining hope for the sailors had been in a rescue submersible that could double as a decompression chamber. Their best, perhaps their only, chance of getting out alive had been the retired Russian submersible commander Andrei Sholokhov, whose remarkable piloting skills almost overcame the defects of the Priz rescue vehicle. We will never know whether the *Kursk* sailors were still alive in the ninth compartment on Thursday, August 17, when Sholokhov scraped over the escape hatch and came so tantalizingly close to docking.

Changing those chemical cartridges could not have been an easy task for men who were badly frightened, shivering violently from cold, and short of practice in emergency drills. In the last glow of emergency light, finding and deploying the chemical kits was difficult; in total darkness, it was a nightmare. What's more, the survivors were in an atmosphere that was rigged for a secondary disaster. The rising pressure meant that a fire would ignite more easily and burn with greater ferocity, and the men were dealing with chemicals that react violently with water.

According to specialists in the Russian Navy's rescue department, at some stage one of the survivors ripped open the packaging around a chemical cartridge and appears to have fumbled and dropped it. As the cartridge fell into the water, with highly flammable oil and lubricants floating on its surface, the chemical reaction was sufficiently violent to ignite a blaze. We know from the fire-line in the compartment that at this stage, the water was nearly waist-high.

In a sealed, high-pressure environment like the ninth compartment, a fire is not just a problem—it is a truly cataclysmic event. This was a flash fire that would have rolled at high speed across the surface of the water. In just a second or two, the fireball would have used up all the precious oxygen the crew had meticulously tried to preserve.

Some of the sailors fought to escape, ducking below the water. Their bodies were later discovered with a distinctive pattern of burns: backs badly charred, chests scarcely touched. Others, it seemed, had been grouped around the spot where the cartridge was dropped— they were found with thermal burns compatible with a violent chemical reaction. The lower limbs of all of the bodies recovered from the aft compartment were untouched by fire, confirming the view of Russian experts that the men had been standing deep in water when the fire erupted.

For those who had managed to duck under the water and emerge to breathe, when they resurfaced they faced an atmosphere no longer capable of supporting life. One of the sailors had a mask seared to his face. The superheated gases would have burned their lungs, and they would have faced yet another killer. As the fire reacted with the paintwork and metals inside the ninth compartment, carbon monoxide was being generated in lethal quantities. Carbon monoxide is known as the silent killer. It comes with no taste or smell; it is not detectable by the human senses. Victims of CO poisoning feel no pain and rarely comprehend what is happening to them. For that reason, using the exhaust fumes of a car is one of the most common forms of suicide. The increase in carbon dioxide must have already left the survivors gasping for air, but when the monoxide hit them, they would have felt an incredible tiredness. Their muscles would have weakened, their vision grayed.

Their last vision of the ninth compartment would have been a rapidly narrowing tunnel surrounded by darkness.

The twenty-three men had certainly faced the hazards of carbon dioxide and drowning, but, as the Russian naval pathologists recorded on the death certificates, all of the *Kursk* sailors in the aft compartments died of carbon-monoxide poisoning. Their lower limbs, which had been underwater at the time of the fire, remained a bright pink, a healthy hue that is a telltale feature of death by CO. Several of the sailors who had avoided facial-burn injuries while ducking underwater wore expressions that appeared so peaceful they looked as though they had just fallen asleep.

After twelve of the twenty-three bodies were recovered and brought to the surface, with winter conditions fast approaching, the decision was made to seal the *Kursk* again. The recovery of the rest of the sailors and the retrieval of the missiles would have to wait for the salvage of the submarine, which would take many months of additional planning.

On the morning of November 7, 2000, all work stopped on the Regalia. The Russian divers, the Norwegian technicians, and all the support staff stood on the deck, heads bowed. A gentle rain washed over them as a minute's silence was held in memory of the crew of the *Kursk*.

One week after the twelve corpses were recovered from the submarine, the coffins were taken through Courage Square in Severomorsk. The ranks of naval officers attending the ceremony dropped onto one knee in the thin layer of snow as a mark of respect. The red coffins, draped in the blue-and-white Russian Navy flag, were carried atop armored personnel carriers, as the High Command looked on. Marshal Sergeyev and Admiral Popov stood together, in their thick winter greatcoats. Finally, Sergeyev stepped forward to the open-air lectern.

"Even the great Russian language fails to provide words for the bitterness of this loss and tragedy. Forgive us, and let the ground beneath you be as soft as down."

A dozen warships riding at anchor in the bay sounded their foghorns. The sirens resonated across the low hills and frozen landscape to the south.

Irina Lyachin, the widow of the *Kursk*'s commanding officer, stood poised and composed in the bitter cold. Not far away was Olga Kolesnikov, braving the weather without a hat or gloves. She watched the ceremony unfold in the gentle snow, with the battle-gray backdrop of Russian warships in the port. The first casket that passed contained the body of her husband. Dmitri had written her a poem before he had left on the exercise that now seemed strangely prophetic:

> *When there is A Time to Die*
> *Although I try not to think about this,*
> *I would like time to say:*
> *My darling I Love You.*

II: OCTOBER 2001
Southern Barents Sea

TWELVE MONTHS PASSED BETWEEN the recovery of the first bodies from the aft compartments and the salvage of the submarine. That time had been spent deciding on the best strategy for bringing the *Kursk* to the surface, while different technical plans were considered. By the time a conclusion was reached, and the Dutch companies Mammoet and Smit International were given the contract, the salvagers faced a race against the onset of winter.

In the early morning of October 8, 2001, the *Kursk* shuddered as the colossal weight of the flooded submarine contested the pulling power of twenty-six strand jacks. Each jack was composed of fifty-four thinner cables and could lift 900 tons. Slowly, the *Kursk* inched upward toward the special pontoon that had been constructed for the salvage. The average rate of ascent was thirty feet every hour. The impact of the swell of the ocean was reduced by heave compensators, which made sure that the force exerted on the cables was always equal.

October frequently witnesses the first storms of winter in the Barents, and already, strong winds had forced some delays in the project. The experts gambled on a window of calm seas, and for once the weather cooperated. Safety engineers gave the international team of divers and heavy-lift specialists the green light.

The first step in the salvage work had been to remove the severely damaged bow section of the *Kursk*, using a special abrasive cutting wire, reducing the risk of loose and unstable torpedoes detonating during the lifting operation. Holes were then made in the hull to allow divers to attach the lifting cables to the submarine. There was still much anxiety about the state of the weapons systems: Even without the bow section, the *Kursk* wreck contained twenty-three Shipwreck missiles, among the most powerful conventional naval weapons in the world.

Several weeks behind schedule and dangerously close to the fierce seasonal gales, the *Kursk* was successfully lifted toward the surface and secured into position in a special cradle below the pontoon. In this position, just below the waves and out of view of the outside world, the submarine and pontoon were towed toward a giant dry dock in Roslyakovo, just outside Murmansk. For the Dutch contractors, the salvage was a stunning technical achievement—the heaviest object ever lifted from such a depth.

With the submarine safely ashore and out of the water, investigators and forensic scientists meticulously combed every piece of the wreckage, finding logbooks, equipment, and the bodies of sailors. Everything they discovered backed up the understanding of events framed by the investigators a year earlier, when the first twelve bodies had been recovered.

A further note was discovered stuffed in a bottle, written in a twilight world in which the sailors confronted their fears, prayed for survival, and thought of their families. The author was Senior Midshipman Andrei Borisov:

If you are reading this note this means I am dead. But your lives will carry on and I am asking that my son becomes a true man, like I used to be.

The widows and family members of the dead sailors watched with horrified fascination as the submarine salvage was accomplished, but they were divided about the value of the operation. Some wanted a chance to bury their husbands; others felt the *Kursk* herself was a fitting cemetery. The widows of the sailors who served in the front two compartments knew that they would at best receive only body parts rather than a recognizable corpse. After fifteen months, many of the emotional wounds were reopened.

Natasha Tylik understood that there was no realistic chance that Sergei would be found in the wreckage. He had served toward the forward end of the command center, close to the bulkhead with the torpedo room. If the reports of the devastation were accurate, his body would have been torn apart by the explosions, and lamprey eels would have entered through the shattered bow. They are normally the first to reach bodies at this depth.

But Natasha's hopes were raised on October 29, 2001, fifteen months after her husband had died. She received a call at her new home in St. Petersburg from the Northern Fleet. A naval officer announced that Sergei's body had been retrieved from the wreck, identified by his face and the tattoo on his hand. She was invited to visit the naval hospital in Severomorsk to formally identify her husband.

Natasha entered the morgue accompanied by three medical officers. The body lay on a table covered by a white sheet. A doctor moved the sheet partially aside to show Natasha first the feet, then the arms and hands. From the outset, she sensed something was wrong. Submariners are discouraged from wearing wedding rings on the fingers because of concerns that they might catch on equipment or machinery. But Sergei had never taken his off. He wore it on the fourth finger of his right hand, but as she stared at the hand of the body in front of her, there was no ring—not even a mark against the white skin. And instead of a tattoo of a submarine and roses, there was an image of a submarine and a flag, along with two dates whose significance Natasha didn't understand. Finally, the doctor removed the sheet sufficiently for her to see the face and upper torso. She gasped. She had never seen this sailor before.

Natasha felt not horror but relief. Had she not made the journey to Severomorsk, she would have accepted the body in good faith and spent the rest of her life grieving at the grave of a total stranger. Later, she learned the body was that of Captain Viacheslav Bezsokirny, an officer from the Ukraine who served in the third compartment.

Natasha felt uncomfortable being back on the Kola Peninsula. As she watched, a bus came up from the docks, unloading dozens of young sailors, many of them laughing. Natasha couldn't take her eyes off their faces. At any moment she half expected to see Sergei emerge, grinning, tall and proud in his submariner's uniform.

In the end, the bodies of nearly one hundred officers and sailors were removed from the *Kursk* and positively identified. During the deep winter of January 2002, the last of the funerals were held in towns across Russia. Fittingly, the final body recovered from the salvaged submarine was that of the *Kursk*'s commanding officer, Captain Gennady Lyachin.

After the mix-up in the morgue, Natasha Tylik was eventually told that no trace of her husband could be found. Along with the men of the torpedo compartment, his body had been lost to the explosions and the sea. A small memorial would be built in Vidyaevo to honor the dozen men who would never have a grave.

In addition to their personal grief, the families of the *Kursk* crew have experienced numerous problems adjusting to life outside the structured world of the Northern Fleet. As part of the package of measures promised by President Putin to the widows during that turbulent night in Vidyaevo's Officers Club, each family received compensation worth about $30,000. By Russian standards, this sum represented a great deal of money. They were also provided with apartments in their native cities. Inevitably, these arrangements aroused resentment among many military families, who felt that the *Kursk* widows had been given vastly preferential treatment by the Russian state. Widows and mothers of the conscript soldiers who died by the hundreds during the Chechen War received almost no compensation—in many cases not even enough to cover funeral and burial expenses. Why was it more heroic and more profitable to die in a submarine accident than on the battlefields of Chechnya? Why had Russian and world public opinion focused on the *Kursk* but not on dozens of other, forgotten military accidents?

In some cases, painful disputes broke out between the widows and parents of the *Kursk* sailors over how to divide the money. There were also several family quarrels about where funerals and burials should take place. Parents wanted their sons buried in their hometown, often thousands of miles away from where the widows were now living. These were difficult, traumatic arguments, conducted behind closed doors.

Today, almost all the families of the sailors of the *Kursk* have left Vidyaevo and returned to their hometowns across Russia. The majority are living in St. Petersburg and the naval towns of the Russian Crimea, where they first met and fell in love with the young cadets who went on to form the crew of the *Kursk*.

Epilogue

SEVERAL WEEKS AFTER THE successful salvage, and a full fifteen months after the disaster, Russia's military leaders gathered in the Kremlin. The time had finally come to exact punishment on those judged responsible for the national humiliation of August 2000.

Chairing the meeting was the supreme commander of the Russian armed forces, President Vladimir Putin. Around the small table were Defense Minister Sergei Ivanov, chief of the General Staff Anatoly Kvashnin, and Navy commander Vladimir Kuroyedov. They invited Prosecutor-General Vladimir Ustinov to brief them on the results of his investigation.

Putin felt betrayed by the Navy, judging that the admirals had consistently misled him over the cause of the accident. He also believed that the collision theory, which the Navy had promoted as the most plausible explanation, was a deliberate attempt to undermine his policy of improving relations with Britain and the United States. Washington had already gone to exceptional and unprecedented lengths to show that no U.S. submarine was involved in the loss of the *Kursk*. Three months after the tragedy, at a meeting in a New York hotel in September 2000, in the wings of the United Nations Millennium Summit, Sandy Berger, President Clinton's national security adviser, met with Sergei Ivanov (who was, at that time, head of Russia's Security Council). Despite the opposition of U.S. Navy intelligence, Berger handed over edited audiotapes from the USS *Memphis* to his Russian counterpart. The gesture was designed to show Moscow that the Northern Fleet was wrong to speak of a collision. The tapes strongly indicated that the explosions were a result of an internal weapons accident.

In the Kremlin meeting, the prosecutor-general supported the view that the Navy had deceived the president, reportedly telling Putin, "You have been audaciously lied to." Putin's close personal friendship with Kuroyedov appears to have protected the Navy commander himself, but others were in the firing line. The purge was announced later that day, November 30, 2001.

Admiral Viacheslav Popov and Vice Admiral Mikhail Motsak were demoted, for "serious shortcomings in the organization of the activities of the Russian Navy." In an ironic twist to his life as a commanding officer of strategic nuclear submarines, Popov was ordered to join the ecology department of the Ministry of Atomic Energy.

Others dismissed on this day were:

- Rear Admiral Gennady Verich, the head of the Navy's search-and-rescue forces;
- Captain Alexander Teslenko, who had been in charge of the operation on the *Rudnitsky;*
- Vice Admiral Oleg Burtsev, commander of the First Submarine Flotilla, the man who had visited the *Normand Pioneer* and given the British rescuers such a burst of hope with his desire to deploy LR5 in a last-ditch effort to reach the *Kursk* survivors;
- Rear Admiral Mikhail Kuznetsov, commander of the Seventh Submarine division;
- and Vice Admiral Yuri Boyarkin, head of the military-training department of the Northern Fleet.

In total, fourteen top naval officers were sacked. All those who had talked of a "collision" with a Western submarine were targeted. The only senior commander who had conspicuously not spoken of a collision, Vice Admiral Vladimir Dobroskochenko, was promoted to take Popov's place, although his tenure would last just a few months. The other category of senior officers sacrificed were those associated with the failed rescue attempt, most notably Verich and Teslenko, and those responsible for the storage and operation of the Northern Fleet's stock of torpedoes. The head of the Armaments Department, Rear Admiral Vladimir Khandobin, chose to resign before he could be dismissed. The cull was a clear signal to the armed forces that the investigation had concluded that the accident was caused by a faulty torpedo and that a heavy price would be paid by those who sought to deceive the president. The collision theory was always seen by hardliners as a coded attack on the president's pro-Western policies, and the purge was interpreted in the Defense Ministry as a warning to Russia's generals and admirals not to interfere with Putin's conduct of foreign policy.

Putin lived up to his reputation as a man who wields power quietly but ruthlessly. As one Russian defense analyst described the president's actions: "Putin refuses to execute his opponents in public, preferring quietly to put poison in their drink."

The purge created a furious backlash in the Northern Fleet and in the search-and-rescue department in Moscow, not least because it came in the immediate aftermath of the widely acclaimed salvage. Moreover, most naval officers believed that the underlying cause of the *Kursk* disaster was the lack of investment and funding, problems for which they could not be held responsible. They felt the victims were being punished, while those guilty of abandoning the Russian armed forces were now sitting in judgment. Thirty well-respected officers took the risk of petitioning the Defense Ministry for a reversal of some of the dismissals, arguing that some sacked commanders had showed courage and determination in the rescue effort and had done everything humanly possible. As a result, admirals Kuznetsov, Burtsev, and Filatov were reinstated. Other appeals were turned down.

In reality, the Navy succeeded in protecting the futures of those publicly demoted and fired. Almost all now have flourishing careers, some having made a seamless transition into politics. Admiral Popov never took up his job in the ecology department. He became a senator in Russia's Upper House of Parliament, representing the Murmansk region. Admiral Motsak took up a senior post in the government for northwest Russia. Deputy Prime Minister Ilya Klebanov, who had been the target of so much fury in Vidyaevo, was moved to become Minister for Industry, Science, and Technology.

The official Russian probe into the *Kursk* disaster ended on July 19, 2002, nearly two years after the HTP 65-76 torpedo exploded in tube number four of the submarine's bow compartment. Investigators revealed that a large number of the Navy's torpedoes were suffering from corrosion and inadequate servicing. In many cases, worn gaskets were found in weapons long after they should have been replaced. The report ran to an astonishing 133 separate volumes of documents and analysis. Even the report's final protocol, signed by Lt. Colonel Egiev on behalf of the Office of the Military Prosecutor, was two hundred pages long. After all of this work, the central recommendation was that no charges should be brought against any official, since no crime had been committed. Relatives of the *Kursk* crewmembers called the investigation report the "final betrayal."

Although we know the horrifying circumstances of the death of the twenty-three men in the aft compartments, it is more difficult to establish with any precision *when* they were engulfed by the flash fire. Kolesnikov's third and final note had no time written next to it. Initially, Fleet commanders declared that the crewmembers in the aft had survived for between eighteen and twenty-four hours. This timeline was politically convenient, for it meant that no one would suggest that the bungled rescue operation had cost the lives of sailors. After all, not even a superbly executed search-and-rescue effort would have reached the ninth-compartment hatch on the first day. But the forensic evidence from the salvaged submarine is more troubling. It suggests that Dmitri Kolesnikov and his colleagues were alive for several days, possibly until Wednesday or Thursday. The evidence includes the large number of oxygen-regeneration canisters that had been opened and used up by the survivors, a quantity that suggests they lived well beyond the first day. Vice Admiral Vladislav Ilyin, who headed the *Kursk* incident cell, is now convinced that the sailors in the aft survived for at least three full days. There is even an outside chance that they were alive when the talented submersible pilot Captain Sholokhov maneuvered Priz over the escape hatch late on Thursday, August 17. But by the weekend—when the *Seaway Eagle* and *Normand Pioneer* specialists arrived on the scene, eight days after the accident—the twenty-three men certainly were dead.

The reason why the Russian rescue vehicles Priz and Bester were unable to secure a "seal" over the ninth hatch is still hotly debated by both Russian and Western submersible specialists. Ultimately, this failure doomed the surviving crewmembers.

Russian experts, both officially and in private, speak of a "crack" on the surface of the upper hatch that distorted the steel rim just enough to make a seal impossible. The huge shock waves in the forward end of the *Kursk* were certainly powerful enough to have caused damage all the way down the hull. But the *Seaway Eagle* divers, highly experienced in evaluating sub-sea damage, established beyond doubt that there were no distortions to the hatch itself, and the upper door swung open once the tide had equalized the pressure with the inside of the escape tower. There does, however, remain the possibility that there was some damage in what is known as the "cofferdam" boundary, the mechanism that rings the hatch. If this boundary was twisted, Captain Sholokhov may have been correct to blame "distortions" for his failure to establish a vacuum with the aft escape hatch.

Other possibilities that have been raised are a defect in the sealing ring on the submersibles themselves or an operator error by the pilots. Certainly, neither Bester nor Priz was well maintained. As the vessels deteriorated, many of the most able rescue professionals left the Fleet out of despair at the lack of resources, wearied by the constant battles with Moscow to retain their tiny budget.

Several Western specialists, including some of those who worked aboard the *Seaway Eagle,* believe that the *Kursk* spent the first few days of the disaster at an acute angle. They suggest that her jagged bow was cutting into the seabed but that her dry aft compartments, possessing positive buoyancy, were high in the water, quite possibly only a few dozen yards below the surface. If this was the case, the body of the submarine would have been pivoting with the movement of the currents and the tide—"weather-vaning," as salvage divers call it. Any attempt at sealing with the ninth hatch in these circumstances would have been extraordinarily difficult.

The odds were stacked heavily against the *Kursk* crewmembers as they clung to life in the aft of the submarine. They were in a submarine designed to hide, making it difficult for rescuers to find her on the seabed. The accident had been so overwhelming that there had been no time even for a distress signal. The emergency buoy had been disabled during previous patrols for fear that it would release accidentally. They were in a compartment that leaked, so that the survivors immediately faced the problem of rising pressure, severely limiting their ability to escape from the ninth-compartment hatch and survive an ascent to the surface. By a tragic and ironic twist, the superoxide chemical kits that were supposed to boost their survival prospects ignited the fire that killed them. They served a Navy starved of the resources to run an adequate search-and-rescue service, and were led by admirals in Moscow who were so preoccupied with issues of pride and secrecy that for the first forty-eight hours they hesitated to accept foreign help.

Russia's military leaders had forgotten that their most valuable resources, the assets really worth fighting to protect, were not the secret weapons aboard the *Kursk* but the young sailors themselves.

Crew List of the Kursk, *K-141*

STATEMENT BY THE KREMLIN IN AUGUST 2000:

For courage and heroism shown during performance of a sailor's duty, the Kursk *commanding officer Captain G. P. Lyachin has been given the rank of Hero of the Russian Federation (posthumously) on August 26, 2000. All 118 crew members are awarded the Courage Order (posthumously) and are inscribed forever in the memory of the 7th Division of the 1st Submarine Flotilla of the Northern Fleet.*

FIRST COMPARTMENT

1. Senior Midshipman Abdulkhadur Ildarov (Dagestan Republic)
2. Midshipman Alexei Zubov (Ukraine)
3. Seaman Ivan Nefedkov (Sverdlovsk Region)
4. Seaman Maxim Borzhov (Vladimir Region)
5. Seaman Alexei Shulgin (Arkhangel Region)
6. Senior Lieutenant Arnold Borisov (Dagestan Republic)
7. Mamed Gadjiev (Dagestan Republic)

SECOND COMPARTMENT

Visiting from the 7th Submarine Division Headquarters:

1. Captain First Rank Vladimir Bagriantsev (Crimea)
2. Captain Second Rank Yury Shepetnov (Crimea)

3. Captain Second Rank Viktor Belogun (Ukraine)
4. Captain Second Rank Vasily Isaenko (Crimea)
5. Captain Third Rank Marat Baygarin (St. Petersburg)

Crew:

6. Captain First Rank Gennady Lyachin (Volgograd Region)
7. Captain Second Rank Sergei Dudko (Belorussia)
8. Captain Second Rank Alexander Shubin (Crimea)
9. Captain-Lieutenant Maxim Safonov (Moscow)
10. Senior Lieutenant Sergei Tylik (Murmansk)
11. Senior Lieutenant Vadim Bubniv (Ulyanovsk Region)
12. Captain Third Rank Andrei Silogava (Crimea)
13. Captain-Lieutenant Alexei Shevchuk (Murmansk)
14. Senior Lieutenant Andrei Ponarin (St. Petersburg)
15. Senior Lieutenant Boris Geletin (Murmansk)
16. Senior Lieutenant Sergei Uzky (Arkhangel Region)
17. Captain Second Rank Yury Sablin (Crimea)
18. Captain Third Rank Andrei Milutin (St. Petersburg)
19. Captain-Lieutenant Sergei Kokurin (Voronezh Region)
20. Midshipman Vladimir Khivuk (Kursk)
21. Captain Third Rank Alexander Sadkov (Amur Region)
22. Captain-Lieutenant Mikhail Rodionov (Crimea)
23. Senior Lieutenant Sergei Yerakhtin (Murmansk)
24. Midshipman Yakov Samovarov (Arkhangel)
25. Senior Midshipman Alexander Ruzlev (Murmansk)
26. Midshipman Konstantin Kozyrev (Murmansk)
27. Senior Midshipman Vladimir Fesak (Ukraine)
28. Midshipman Andrei Poliansky (Krasnodar Region)
29. Midshipman Sergei Keslinsky (Kostroma Region)
30. Midshipman Sergei Griaznykh (Arkhangel Region)
31. Seaman Dmitri Mirtov (Komi Republic)
32. Petty Officer Dmitri Leonov (Moscow)
33. Senior Lieutenant Maxim Rvanin (Arkhangel Region)
34. Seaman Andrei Driuchenko (Arkhangel Region)
35. Senior Lieutenant Alexei Ivanov-Pavlov (Ukraine)
36. Midshipman Viktor Paramonenko (Ukraine)

THIRD COMPARTMENT

1. Captain-Lieutenant Dmitri Repnikov (Crimea)
2. Captain Third Rank Andrei Rudakov (Moscow)
3. Captain-Lieutenant Sergei Fiterer (Kaliningrad Region)
4. Captain-Lieutenant Oleg Nasikovsky (Kaliningrad Region)
5. Captain-Lieutenant Vitaly Solorev (Bryansk Region)
6. Captain-Lieutenant Sergei Loginov (Ukraine)
7. Captain-Lieutenant Andrei Koroviakov (St. Petersburg)
8. Captain-Lieutenant Alexei Korobkov (Murmansk)
9. Captain-Lieutenant Alexander Gudkov (Kaliningrad Region)
10. Captain Third Rank Viacheslav Bezsokirny (Ukraine)
11. Senior Midshipman Igor Yerasov (Voronezh)
12. Senior Midshipman Vladimir Svechkarev (Nizhny Novgorod Region)
13. Senior Midshipman Sergei Kalinin (Ukraine)
14. Senior Midshipman Igor Fedorichev (Tula Region)
15. Midshipman Maxim Vishniakov (Ukraine)
16. Midshipman Sergei Chernyshov (Crimea)
17. Midshipman Mikhail Belov (Nizhny Novgorod Region)
18. Midshipman Pavel Tavolzhansky (Belgorod Region)
19. Senior Midshipman Sergei Vlasov (Murmansk)
20. Midshipman Sergei Rychkov (Uzbekistan)
21. Petty Officer Yuri Annenkov (Kursk Region)
22. Seaman Dmitri Kotkov (Vologda Region)
23. Dubbing Seaman Nikolai Pavlov (Voronezh Region)
24. Seaman Ruslan Trianichev (Vologda Region)

FOURTH COMPARTMENT

1. Senior Lieutenant Denis Kirichenko (Ulyanovsk Region)
2. Captain of Medical Service Alexei Stankevich (Ukraine, St. Petersburg)
3. Midshipman Vitaly Romaniuk (Crimea)
4. Senior Midshipman Vasily Kichkiruk (Ukraine)
5. Senior Midshipman Anatoly Beliaev (Ryazan Region)
6. Chief Ship's Petty Officer Salovat Yansanov (Bashkortostan Republic)
7. Seaman Sergei Vitchenko (St. Petersburg Region)
8. Seaman Oleg Yevdokimov (Kursk Region)

9. Seaman Dmitri Staruseltsev (Kursk Region)
10. Seaman Alexander Khalepo (Komi Republic)
11. Seaman Alexei Kolomiytsev (Komi Republic)
12. Seaman Igor Loginov (Komi Republic)

FOURTH (B) COMPARTMENT

1. Captain Third Rank Dmitri Murachev (Crimea)
2. Captain-Lieutenant Denis Pshenichnikov (Crimea)
3. Captain-Lieutenant Sergei Lybushkin (Nizhny Novgorod Region)
4. Captain Third Rank Ilya Shchavinsky (St. Petersburg)
5. Captain-Lieutenant Alexander Vasiliev (Crimea Republic)
6. Captain Third Rank Nikolai Belozorov (Voronezh Region)
7. Senior Midshipman Ivan Tsymbal (Ukraine)
8. Midshipman Oleg Troyan (Azerbaijan)
9. Chief Petty Officer Alexander Neustroev (Tomsk Region)
10. Seaman Alexei Larionov (Komi Republic)
11. Midshipman Vladimir Shablatov

FIFTH COMPARTMENT

1. Senior Lieutenant Vitaly Kuznetsov
2. Senior Midshipman Nailkh Khafizov (Bashkortostan Republic)
3. Senior Midshipman Yevgeny Gorbunov
4. Midshipman Valery Baybarin (Chelyabinsk Region)

SIXTH COMPARTMENT

1. Captain-Lieutenant Rashid Ariapov (Uzbekistan)
2. Midshipman Alexei Balanov (Chuvash Republic)
3. Senior Lieutenant Alexei Mitiaev (St. Petersburg)
4. Chief Petty Officer Viacheslav Maynagashev (Khakass Republic)
5. Seaman Alexei Korkin (Arkhangel Region)

SEVENTH COMPARTMENT

1. Captain-Lieutenant Dmitri Kolesnikov (St. Petersburg)
2. Midshipman Fanis Ishmudatov (Bashkortostan Republic)

3. Petty Officer Second Class Vladimir Sadovoi (Nizhny Novgorod Region)
4. Seaman Roman Kubikov (Kursk Region)
5. Seaman Alexei Nekrasov (Kursk Region)
6. Petty Officer First Class Rishat Zubaydullin (Ulyanovsk Region)
7. Seaman Ilya Naletov (Vologda Region)
8. Petty Officer Second Class Roman Anikiev (Murmansk)
9. Senior Midshipman Vladimir Kozaderov (Lipetsk Region)

EIGHTH COMPARTMENT
1. Captain-Lieutenant Sergei Sadilenko (Ukraine)
2. Senior Midshipman Viktor Kuznetsov (Kursk Region)
3. Chief Ship's Petty Officer Robert Gessler (Bashkortostan Republic)
4. Senior Midshipman Andrei Borisov (Ryazan Republic)
5. Seaman Roman Martynov (Komi Republic)
6. Seaman Viktor Sidukhin (Komi Republic)
7. Seaman Yury Borisov (Komi Republic)

NINTH COMPARTMENT
1. Senior Lieutenant Alexander Brazhkin (Crimea Republic)
2. Midshipman Vasily Ivanov
3. Midshipman Mikhail Bochkov (Crimea Republic)

Acknowledgments

MY DEEPEST GRATITUDE GOES to the wives and families of the *Kursk* officers and sailors, so many of whom offered me unfailing assistance and friendship in the two years following the tragedy. Their enduring pride for lost sons and husbands and their belief that Russia deserves a military leadership that is open and honest remain an inspiration. To them, especially to the families of Sergei Tylik and Dmitri Kolesnikov, I offer my humble thanks. The spirit of these families is remarkable. Seventy children lost fathers in the *Kursk* accident, and many of the young boys have a single aim: to follow in their fathers' footsteps and join Russia's submarine flotillas.

There are many people in a number of countries who have assisted me in understanding the circumstances surrounding the *Kursk* accident and the subsequent multinational rescue effort. In particular, this book would not have been possible without the scientific curiosity and patience of two men who generously shared their thoughts and technical knowledge.

Garry Ball, a dive supervisor who worked aboard the *Seaway Eagle* during the *Kursk* disaster, has provided me with constant support, guiding me through the world of saturation diving and explaining the technologies and operating culture of the breed of men who work offshore. He dealt with a torrent of questions—not least about the workings of the *Kursk*'s escape hatches and valves—with great patience. Ramsey Martin, a marine engineer specializing in submarine escape-and-rescue systems, has been of enormous help. His startling breadth of scientific knowledge and understanding of Russian naval engineering—as well as of the physiological issues that faced the *Kursk* sailors—helped unravel what happened in the submarine's ninth compartment.

The Russian Navy has forbidden Northern Fleet officers from discussing the events of August 2000. But there were several officers, including in the search-and-rescue department, as well as Navy doctors and torpedo engineers, who agreed to speak privately about the accident and its aftermath. They must all remain anonymous, but their help was invaluable.

I owe a great deal to the researchers who worked with me in Moscow, St. Petersburg, and Murmansk, Lisa Gusarova and Constantine Miniar-Beloroutchev, whose good humor, energy, and sharp intelligence helped to open doors in the closed world of the Kola Peninsula, and who sorted through a wealth of often-contradictory information.

In Moscow, I was greatly assisted by the insights of a number of military analysts, especially Alexander Golts, Sergei Vasilyev, and Igor Korotchenko, and by the thoughts of two retired Oscar II submarine commanders, Captain Arkady Yefanov and Captain Konstantin Astafyev. In Murmansk, I received the help and support of Alexander Raubee, Igor Zheveluk, and Vladimir Shkoda.

In the United States, I have benefited enormously from the patient advice and generous guidance of Norman Polmar, co-author of *Cold War Submarines* and the West's leading authority on Soviet/Russian submarines, and the assistance of Rear Admiral Tom Evans, whose own Cold War patrols aboard the USS *Batfish* are already a legend. Robin Pirie, a former acting secretary of the Navy and former commanding officer of the USS *Skipjack*, assisted with understanding the political background to the U.S. reaction to the accident.

In Britain, I am grateful to Commodore David Russell, who spent many hours talking to me about his experiences in the Barents Sea during the *Kursk* rescue and who permitted me to see the Royal Navy files and the "situation reports" from the summer of 2000, which were unclassified. His openness—as well as his instinctive desire to try and save the *Kursk* submariners—was in the finest tradition of the Royal Navy. Martin Macpherson, a retired Royal Navy submarine commander, was exceptionally helpful and provided me with numerous invaluable suggestions, as well as agreeing to read a draft. Jim Ring, who has written his own book on submarines, *We Come Unseen,* was a source of great encouragement and assisted in numerous introductions.

In addition, I am grateful for the time and cooperation of many of those directly involved in the events who agreed to speak to me. From the Royal Navy: Captain Simon Lister and Captain Geoffrey McCready, both of whom have worked so hard to improve and foster links with the Russian Navy, and Lt.-Commander David Green at the submarine-escape training tank. From Stolt Offshore: Graham Mann, Bob Rose, Graham Legg, Mark Nankivell, Tony Scott, Dag Rasmussen, and Matt Kirk. Many of these discussions were arranged by Stolt's Julian Thomson, whose goodwill and refreshingly open view of corporate information proved invaluable. From the Norwegian Navy: Admiral Einar Skorgen, who provided a candid and compelling account of his dealings with Admiral Popov throughout the rescue efforts, and Captain Paal Svendsen, the liaison officer on the *Seaway Eagle.* In Oslo: Frode Ringdal explained with patience the seismological detective work that followed the underwater explosions.

This book was possible only with the kind support and encouragement of Nigel Dacre, editor of ITV News, and ITN's editor-in-chief Richard Tait.

My editor at Crown, Emily Loose, believed in this book from the outset and invested an extraordinary amount of her time and effort in the project. Her unfailing support and exacting standards have improved the book at every stage.

Finally, none of this would have been possible without my parents, John and Avril, who taught me the value of curiosity, and my wife,

Liz, who tolerated with infinite patience my long absences in Russia. Her good humor and support never wavered.

Many people have helped me, but any mistakes are mine alone. I ask for the forgiveness of submariners and professional divers—who, after all, spend their entire working lives under the ocean surface— if they judge that there are omissions and oversimplifications in this account.

Index

About the Author

Robert Moore is currently the chief U.S. correspondent for England's ITN News, based in Washington, D.C. He is the recipient of numerous journalism awards, including an international Emmy for Best News Coverage in 2000 and the New York TV & Film Festival Gold Medal for Reporter of the Year in 1997. He lives in Washington, D.C.